For

my dearest Gertrude and Emil
with my sincere love —
and all good wishes from
Helen Dreiser

Hollywood, Calif.   Feb. 18, 1951

My Life with D R E I S E R

THEODORE DREISER

Portrait by Wayman Adams

by HELEN DREISER

My Life with DREISER

Cleveland and New York

THE WORLD PUBLISHING COMPANY

Published by The World Publishing Company

FIRST EDITION

TO *the unknown women in the life of*
Theodore Dreiser, who devoted themselves
unselfishly to the beauty of his
intellect and its artistic unfoldment.

PREFACE

The following pages reveal a personal record of my life with Theodore Dreiser. It is my small contribution to his biography, but one of many that will be written. My sole reason in presenting it is that I feel the story of Dreiser would otherwise be incomplete. Perhaps by holding fast to my own personal reactions to such a vital force as he was, I may throw some light upon him which will have some value in the over-all picture when his comprehensive biography is written.

Dreiser was not an ordinary man and he did not live an ordinary life. He wrote honestly and frankly about himself when he was among us and he would expect no less from me. As his great friend J. G. Robin so often said: "When Dreiser puts his pen to paper he tells the *truth*."

This is what I have tried to do in relating my story. If I have failed, it will not be because I did not try to cleave to the truth—or as near as anyone can define the truth about so intimate a record.

Helen Dreiser

FACSIMILES

ILLUSTRATIONS

1

It was a late September afternoon in 1919 when Theodore Dreiser and I faced each other at the door of his studio at 165 West Tenth Street in New York.

I remember the breezy, challenging quality of that day, which somehow matched my own restless mood as I walked down the steps of the rattly old El at Eighth Street. I never pass that corner now without recalling my frame of mind at the time—emotionally free, blindly unaware of the influence that a few moments later was to close in on me, to affect and change the entire course of my life.

As Dreiser later told me, he had not been answering the doorbell for days, owing to the fact that he was concentrating on his book of essays, *Hey Rub-a-dub-dub!* When I rang a second time, he hesitated. And then he went to the door, opened it and stood there gazing at me, much to my bewilderment and confusion. I saw a tall man with powerful build, large features, leonine head, deep-set eyes and sensual mouth. I knew him instantly because he bore such a striking resemblance to his brother Ed, whom I had met previously. And while it had seemed perfectly natural for me to make the

3

acquaintance of Ed, as I stood gazing at Dreiser I suddenly wondered why I had come and what in the world I would say to him.

I stammered, "Are you Ed's brother?"

"Yes, I am," he said.

"Well, I am his cousin," I replied.

He chuckled and said what he could not very well avoid saying: "Well, if that is so, then you are my cousin, too," and cordially motioned for me to come into his studio. He quickly put me at ease, and I found myself talking of trivial things.

Something was happening. I certainly did not know what, and I laughed a little nervously. During the course of the conversation I asked if I could meet Mrs. Dreiser. He said, "No, I live alone." We talked awhile, about what I could never remember. He finally got up and walked over to a bookcase and took out a copy of one of his books. It was *The Hand of the Potter*. He autographed it to his "little Oregon cousin." Then he asked me to write my name on a sheet of paper which was lying on his desk. I could scarcely hold the pen, my hand trembled so, and I had a keen desire to run away to the safety of my own room so I could think about this meeting, for I felt that something different and important had happened to me. After a few moments, I started to leave, inwardly more nervous and excited and bewildered than I had ever been in my life.

What combination of chemicals had been carelessly or carefully, intentionally or accidentally, thrown together at this psychological moment and why?

But here I will insert Dreiser's own version of our meeting. It was written five years later, when I was in California, but

Helen

With what words may one pen
ones deepest Emotions   With what
colors paint that which appears to
be the essence and hence the meaning
of all sharp shades.   I can
begin in no better way I think
than is by referring to a certain
grey windy day in September

Facsimile of the first page of Dreiser's composition on Helen.

never finished. As he wrote me, it would have to be a book, not a sketch.

HELEN

With what words may one pen one's deepest emotions. With what colors paint that which appears to be the essence and hence the evasion of all sharp shades. I can begin in no better way, I think, than by referring to a certain gray windy day in September of a certain year when seated at my desk in 10th Street, New York, writing, my door bell rang, and I sat there for a few moments wondering whether I should answer. The drag and almost despair of a dreary interlude was upon me. At best one feeds so much on husks. Affairs begin and affairs end. But before they end, whatever they are, there is a period of wretched retrospect and dark foreboding, than which there could be nothing darker or more dreary. I have described various personages and identified myself with them. Among them, if one looked sharp, might be several of those —the romance with whom had paled to greys and sombre days. My soul was really sick of this malaise that concerns the black lees of once sparkling cups. Must romance ever end in disillusion? Must my dreamful searchings for delight end where black night was settling upon a bleak and pathless moor? I was thinking so— as I wrote.

And then this ring.

It was repeated.

I got up, and slipping on a blue Chinese working coat that lay near me—in order, always, to make myself somewhat more presentable if needs must—I strode to the door. In doing so I noticed I had slipped on the coat wrong side out—a most drastic and inescapable and invariable sign of change. I had never known it to fail. Yet since it looked well either way, the inside as well stitched as the outside, I left it. The bell rang again, and peeping through a dark brown silk curtain which protected the panes of the outer door I observed a girl of not more than nineteen or twenty, I would have

6

said, at the most. She was dressed in a long slate blue afternoon frock, with a large, floppy slate blue hat, in which was fastened a single, immense and very faintly tinted but delightfully harmonious old rose-tinted rose. I opened the door. At once visiting me with such a youthful, gladsome, innocent-seeming smile, such as I had not (I would have said at the moment) seen in years, she inquired if I knew where I lived, reciting my full name.

"Here, and I am the person."

"Well, then, I am your cousin, V's niece," she promptly trilled, "and she made me promise—"

"If you're my cousin V's niece or any relationship to me near or far, come right in," I interrupted, welcoming her as I would a beautiful light in a dungeon. And her smile and her eyes were all light. I would scarcely have imagined up to that moment that any so glorious a maid could have been kin to me. A painted flower in a meadow, say, as contrasted with a coarse weed in a city lot. A little mincing gazelle and a tusked boar, wild and evil—Pierrette decked for a May party and old Boreas scowling darkly by her side. And yet I was trying to smile, and be young of heart, and was achieving something, I would scarcely venture what. Who is it that has written "Making a gay sun to shine in the dim hearts of those who find beauty a need."

That evening I read his book *The Hand of the Potter*. What a powerful impression it made on me at that time! I decided I must get all of the Dreiser books and read them.

I slept very little that night, finally getting up to reread parts of his book and study a photograph of him in a pamphlet he had given me, containing the following poem to Dreiser, by Edgar Lee Masters:

Soul enrapt, demi-urge
Walking the earth,
Stalking life.

7

Jack o' lantern, tall shouldered,
One eye set higher than the other,
Mouth cut like a scallop in a pie,
Aslant, showing powerful teeth,
Swaying above the heads of others,
Jubilant, with fixed eyes scarcely sparkling,
Touching fingers together, back and forth,
Or toying with a handkerchief,
And the eyes burn like a flame at the end of a funnel,
And the ruddy face glows like a pumpkin
On Hallowe'en!

Or else a gargoyle of bronze
Turning suddenly to life
And slipping suddenly down corners of stone
To eat you:
Full of questions, objections,
Distinctions, instances,
Contemptuous, ironical, remote,
Cloudy, irreverent, ferocious,
Fearless, grim, compassionate yet hateful,
Old yet young, wise yet virginal,
To whom everything is new and strange,
Whence he stares and wonders.
Laughs, mocks, curses—
Disordered, yet with a passion for order
And classification—hence the habitual
Folding into squares of a handkerchief.

Or else a well cultivated and fruitful valley,
But behind it explored fastnesses.
Gorges, precipices, and heights
Over which thunder clouds hang,
From which lightning falls,
Stirring up terrible shapes of prey

That slink about in the blackness.
The silence of him is terrifying,
As if you sat before the Sphinx.
The look of his eyes makes tubes of the air
Through which you are magnified and analyzed.
He needs nothing of you and wants nothing.
He is alone and content,
Self-mastered and beyond friendship,
You could not hurt him.
If he would allow himself to have a friend
He could part with that friend forever
And in a moment be lost in wonder
Staring at a carved rooster on a doorstep,
Or at an Italian woman
Giving suck to a child
On a seat in Washington Square.

Soul enrapt, demi-urge,
Walking the earth,
Stalking life.

I felt as if I had been looking for Dreiser all my life. I recalled a conversation I had had a few months before with a young man who had been paying considerable attention to me. We got to talking about men, and he asked me rather impatiently what kind of man I wanted anyhow. When I told him, he said contemptuously, "You don't want a man, you want a god!"

"Maybe so," I replied, "but I'll meet him one of these days; I know I will."

And now I realized that the outline of the man I had drawn in the empty frame was a perfect likeness, spiritually, mentally and physically, of Dreiser himself. Many people would dismiss this sort of thinking as nonsensical. But to me these pictures that we draw out of some etheric essence take strange forms. They are like signposts in the road that seem to indicate a sharp turn ahead. Never do I see one appear that I do not hesitate, trying to grasp the meaning or the direction. "Runic handwriting," John Cowper Powys calls it.

The next morning at eight o'clock my telephone rang. I knew it was Dreiser calling. His voice was soothing yet commanding, and there was a sadness about it that held an intimate sensual appeal which moved me deeply.

"I haven't slept all night," he said. "I must see you. Won't you please have breakfast with me? Come down to the Pennsylvania Roof. I want so much to talk to you."

I recall little of our conversation over the breakfast table that morning, but I do know that all the while we seemed to be probing, subconsciously, in an effort to reach some hidden mystery. One question he asked remains with me. Was I religious? I was puzzled at the time, for I could not imagine of what earthly importance it could be.

Formal religion, as such, had never meant much in my life. I had gone to Sunday school as a child to please my grandmother. But I had never had religion deliberately imposed on me to a degree of discomfort, and although my grandmother was a deeply religious woman in a very large sense, she had nothing of the narrowness that so often goes hand in hand with religion. I had never questioned it or thought much about it. But to Dreiser, as I found out later, organized religion was something one approached through a closed door and once through the door, one's vision of life was forever blurred unless one could fight his way back and out again. Religion to him meant childhood torture, for his mind was one that reached out in every direction for intellectual nourishment, expansion and freedom, and this the Church denied him. No one with organized religious training or prejudice could ever be of any constructive value to him.

"No, I don't think so," I answered.

He looked at me in a searching, almost doubting way, as if to probe deeper for a trace of conventional prejudice.

Later we went downstairs and sat in the hotel lobby for a little while, and then he asked me if I cared to go to his studio.

"No, I would rather walk somewhere," I said. With this he seemed delighted, and we started out, arm in arm, up one street, across another, until finally we reached upper Park Avenue. Swinging along rhythmically and harmoniously together, we did not care where we walked. But all the while, from a little distance, a part of me was continually observing this man who strode beside me. He seemed so powerful and vital, in his mood so much of the rebel. To my young, inexperienced mind, he was an encyclopedia of knowledge, a whole constellation of suns rolled into one, and I was impressed to the point of wonder.

We walked for two hours and he made me promise that I would dine with him the following Tuesday evening. Then he stopped at the door of my home near Morningside Park and bade me goodbye, after thanking me for coming and assuring me that he felt much more cheerful after our refreshing and stimulating walk.

2

After days of anticipation, Tuesday finally arrived. I remember the dress I wore that evening: a simple pearl-gray georgette embroidered with large circles of small dull beads, which weighted the skirt just enough to make it cling to the form as one walked. Gray shoes and stockings, a little gray poke bonnet, and a soft brown cloth coat trimmed with gray squirrel completed the ensemble.

When I entered the studio I was greeted warmly and eagerly. Would I come in? Would I have a cocktail before dinner? And, as Dreiser noticed my interest in and admiration for his studio, would I like to look around while he mixed the drinks? I would and did.

Dreiser's studio was on the parlor floor of an old red brick house and consisted of a large living room and bedroom. Along the lower part of the walls were filled bookcases, and on the walls hung some arresting paintings, two of which dominated the studio. One was a decorative painting in which there were two Egyptian dancers; a black figure in the background held a huge tray of fruit. Almost the entire painting was made up of triangles. The other painting was a back view of a voluptuous nude woman, her red hair twisted in a heavy knot at the back of her neck. She was reclining in a sensual pose while a heavy Negress stood before her offering her a large plate of luscious fruit. Then there was his desk which he had had made from a square rosewood piano. Near it stood a lectern on which rested a large dictionary. There was a day-bed of Madame Récamier influence in his front studio, filigree candlesticks, Windsor chairs, and, of course, an old-fashioned simple rocker which I afterward learned he could never do without, even in a hotel room. But I returned again and again to his beautiful desk at which I knew he had spent the most important part of his life.

We lingered in his studio over the cocktail, and then he took me to Paula Holliday's restaurant in Greenwich Village. During dinner he pointed out the interesting people around us, among them Hippolyte Havel, an anarchist of distinction among liberals; Harry Kemp; and Edward Smith, Dreiser's devoted friend of many years. Each time I looked around I noticed Edward Smith studying me. Smith had a deep and lasting affection for Dreiser, and years later as I stood with Theodore at his bedside when he was dying of pneumonia, one of his last gestures was to pretend to be drinking a toast to Dreiser. He lifted his hand holding an imaginary glass and whispered in his delirium: "To Dreiser." The story of "Olive Brand" in Dreiser's *Gallery of Women* reveals the significance of this man's life in its beauty and tragedy. He was one of those rare few who had the capacity for deep and lasting love and friendship.

During dinner Dreiser asked me to tell him something of

my own life. As I look back, I wonder if there was ever a man who so evoked the desire to confide one's joys, sorrows and secrets as did Dreiser? I couldn't understand his interest in my simple story when he was familiar with so many dramatic experiences. But he *was* interested.

"So you're a real little Western girl," said Dreiser. "Well, I, too, am a Westerner. I think they are pretty nice people, but you have me beaten by half a continent." At another point, he said, "And you say that your grandmother was my mother's sister? Now that *is* interesting. Tell me about yourself. I want to know more about this relationship between you and me."

Encouraged by Dreiser's questions I recounted my grandmother's stories of her girlhood in Indiana, her tales of encounters with Indians, and how she married a descendant of the Quakers, David Parks, who had been a Forty-Niner in California where he had made a fortune. They subsequently moved to Wisconsin where my mother, Ida Viola, was born. When I told of my grandmother's voyage around the Horn on her way to San Francisco with her husband and two children, and how she attended a woman in childbirth on the ship during a storm which lasted three days and three nights, Dreiser exclaimed: "Sounds like my own mother. They must have been much alike in temperament and experience." And as I came to know more about his mother, through Dreiser and his love for her, I realized how true this was. Through the years that followed, this bond between us became one of the strongest. In his book *Dawn*, which he did not finish or publish until 1931, he describes his mother's home:

It was while working his way from Connecticut and New York to Dayton, Ohio, that not far from Dayton, he (Theodore's father) met the girl who became my mother. She was the daughter of a prosperous Moravian farmer, of Dunkard or Mennonite faith, who was a unit of the sect that then centered about Bethlehem, Pennsylvania. The world of her rearing must have been a pleasant one, for often I have heard her speak of her parents' prosperity as farmers, of orchard and meadow and great fields of grain, and of some of the primitive conditions and devices of pioneer life that still affected them—neighbors borrowing fire, Indians coming to the door to beg or be sociable, the spinning of wool and cotton on hand looms, the home manufacture of soap, shoes, and furniture.

I went on to tell of my grandfather's death which left my grandmother alone on a huge farm in Fairview, Oregon, with six daughters. My mother was the eldest of the six. Gentle, kind and understanding, she married a handsome, temperamental Dane, George Christian Patges, who had been driven out of Denmark by his stepmother. His sole ambition was to become a fine musician and he had progressed considerably as a violinist before leaving Denmark. He was very honest and had no difficulty in securing and holding a position as superintendent of a property, but whenever a real problem appeared he usually left it for my mother to solve; so, after a time they decided to live separate lives.

The farm life of my grandmother became too difficult for her and she was forced to sell her Fairview farm and try the hotel business in Portland. She took my mother into this venture, and thus I was raised in a matriarchy of which my beloved grandmother was the head. I went to her for everything: affection, advice and spiritual guidance.

Being stagestruck, I spent much of my time hanging out of a back window of the hotel, which faced the stage door of the

Marquam Theater in Portland. All the stars of the day appeared here, and I took every opportunity to lend my dog, my pony or even myself whenever the need presented itself. During summer vacations from school, I played small parts in stock companies and once even achieved a trip to Boise, Idaho, with a company, which my mother finally approved when she learned I would be heavily chaperoned by a most reliable elderly couple traveling with the company.

At sixteen I fell in love with a handsome young Southerner of nineteen who was also interested in the theater. He came from Charleston and was visiting an older brother in Portland. My sister, Hazel, was planning to be married at the time and I wanted to make it a double wedding so that I could leave school and go on the stage. If I could not marry I would run away. My relatives made my life miserable with their discussions as to the absurdity of it, but my mother, sensing my determination, finally said, "Why not? She insists on going on the stage. I can't let her go out in the world alone. It would be better for her to go with him." So I did, and never regretted the step.

The day I married Frank Richardson was the day my real education began. We were young, gay, hopeful and very much in love. He was as devoted to the theater as I was. We studied singing and dancing together and eventually worked up a routine that landed us bookings in small theaters in Washington and Oregon. While the going was difficult at times and our financial condition far from satisfactory, we refused to acknowledge defeat.

Our ultimate goal was San Francisco, and when we finally

arrived there we fell in love with that romantic city—the foggy evenings, the hilly streets, the little cable cars, the Barbary Coast with its swarming streets filled with sailors and people of every nationality and description. But here a situation arose that troubled me. The booking agents preferred to book me as a single, and as a consequence we had to refuse several engagements because we could not bear to be separated. Our funds gradually diminished, and soon we were pawning everything of value that we possessed. There seemed to be no way out except for me to accept a few engagements alone for a while, and much against his will my husband finally consented. However, the realization that we were both too young, too untrained, too poorly equipped for the struggle began to take place in my mind.

Our troubles were finally partially solved by Frank's return to his family in Charleston. I would remain behind temporarily in San Francisco, where I was singing in a centrally located night club. We were both badly shaken by our separation but consoled ourselves with the thought that it would be only temporary. Two months later he sent for me and I was on my way south, to a way of life vastly different from anything I had ever known.

To one born in the West with its youthful aspect and unsophistication, the older and more conservative East and particularly the provincial South offered a startling contrast.

I was nervous and uncertain about the reception awaiting me from my husband's family, for they felt he was much too young and should have waited to establish himself before marrying. But my first meeting with his mother dispelled all doubts. She loved her son deeply, and that was all that mat-

17

tered to me, for I loved him too and felt this common bond would enable us to reach an understanding.

No sooner did I arrive in Charleston than the entire household was turned over to me. With a few explanations and directions I was to be left all summer to run the house while Frank's mother visited her son at West Point. While I was flattered by this display of confidence, I was most uncertain as to my ability to carry it out. For one thing, the Negro servants were a new experience to me.

The summer went smoothly, although the stifling heat was almost too much for me at times. However, in many ways I enjoyed the change, and Charleston fascinated me. To hear the criers musically calling their wares as they passed, each with his own peculiar cadence, was almost hypnotic. To this day I can close my eyes and hear those haunting melodies as they fell on the sultry, still, early morning air. But Frank had accepted a position as a traveling salesman and I was alone a great deal. Although I spent much time reading, this could not keep me from growing weary of the heat, the conventionality, the provincial atmosphere. I could feel no sense of growth in any direction. I lost weight, had no appetite and was verging on anemia. It was then that Frank's mother thought I had better take a short trip to visit my family, which I did. When I returned to Charleston a couple of months later, my health was noticeably improved.

It was the summer of 1918 and most of Charleston had moved over to Sullivan's Island. Many soldiers were stationed there at different periods prior to their embarkation for France. There were dances, parties, clambakes, a continuous round of pleasure which infected me with restlessness. I began to dream of going away, perhaps to New York; I might obtain a position there, replace someone being drafted. Instead of stagnating here in the South, I could be of some real use.

It was at this time that W. E. Woodward, senior vice-president of the Industrial Finance Corporation of New York, visited my husband's family. After dinner one evening, as we walked along the beach, I asked him if he thought there would be any opportunity in New York for me, now that the war was on. He looked at me searchingly.

"I believe I understand how you feel," he said. "You really don't belong in the South. You want to be where things are happening, don't you? I know; I was born in the South and I know all about it."

"Yes," I told him, "I'm stifling down here. I can't adapt myself to the atmosphere even though everyone has been wonderful to me."

"Well, I don't know," he continued. "New York is very hard and commercial for a newcomer to face. I don't know what to advise you, but if you ever do come to New York, look me up. One never knows when an opening may occur."

To me, filled with ambition and the desire to grow, this meant a great deal. It was a small opening wedge, and as the months passed I not only remembered this conversation but exaggerated its importance. Being alone much of the time now, as Frank's work compelled him to be away for long intervals, I had plenty of time to evaluate my situation. Long stretches of inactivity have always been unbearable to me, and with the entire world seemingly on the march it became impossible for me not to move with it. And so the decision to go to New York crystallized in my mind.

During these last few months in Charleston Frank and I had been gradually drifting apart. My actual departure for New York marked the beginning of the end of our marriage, which a few years later culminated in divorce.

On arriving in New York I secured a room in an apartment near Columbia University, adjoining one occupied by Lucile Nelson, a girl with whom I had become friendly in Charleston. She was a beautiful girl with a voluptuous poppy-like personality, whose warmth and generosity had appealed to me from the moment I first met her.

Soon after I was settled, I called Mr. Woodward on the telephone and he invited me to come down to his office at 52 William Street—the Industrial Finance Corporation which was the parent company of the Morris Plan Banks.

After greeting me cordially he informed me that his secretary, a young man, had just been drafted. Did I think I could do the work? I was terrified at the idea, but so desperate was I to establish myself that I said I would like to try. I would go to night school and brush up on my shorthand and typing, which I had learned in high school.

"All right," he said, "I'd like to have you try it. I like your cheerfulness. I need the sunshine you'd bring into the place. Suppose I keep the position open for about a month, and we'll see what you can do."

He stood up and shook hands with me, and as I left his office I felt that I must succeed in this undertaking, for here was an opportunity to work for a man whom I immediately liked, respected and admired.

Lucile Nelson helped me find a job as cashier in the Uni-

versity Cafeteria, and in the evenings I attended business
school. It was Armistice Day, November 11, 1918, when I
walked into Mr. Woodward's office prepared to begin work
in earnest.

I knew nothing about the Wall Street world of finance, and
I was impressed with the atmosphere which was laden with
importance, initiative and the necessity for quick decision,
and with the men of importance who floated in and out of
A. J. Morris' office. There was John Markle, the leading
anthracite coal operator in the United States; Coleman Du
Pont of the famous Du Pont family; Robert J. Bulkley, who
belonged to a Cleveland law firm and had often been mentioned as a possible candidate for President of the United
States on the Democratic ticket; Edwin Holter, a financier
reputed to be the largest wheat farmer in the United States,
and many others.

A. J. Morris, the president, was a short, forceful-looking
man. He had been a lawyer in Norfolk, Virginia, where he
was born, and commanded a brilliant, fluent and descriptive
English. Many times, in the absence of his secretary, Mr.
Carter, I took his rapid dictation, dashing along with him,
alert to his every expression; and while often I did not know
the meaning of a word, still I caught something that sounded
like it and later went in distress to the secretary of the organization, Joseph B. Gilder, a grand old man whose knowledge
of the English language was, to me, astounding. He never
failed to find the word I was looking for and to explain its
meaning.

At this point Dreiser interrupted to say: "So you worked
with Joseph B. Gilder! That is *something*. I knew all of the

21

Gilders in my early editing days. They were wonderful people."

A. J., as Mr. Morris was often referred to, was a force. When he entered in the morning, one could feel his presence vibrate throughout the office, even though he was not seen. And when, in the evening, he finally and reluctantly walked out with his pronounced limp and shifting of the body, one immediately felt the let-down of the office force.

Later, when I was well into the work, I was often called into meetings of the Board of Directors, where among all these important and severe-looking men I, the only woman present, sat taking notes. To one who had had no business experience, this was a most impressive task.

Everything in the office was precise, accurate and sophisticated, moving smoothly with no lost motion. But the human element intrigued me psychologically. The personalities surrounding me were all part of a fascinating pattern. I became interested in my position from many points of view, and it wasn't long before I came to live my job.

During the year that I worked for Mr. Woodward I came to know in him one of the most cultured, sympathetic and just men I had ever met. He was always patient, kind and appreciative, as well as exacting, and I worked hard in an effort to please him. He directly influenced my reading, for he was continually recommending some specific book in his correspondence, or making lists of books for himself which I took advantage of. English literature had always been my favorite school subject, and I loved Greek mythology, but Mr. Woodward enlarged my vista of poetic literature.

One day, while he was dictating, he stopped and looked out

of the window. "When I am fifty," he said in his character-
istically decisive way, "I shall chuck this financial game completely . . . I shall *write* . . . when I am fifty," he repeated,
as he continued to gaze out the window. True enough, Mr.
Woodward did eventually quit the financial world when he
was fifty to become a distinguished writer of biographies.

At this particular time it was Dreiser who was his enthusiasm. He had just finished reading *Twelve Men* and he made
it a point to have me add a postscript to each letter he wrote:
"If you have not read *Twelve Men*, get it and read it." On
the strength of this, I purchased a copy of the book and read it.

I thought it was a wonderful book; the twelve portraits
were all so different. I especially liked the story "My Brother
Paul," which was a revelation to me in the light of what I
knew about this cousin already. It gave me such an insight
into Dreiser's relationship with his brother that I looked forward to meeting him. One day after reading the book I commented casually to Mr. Woodward that Dreiser was my
cousin, a remark which had a startling effect on him.

"Well," he said, "why don't you go around and see him?
If he were *my* cousin, I certainly would."

The decision to see Dreiser, so casually made on Mr.
Woodward's equally casual suggestion, had brought me to a
turning point in my life—this dinner at Paula Holliday's,
with Theodore Dreiser sitting across from me and listening
eagerly to my simple story, was only the beginning.

"What do you intend to do now?" Dreiser asked me when I
had finished.

"My trunks are all packed," I replied, "and I am leaving

for California in a few days. However, I thought it would be nice to see you before going, so I could tell the folks back home that I had met Theodore Dreiser. I've saved some money and have decided to take up the theater again. This time I will try to connect with an experimental dramatic group which will give me the training I need, and then I might even try for the movies!"

"Well," observed Dreiser, "you are one girl, I would say, who might easily succeed."

Perhaps some humans swing in large orbits, gathering unto themselves lesser planets as they pass, like great suns. Others seem like smaller planets absorbing small ideas and limited experiences. Theodore Dreiser seemed to me to move in a large orbit and for me, at my age and with my limited background, to have come into contact with a man of his caliber was an astounding experience. The emotional depth plumbed by this meeting set in motion an intense vibration between us. While the outward complexion of it was to change as time went on, still, at the slightest provocation a real emotional disturbance or great stress might develop which would cause both of us acute suffering. So much so, in fact, that we soon came to know that above all, things had to be right between us at all times.

After leaving Paula Holliday's we went over to Dreiser's studio on Tenth Street, where we continued talking for an hour or so. He showed me a collection of woodcuts that he thought much of, as well as several other small objects of art in which he felt I would be interested. Suddenly he gently took me in his arms. I felt my heart sink, for I knew that my

fate, good or bad, lay in that gesture. And yet I resisted him.
Not wanting to offend or frighten me, he tried to restrain himself. But there was something so groping in his movement, so
grayish in the tint of his complexion, as a man who had been
long confined in a darkened cell and was fumbling eagerly
toward a light, that I felt who was I to deny him what I could
easily sense he needed most—the love of a young, happy,
sympathetic girl. My affectionate nature was so stirred that
I did not hesitate.

Up to that time, I had always believed I would never make
such a decision without considerable deliberation, but in
thinking as I did, as suddenly, I realized for the first time how
differently one acts in the face of a real emotion. Still, I
wanted to set aside a day—a sort of consecrated betrothal—
no matter how brief. I do not think he knew just how to inter-
pret my hesitation. He said: "I would give *you* anything—
anything in the world that I could. If it is marriage you want,
you can have that too. I will get a divorce and marry you as
soon as it can be arranged, because I want *you*."

But I was not bargaining for anything. I told him I did not
feel that way about love. I just wanted to wait a few days.
Then I would surely come to him in complete surrender. It
was a promise. A sigh of relief escaped him and he pressed
me to name the day.

Life for me during the next few days was a state of intoxicating anticipation, and all preconceived plans of action were,
for the time, discarded. At last I had found a man whose response to beauty was deep and true. Later, I felt that he often
read more beauty into things than existed. But for this I loved
him all the more. Perhaps this gift of reading so much beauty

into life is the quality that raises the poet above the commonplace.

The end of our brief betrothal marked the beginning of a whole new world for me. During the days that followed, we could not endure being apart for more than an hour or two. If I tried to leave his studio for a few hours, I would be seized with a sharp and poignant pain, as if we were connected by a taut violin string on which every vibration registered. Relief came only when I rushed back to him. For weeks, no harmony or synchronization resulted from our relationship. Instead, there was a combustion of two forces, with some doubt as to which one was to be annihilated.

Dreiser now decided to close his New York studio and accompany me on my trip to the west coast, and while an orderly practical program of packing seemed impossible at this chaotic time, yet, in about ten days we were boarding a ship together bound for New Orleans, on our way to Los Angeles.

3

Our trip to New Orleans was a glorious experience. The weather was perfect. Every night the moon's witchery evoked an ecstatic response in us.

Upon our arrival, we found the city sweltering in a consuming heat wave, although it was now the last of September. The atmosphere was suffocating and the humidity unbearable. The streets, littered with indifferent people ambling to and fro, infected one with the languorous feeling of a southern city at the end of a long, hot and almost lifeless summer. But the charming century-old Creole homes with their exterior balconies and galleries decorated with wrought-iron railings imported from Spain in the late Eighteenth Century, and the cast-iron lace work which came in later, lent a peculiar fascination to the city. Everywhere there were flowered patios and courtyards of the most artistic and inspiring designs through which one would occasionally glimpse a window or an architectural bit that took one's breath away.

We found a room in an old-fashioned hotel in the heart of the city with a large window looking out on an enchanting square. Through the warm sultry air came the light and pleasing refrain of *Cielito Lindo*, played by an organ grinder in the street below. The romantic melody set us both reeling in an ecstasy of delight. Catching each other's hands, we danced around the room in a delirious moment of gaiety.

We were in the room only a few moments when Theodore spied a picture hanging on the wall—a colored print of an old-fashioned farm scene.

"Now that is peculiar," he said. "I haven't seen that picture since I was a small boy at home. It was a picture that mother had in her room and liked so much," he continued, as he stood studying it in an interested and affectionate manner. It was easy to see that he had loved his mother deeply. Having lost her when he was only nineteen, I think the loss of her grew on him considerably as the years went by, for she was a woman who would have understood his temperamental difficulties. When I came to know Theodore better, I often wondered what she thought of this strange child as she observed the idiosyncrasies that made him so different from the rest.

As I came to learn, Dreiser had a fear of losing anything he loved very much. And certainly this applied to his mother when he was a boy. In fact, that is probably where the fear was born. For one day when he and his younger brother Ed had been displeasing her by doing things they shouldn't have, she threatened to go away and not return. And when they continued, she suddenly started walking in the direction of an adjoining wheat field. When she had walked about a hundred feet and was well into the tall swaying stalks of wheat, she sat down so that they could no longer see her. Theodore watched and waited for a while—even called to her—but when he received no answer, nothing but the soft swish of the wheat as it gently rippled in the breeze, he suddenly went into a convulsion. When she heard his terrifying hysterical screams, she hurried back and vowed she would never repeat the experiment.

From what I have gathered from the different children of the family, she must have held them with the inspiration of a great love, which included no trace of fear. She enveloped them in it, and yet it was not the smothering type of mother love that in the end kills its young, or stifles them to the point where they fear to face life alone. On the contrary, she was the kind of woman who dared for her children to attempt the difficult—to go out into the world and do things. She strengthened them for the battle of life. Theodore has described his mother in *Dawn*, as no one else in the world ever could.

Among the many places of interest that we visited in New Orleans, was the Old Spanish Fort, where Theodore contracted a strange kind of fever from the ground on which he had been lying. That night he awakened from a sound sleep dripping with perspiration and burning with fever. The next day he was too weak to get out of bed. I called a doctor, who was evidently unable to diagnose his case. However, he said it was not malaria. I knew no one in the city to appeal to, and I felt terribly alone and helpless. Fortunately, by that time we had moved into a suite in a private residence, which made it easier for me to take care of him. I was even able to prepare the clear broths which were the only nourishment he was allowed to take. To me it seemed perfectly natural to nurse him when he was ill, but Dreiser commented on it for years afterward. He seemed to think it unusual that a girl so young could do this sort of thing so efficiently, as he put it.

He did not improve. I was baffled and very much afraid if I did not get him out of that climate he might even die. Finally I decided to get him aboard a train going north, if he could possibly make it. It seemed a dangerous thing to do, but the thought persisted, and when I told him what I had in mind, he made one final attempt to get up out of his sickbed and board a train headed for St. Louis, where we knew it would be cooler. And curiously enough, the moment we arrived in St. Louis he was entirely well, and no trace of the fever returned. We went out and bought an overcoat for him and started for the West, happy and thrilled that he was actually better and that we were going to a new land which neither of us had ever seen—Southern California.

4

California—youthful—exotic—a playground for lovers. We came like two children, hand in hand, united in a common bond—the love of beauty. What one did not see the other was quick to observe and present for approval.

As the train crossed the desert, we caught a glimpse of orange trees, the first we had ever seen. We were standing on the observation platform, when we first saw them, and they held promise of a strange and wonderful land to be explored.

On arrival, Los Angeles struck us as extremely commonplace as cities go, and after two weeks in a hotel, during which time we explored the city, we settled on the Westlake Park district as a desirable place to live. Our suite, in a very nice private home on Alvarado Street, had an attractive balcony overlooking a typical California courtyard filled with flowers and sunshine. A balcony in the sun! What could be more pleasing after being so long in New York with its canyons of brick and pavement? Dreiser opened to the sunshine like a flower confined too long in artificial lighting, and the effect of those warm rays, combined with the harmony produced by this surprisingly beautiful romance, flooded his entire being with a glow of new life which was soon reflected in his eyes and complexion.

In the evenings we often strolled through Westlake Park, and on one lovely moonlit night, as we were walking down the tree-shaded paths, I noticed there were tears in his eyes. I asked him why he was crying.

"It's all too beautiful," he said. "Why should this have come to me? Why has life given me this exquisite beauty?"

And as time went on, I noticed that every passing phase of beauty moved him to despair at its transient quality. He fairly prostrated himself before beauty in any form.

For weeks we explored far reaches of the city, by trolley, bus, or on foot, as we had no car. Streets ran for miles through meadows and out again into small developments or communities and many of the sections through which they passed were not cut through. It was not until four or five years later that most of these sections were connected by cross streets.

Perhaps we would encounter an oil field of great proportions which resembled a forest, and it might well be adjoining a residential quarter very near the civic center of the city. One or two of the major motion picture studios, as well, were centrally located but were pushed out into more open country as the city grew up around them.

I remember how a trip to the ocean then seemed like quite a journey, while today one rides on a wide boulevard past smart shops directly to the shoreline in about twenty minutes. Wilshire Boulevard then was not much more than a widened road with real estate signs posted all along the way, advertising footage at so much a front foot. Today it is a western Fifth Avenue.

On our numerous walks through the West Hollywood section, we marveled at the enormous eucalyptus trees imported from Australia, that so often looked like powerful human bodies in their nakedness as the bark stripped itself off and dropped to the ground. At times the sidewalks were literally carpeted with red peppers which had fallen from overhanging pepper trees, used at that time to shade the walks. We could not avoid crunching the peppers beneath our feet, and we could hear them pop as we trod on them.

After being together constantly for months, the day finally came when I felt the urge to investigate the possibilities of work for myself, as I had originally planned. While Dreiser understood and appreciated this desire of mine for artistic expression, he could not hide his reluctance to consent to anything that would take me away from him. He was not yet ready for a change. On this particular day, when I started to dress he came over and, affectionately laying his hand on my arm, said: "Now you are going to leave me. This is the first time we have been separated."

"Yes," I replied, "but it seems there has to be a first time for everything. Anyway, we must go forward, and this may be one of the ways."

And so I left for the afternoon, to call at a few of the studios which were scattered all over the town and had to be reached by different trolley lines. Not having any introductions, I realized that it would not be easy and probably would take a great deal of persistence. However, I felt that if I did anything at all, it would have to be done on my own, as I did not want to run the risk of spoiling my relationship with Dreiser by putting it to a single use. We decided, therefore, to keep our connection a secret, and we succeeded, except in the case of a few close friends, for all of the first three years we spent in Los Angeles.

Although I expected difficulties where I was so unknown and inexperienced, little did I realize the ramifications of the fortified studio and how little registration on their over-crowded books meant. Dreiser painted a vivid picture of the Hollywood of that day in a series of articles he wrote for *Shadowland** and *McCall's,** which created quite a stir for they presented Hollywood through the back door. Much of this data I related to him from my experiences in the movie world, for I always came home full of stories of the day.

One Sunday, on one of our customary excursions, we came across a small community called Highland Park, which we had reached via the big red car of the Pacific Electric Railway system. It was a simple little place with a cluster of ordinary stores and houses, but there was something in the quiet and peaceful atmosphere that appealed to Dreiser. We crossed a low wooden bridge spanning a small waterway which, like so many rivulets and rivers in California, had become a sandy gully. There was a rustic charm about this bridge and the *arroyo seco* over which we passed toward soft green hills in the near distance. Almost instantly, Theodore decided he would like to live there. We looked around all afternoon until we found a lower flat in a two-story house. The brown house

* *Shadowland*, November, December, 1921; January, February, 1922. *McCall's*, September, 1921.

was situated at the foot of one of the green hills, and we thought what a thrilling thing it would be to run to the top of this rolling hill in bright morning sunshine. The very thought was too appealing for deliberation and we decided at once to take it. We soon settled ourselves and our few belongings in this quaint but interesting neighborhood.

The neighborhood, however, turned out to be a fanatically religious community. Not far away, perhaps a thousand feet, was a settlement of unique character. In fact, there was an actual Ark built in the tops of the trees of the *arroyo seco* where meetings were held by members of the organization— men with long hair and beards, who wandered about the neighborhood during the day. Most of them lived in poor little houses scattered along the flats bordering the dried-up water channel. Thin domestic animals of all kinds could be seen hovering near these shacks.

Our landlord, who occupied the upper flat, did not belong to this sect but was equally fanatic in his own religion, being an active worker in one of the principal village churches. He was a small, intense man who had taken religion all the way and who wanted to do a great deal of shouting about it. Whenever we met him of a morning, he would call out loudly in his most profound tone of voice: "PRAISE THE LORD" and "I hope you are well on this, the Lord's day. PRAISED BE HIS NAME!"

Often in the midst of a conversation between Theodore and myself in the quiet of our apartment, or perhaps during working hours when he was trying to concentrate on his writing, a great shouting would reverberate throughout the house. It would be our landlord who had just received a caller and during the talk which invariably centered on religion, they had gotten "the spirit" as it were, and had become oblivious to the rest of the world.

The landlord's wife was a large, bony, physically hardened and angular woman who had probably worked hard all her life, trying to keep the family going. Her body, when she walked, swayed awkwardly to and fro as she set her heavy feet down, one after the other, with a decided firmness. Her voice startled one with its shrill, metallic, nasal quality as she called out, "Henry!" But if Henry came, he did not linger long, as he usually had to meet some fellow religionist at the corner or do something equally important.

Every Sunday morning, as regular as the clock, he could be seen scurrying to the church to ring the bell, one of his sacred and solemn privileges, which, he thought, elevated him far above the average churchgoer, to say nothing of the miserable sinner outside the fold.

There was a daughter, too, not more than fifteen years old, plain, but with a certain radiant physical self-consciousness. On seeing her come home in the evening with her mother from the laundry where they both worked, you felt that her chance to extricate herself from such a life was so slight as to be almost nonexistent. But occasionally the sheer force of her youth would break through the veil of misery and drabness and we would see her darting out with a neighbor boy, her face aflame with excitement and anticipation. Always this mood of hers caught the attention and sympathy of Dreiser, and she responded by taking advantage of every opportunity to talk with him.

While he was naturally fascinated by the youthful, vital

mood in her toward sex, which is a considerable attraction in itself, she was so removed from his standard of beauty that she was not a compelling temptation to him, personally. Still, it was interesting to note that the male instinct had been aroused enough at least to turn over in his mind, and even to voice, the possibilities in connection with her, and their probable result. I began to realize how very susceptible he was to a certain mood in the opposite sex, and for the first time felt a slight foreboding as to what might lie ahead of me should beauty be linked with this identical expression of female temperament.

Of all the households that we could have chosen, I thought this was one of the most singular, and yet, perhaps it supplied the necessary climate for the engendering of the soon-to-be-born *An American Tragedy*.

Although the new locality was definitely inconvenient for me, I occasionally went to Hollywood to make connections in the studios which I could follow up later. But I soon came to realize that we were too far away from the studios to do any good, my trip to Hollywood taking up the greater part of the day. So I gave it up for the time being and settled down to housework and typing for Dreiser. He was working on a dramatization of *The "Genius"* for Leo Ditrichstein, who was then in New York. There were letters, and more letters; typing and retyping of the play. However, after months of negotiation, the producers decided on another vehicle for their star.

I kept up my dancing, going twice a week to Theodore Kosloff's school. Natacha Rambova, who subsequently became the wife of Rudolph Valentino, was one of the teachers. Later I studied at the Italian School of Rossi for several months.

But what a joy it was to walk across the *arroyo seco* bridge through the fog which usually settled over this low spot, and up the hill on the other side to Theodore and the little flat where I always felt the heightened pulse beat of life. Life had never before seemed so beautiful.

It was during this period that I came to realize how futile the attempt for two people, no matter how much they are in love, to possess each other. The more intense the desire on both sides to become as one, the more frantic the attempt to merge one's identity in the other—the more exasperating the failure to do so. In spite of ourselves, we found that we were desperately trying to possess each other and were invariably thrust back upon our own individualities. I think now that if this oneness ever takes place between two people it is the outgrowth of a physical and spiritual union developing over a period of years of association; the desire to be or to draw from the other those qualities which appeal to us most, compelling us to take a different form and coloring as time passes. However, I think this is a subconscious desire ever present where real love exists: "As thou desirest me, so shall I be."

One day I brought home a lovely tortoiseshell kitten someone sold me, which soon became a major member of the household. She was the most appealing little kitten I ever had and would perform a number of cute tricks that made us love her. For instance, she had an endearing way of standing up to look at herself in the long mirror on the back of one of the doors. But instead of being a nice mild little Persian cat, as we thought, she was a devil, spending most of the day quarreling with the mockingbirds. She would creep along one of the horizontal clothesline rails stretching between upright poles in the yard, and when she reached a dangerously exposed and helpless position, they would swoop down on her, striking her on the back so hard that she would scream for help. And then the mockingbirds would scold back at her as only a mockingbird can. But if she were the conqueror, she would bring one back in her mouth and proudly place it on the back porch for our observation and approval! How could she know that Dreiser made a bird sanctuary out of every garden, large or small, that he ever had! He would scatter breadcrumbs for them all through the winter months, whether it was in some small back yard adjoining an apartment in New York City, or on the ledges and cornices of a hotel in which he might be wintering.

And so we lived for months with work, play, wandering over the hills at the back of the house, laughing at the funny long-haired religionists, reading to each other, and gathering the sweetness of life.

I remember one particular late afternoon—one of those dreamlike evenings that seem to settle down so often in and around Los Angeles. The clear, blue sky, the undulating hills, the stillness blended perfectly with a mood simultaneously harmonious in both of us. We were walking along the ridge of one of the hills, when, of a sudden, floating on the quiet evening air, we heard singing. It was a kind of chant, and, as we looked down the slope into a little pocket between hills, we saw some picturesque Japanese figures, women and men, singing as they worked. It was spellbinding, seeing these little figurines, so happy in their work as they moved rhythmically to and fro, the warm golden glow of a fading sun lingering on them as it began to disappear over the top of one of the hills. And Teddie, caught by the mood of the scene, running to me and taking my hand in his, saying with a sob in his voice: "I shall never leave you, Helen! Never!"

It was a promise I took to my heart to be remembered in my saddest hours. It was the nearest thing to a promise that he ever made me; it sprang purely from his heart, and I could not resist locking it in mine, forever.

5

After a few months we moved back to Hollywood. We had found an attractive front suite in a large white stucco house on the southeast corner of Larchmont Boulevard and Clinton, within walking distance of Hollywood and Vine, which was then, as now, the center of the movie colony.

Here, for the first time, we were in the very heart of moviedom, which encompassed romance, illusion and mystery. Just to be in the neighborhood of such centers of activity seemed to shed a bewitching light on all that we saw and heard. Even Maurice Maeterlinck, the famous Belgian poet, was our close neighbor and often could be seen walking past our house with his very young wife.

I anticipated the adventure of going into this world and learning something of it, of rubbing shoulders with famous stars. Better yet, I would come in contact with all sorts of people, an experience out of which I would gather color, romance and drama. Theodore seemed as interested as I, in all this—maybe more so, for he wanted me to enter this world, to win for myself what I could. In my round of visits to the studios, my costume depended somewhat on the part I was applying for, as I soon learned that one had to study the classification of parts, and, to a certain extent, how to dress for them.

After working as an extra for a couple of months, I made a number of acquaintances and discovered that one of the best casting directors in Hollywood was a man I had known in the past as a booking agent. He gave me small parts to play, and I soon found myself being called for special type casting. I started out at $7.50 a day, and at the end of the first year I was being paid $20.00 a day and thought I was doing pretty well. I was dressed and made up for the set by eight o'clock in the morning. This meant that I had to arise at six o'clock, for I had no car. Theodore watched this consistent procedure with the most intense interest and curiosity. To me it seemed the natural thing to do, if I were going to do it at all; but to him it seemed wonderful and he talked about it for years.

The interest and drama of it all absorbed me, and many a night when I arrived home after working all day in the studio, I could hardly eat my dinner. There was such excitement, such tension in the presence of so many personalities on one lot at the same time, each with his particular interests, habits, love affairs, ambitions.

Many of the extras accepted their lot as just another day's work, as any laborer might. Some had worked in the movies for years and no longer hoped for anything more. If they had the good fortune to receive a consecutive week's work, they considered themselves more than lucky. And yet some of them were exceptionally clever and versatile. But they had been seen around the studios too long and were shelved forever as extras.

The leading ladies, many of them ex-Follies girls, received as much as $500 or more a week. Competition was so great that most of their salaries had to be spent in trying to keep up a certain standard; yet they seldom advanced any further, eventually being replaced by younger girls. Many became disillusioned and hardened. Once in a while luck smiled on one and she would suddenly become a star. But it did not happen to many. Most of them lived in the sun for a day and then disappeared.

It was not very different with most of the directors. Some of them showed great promise, and perhaps after a fine picture would be on their way to independence and freedom of individual expression. Then, after doing two or three good pictures, they would find themselves classified or pigeon-holed for a certain type of work, never getting another chance to do anything really outstanding. Instead, they received salaries as staff directors when finally their initiative and inspiration were gone. Some of these directors were men of considerable ability and creative force. To watch a good director work was the greatest experience of all for me: Victor Schertzinger, Fred Niblo, Frank Lloyd, Rex Ingram, Allan Dwan; and the stars of the day: Mabel Normand, Douglas Fairbanks, Rudolph Valentino, Lillian Gish, Alan Hale, Bebe Daniels, Charles Ray and a host of others.

At this time we moved again, to a little brown stucco bungalow on Sunset and Detroit Streets. It was hardly large enough for Dreiser to turn around in. He wrote every day in the tiny living room or in the little breakfast nook while I worked in the studios. But every free moment we took off to explore the surrounding country by foot and on streetcars: Glendale, Pasadena, the beaches north and south. Occasionally we rode horseback in Griffith Park.

It was at this period that I noticed in Dreiser a definite poverty complex. Although he had already written *The Financier* and *The Titan*, and had some years before been editor-in-chief of the Butterick publications at a large salary, he believed that money would never come to him in a big way. He wanted money for the freedom and privileges it would bestow on him, but he persistently held to the belief that this kind of money was not for him.

One day, in reply to his comment that everyone in California seemed to own a car, and how delightful it would be to have one, I said: "Well, most of them aren't paid for. They'll be worn out before they are; don't you know that?" My experience with Mr. Woodward and the Industrial Finance Corporation, in the financing of washing machines, refrigerators, automobiles, etc., had taught me this. But this was not his way, he said; he had always paid cash, as his father before him had, and guessed he always would.

"Well, someday I'll drive up to our front door in a car!" I announced, half-jokingly. "I don't know exactly how I'll get it, but I'll get it!"

"I wouldn't be surprised," he said, wonderingly. "That's the way you'd do it, all right."

And that's the way I did do it a very few weeks later. I found a little 1917 Overland club car, with seating capacity for four, for only $385. It was green with red wire wheels.

The day I appeared with the car, Teddie heard a loud honking as I tried desperately to drive it into the garage, a feat I found impossible because of a slight curve in the driveway. Whenever I stepped on the starter, the car lurched forward, making such a noise that a neighbor had to come out to inform me that I was trying to start the car in gear. Up to that time, the only knowledge of driving I possessed was the principle of gear shifting which I had observed as a passenger in other cars. I hadn't even a license to drive a car, and I didn't know when I left the car lot how I would ever get across an intersection alive. But Teddie came out to the curb with surprise and delight. And then, of course, I was determined to show him that I could drive it, although it took me two days to make the garage.

To get control of a car with Theodore Dreiser giving directions with typical Dreiserian emphasis at every turn in the road was almost an impossibility. I was kept so busy defending myself from his suggestions at every traffic problem which presented itself that I soon became discouraged.

"Look out! For God's sake, don't you see that man?" he would scream. "Why don't you turn to the right? Now you go to the left. Now you can go ahead."

Occasionally when I would explain that it was difficult for me to concentrate when he made remarks, he would try to sit quietly. He would even smile in an attempt to make me feel confident, but I was too nervous with Dreiser sitting in such proximity. I shall never forget one evening when he, my sister Myrtle, who was visiting us, and I were riding along quietly down the main street of Glendale, which had an elevated car line running along the center of the street. A train two blocks away blew a long shrill blast in our ears. In the quiet of the night, it almost deafened me. And as I was trying to cross the elevated track, Teddie yelled at the top of his voice: "Look out for the train."

Instantly I thought the train was upon us and suddenly wheeled the car around in a circle over the embankment, almost turning it over. The car stalled on the bank, heading downward. Dreiser immediately fumbled with the door handle, trying to get out as he shouted: "For God's sake, let me out of this damned death trap. What are you trying to do? You'll never learn to drive a car."

By this time, seeing him safe on the ground, I began to laugh hysterically and could not restrain myself. There he stood, saying that he would walk home and stay on the ground from that time on. It was then that I asked my sister to take the car and drive it and when I had recovered my poise I would take it over and drive it with no further interference from anyone, especially Dreiser. He finally came to realize that I meant exactly what I said; from then on there was no more front seat screaming.

Later, the little Overland was traded in for a new Maxwell, which eventually evolved into a nine passenger Imperial 80 Chrysler, in which we toured the States and Canada, north, south, east and west. But no automobile tours were happier or more delightful than those first ones in the little Overland.

The first time I encountered the full force of Teddie's wrath was in our little bungalow on Sunset and Detroit Streets. One day, suddenly without the slightest warning, dark clouds gathered on the horizon of his countenance, passed and repassed; then a flash of lightning and a peal of thunder that seemed to shake the house to its foundation. And as the force of his anger reached an unbearable pitch, he grabbed his coat and, cramming his hat well down over his forehead, rushed out of the house, slamming the door so hard I thought it would break.

The whole thing started over a triviality, as most of our later quarrels did, but I was left trembling with weakness before the outburst. I could scarcely realize what had happened. I only knew I was stunned with the realization of what I might experience in the future, and yet was tortured by the thought that he might not come back.

However, after several hours he returned, calm and controlled as though nothing had happened. He had gone for a long walk, which had clarified his thoughts. Now he was himself again. But I had felt the electric charge and decided then and there that as little of it as possible would be agreeable to me. I was young and compellingly attractive to him, so he was more than willing to forget the episode as quickly as possible. I must dress and we would go out for a ride. Anxious to mend things between us, I put on my most attractive dress and off we went.

We decided to drive to Pasadena, and as we passed through Glendale, we were taken with its homelike quality and nearness to Hollywood. Teddie suggested that Glendale might be a pleasant place in which to live. So we drove up one street and down another, finally coming upon a charming white cottage with green shutters, adjoining a large vacant corner lot. Looking up the agent, we were informed that the house and lot could be had for $4,500; $1,000 down and the balance payable at $50 a month. As we were then paying $90 a month for our tiny house in Hollywood, this impressed us as an attractive proposition. Consequently, two weeks later Dreiser's investment of $600 and mine of $400 secured the house and ground for us. Having no furniture, we purchased a bedroom suite, but we lived in the little house a year before the living room was furnished. The kitchen, being mostly built in, included a small breakfast nook which nestled into one corner. This was where Teddie loved to sit and write. I often wondered what his New York friends would have thought to see him writing down his cosmic thoughts in that tiny nook. He was working on *Moods*, his book of philosophic poems; *Newspaper Days; The Color of a Great City;* and beginning *An American Tragedy.* He was trying to substitute this last for *The Bulwark*, for which his publisher, Horace Liveright, had contracted and was impatiently waiting.*

Here it was that he took a special interest in gardening, planting the corner lot with zinnias which he nursed along like a mother with a large brood of children. And soon a horned toad appeared from somewhere and Teddie made a pet of him. Each day the toad would come out and follow him around as he moved about the garden. Many an evening, as I turned into the driveway, tired from being in the studio all day, I would see Teddie working with the flowers, which seemed to feel the love he extended to them and produced the most beautiful blooms. In fact, they were so unusually attractive that several of the neighbors used to come and exchange opinions with him about the care of them. It seemed to me

* Dreiser-Liveright correspondence regarding this change is now at the University of Pennsylvania.

that his mother's temperament was expressing itself through him, for so much of the time he was like a big warm grandmother, and I never tired of marveling at this gracious side of his personality.

Our life together in Glendale was an interlude of harmony and contentment. We reveled in our solitude, and as I could plainly see, he was not inclined to welcome any intrusions. When friends came to Los Angeles from New York, he would meet them downtown. He maintained a post office box address (P. O. Box 181) at the main office in Los Angeles, where we drove every other day or so to pick up his accumulated mail. Even when his good friend J. G. Robin, author of *Caius Gracchus*, written under the pseudonym of Odin Gregory, came from New York to ask him to write an introduction for this distinguished book, Dreiser met him in the city. I did not meet Robin until several years later in New York.

By then I was doing rather well in the movies, and we turned our Overland in for a new Maxwell. Soon we were touring all over—Mexico, La Jolla, Coronado, Santa Barbara, Yosemite, Portland, Seattle, British Columbia, etc. Dreiser was becoming conscious of a new horizon and was expanding, developing new tastes and attaining a new growth. I could not analyze these things, but I sensed them with an instinctive understanding of what they meant to him, for I was held to him by a magnetism that drew its power from his need for me, which likewise became my need for him. "And love that need is, and would love its need."*

* Theodore Dreiser, "To A Wood Dove" from *Moods* (New York: Boni & Liveright, 1926).

6

The picture in which I was working at the time was scheduled to go to San Francisco on location. Naturally, I had to leave with the company. A few days later came a letter from Teddie, arriving almost simultaneously with Teddie himself, enthusiastic to see San Francisco with me.

Following is the letter I received from Teddie:

Yes, I felt lost after the train pulled out.

Yes, at two A.M. and at three, I wondered if you were awake or sleeping.

Yes, the bed was very lone and cold,—no one to plaster me warm.

Yes, I sighed heavily.

Yes, I'm sighing now.

Yes, I'm going to work to try to forget.

You said it.

I say it.

I mean it.   Wednesday, April 20, 1921.

To My Golden Girl:

What's the good of anything in this burg now?

Nix.

And are we downhearted?

We are.

The sun riseth and setteth, but, it cuts no ice.

The days are just one gloomy hour after another.

I get up at eight A.M.—reformed time.

I fry my mush.

I make my own coffee, such as it is.

I dry my own dishes and polish my own spoons.

What's the good of anything?

Nix.

What's the good of anything since my baby's gone away?

Nix.

Yesterday I wrote one chapter.

I cussed out the telegraph co. because it didn't bring
me a message sooner.

I went to the store and bought me a loaf of bread.

I went to the store and bought me a bottle of milk.

I went to the store and bought me a bottle of malted milk.

What's the good of anything?

Nix.

What's the good of anything now that Helen ain't here?

Nix.

I read the morning paper in silence.

I talked to Myrtle over the phone. (Her call.)

I went to the P.O.

I went to a lousy movie.

I walked far west on Seventh, just to kill time.

I hated to enter the lonely house.

I ducked into bed and listened to a mocking bird talking
all night in a tree.

I wondered how my girl was making out and what she
was really doing.

I said:

What's the good of anything.

Nix.

Oh, nix, oh, nix, oh, nix, oh, nix.
Oh, nix, oh, nix, oh, nix, oh, nix.
Oh, nix, oh, nix, oh, nix, oh, nix.
Oh, nix, oh, nix, oh, nix, oh, nix.

Oh, nix, oh, nix.

Oh, nix, oh, nix.

Oh, nix.

TEDDY D

We stayed at the St. Francis Hotel, where shortly after our arrival George Sterling called on us. He was a tall beautiful person with gray hair carefully arranged over his forehead to cover some imaginary defect, so he said, but framing in a most effective way his lovely face, the duplicate of one that might have graced an old Greek coin—sensitive, exquisitely molded in its classic lines, poignant, childlike. I felt as I looked at him that he was the embodiment of all poetry. His mind, juxtaposed with that of Dreiser's, seemed to soar to the utmost peaks of abstract thought, and irrespective of what they were discussing—literature, sculpture, life, science, philosophy, astronomy, art or any other subject—the height was sustained for hours. Here were two minds in genuine accord in their esthetic perception. As young and inexperienced as I was, I found, much to my delight, that in the midst of such brilliant conversations, I understood the essence of all that was said and was able to follow them in their flights of imagination. To this day, the recollection of having sat between Sterling and Dreiser during several intense discussions stands as the most thrilling intellectual experience of my early life.

Sterling had a room at the Bohemian Club in San Francisco, where he was looked upon as an honored and permanent guest, and because he was invited out so much of the time, his expenses were very low. Still, when anyone like Dreiser came to town, he hastened to some chef with whom he was personally acquainted, persuading him to prepare some particular dish for which he was famous, and although he may have been indebted to the man for past favors, he received the choicest service. Each dish was a masterpiece, and Sterling radiated with pride at his own worth as an epicure. And well he might have!

One evening Sterling insisted that we go to Taits at the beach. On the way back, about three o'clock in the morning, we passed through Golden Gate Park, over which hung one of San Francisco's very own dense salt-laden fogs. In driving through the park, we came upon a lily pond and were so enthralled with its beauty that we stopped the car to look at it. Immediately, Sterling leaped out of the car, announcing he was going to gather some of the lilies for me. Undressing on the bank, he plunged into the pool, his beautiful slender body moving rhythmically through the water with ease and grace. And as his long, thin, shapely hands reached out here and there to pluck each lily, he made a living moving picture that one could never forget. It was like a water dance that Nijinsky or Shankar or Mei Lan-fang might have dreamed up. Unfortunately, a prowling policeman broke in on the scene determined to investigate such unconventional goings-

53

on, but when Sterling identified himself, we were released. The next day a newspaper headline announced: "George Sterling Gathers Lilies in Golden Gate Park for Beautiful Lady at Dawn."

A few days later, I became ill at the hotel, suffering from a slight stomach disorder probably brought on by the nervous tension incident to my picture work. It was Sterling who insisted that I consult a friend of his, a Doctor Abrams, who was creating quite a stir with his experiments in electric vibrations to combat disease. He made the diagnoses from blood of the patients and his electrical machine did the rest. It was set for a certain vibration, so he said, to offset the disease vibration, after which the patient would take a regular course of treatments. The electric wave, being of high frequency, caused no sensation, no pain or heat, and patients all over the country were being treated with these machines. Abrams had a tremendous following; his patients were almost worshipful in their attitude toward him and believed that only in his presence and by his method lay any hope of recovery for them. There were also many physicians, osteopaths, chiropractors and practitioners of various kinds studying the technique of working with his machine.

Dreiser went with me to Abrams' office. The moment Abrams entered I was impressed with his amazing energy and vibrant personality. He was of medium build, and as he moved about the room, his manner was punctuated by quick, sure movements. After submitting ourselves to the machine, we were told that I had sarcoma in some form or another, and that Teddie had tuberculosis. I never believed either diagnosis. Still, on returning to Los Angeles, we took a course of treatments and thought we had been helped. A few years later Teddie had a thorough examination at the Mayo Clinic, where they assured him that no trace of tubercular germ existed in his entire system, although there was a trace of scar tissue from the early stages of a serious condition which developed when he was only seventeen years of age, while working in the basement of Hibbard, Spencer, Bartlett and Company of Chicago. His job consisted mostly of the dusty task of bin-cleaning, which was telling on his lungs. His old teacher of Warsaw days, Miss Mildred Fielding, rescued him from a possible sorry fate, insisting that he quit his job at once and go to the University of Indiana at her expense. What a wonderful thing for a schoolteacher to have done!

Although Abrams was denounced by most of the leading doctors and scientists of standing, he died a few years later leaving a large sum of money to his cause. I encountered him only this one time, but never forgot the effect he produced on me.

I returned to the hotel. While I was confined to bed, one of our most pleasant experiences came to us in the appearance of the two Powys boys. The door opened and in walked the incomparable John Cowper Powys, with his equally distin-guished brother, Llewelyn, at his heels.

It would be useless for me to attempt to describe John Cowper Powys. To appreciate him, one must know him in person, and contact his mind and extraordinary reactions to life, so cosmically and psychically old and yet so eternally young was he. To see him—his swift, smoothly rhythmic movements as he walked along, cane in hand, head up; leav-ing the lecture room after an inspired and brilliant lecture on

Goethe or Shakespeare, Spengler, Conrad, Dreiser; or in an old deserted Indian cemetery, against the sky or trees as an appropriate background for his rare profile—was something never to be forgotten. Each tree he passed on his daily walks through the woods—with his black cocker spaniel, "The Very Old," as he named him—was a special symbolic landmark to Jack. One group of trees was his beloved Tintern Abbey, another Stonehenge, still another Glastonbury.

We often saw him sitting at rest, his hands and chin on his heavy crooked walking stick. His little home, "Phudd's Bottom" as he liked to call the bottom of the hill where it was situated near Hillsdale, New York, and in which he lived for several years before leaving the United States for good to return to his birthplace in North Wales, was in the center of three graveyards—one Lutheran, one Baptist, and one supposedly Indian. The Indian graveyard is situated on the flat at the top of a hill where rows and rows of crude heaps of large stones are piled to high peaks. The front row, as Jack imagined it, was made up of the graves of the big chieftains, while the others were scattered here and there over the plateau. And as he contemplated the existence of the departed chieftains, he would suddenly burst into poetry which, as he stood with arms extended in exaltation, he seemed to hurl into space.

The little house seemed to ramble along, one room after another, with two bedrooms upstairs. The general furnishings were early American, and the atmosphere, as well as the character of the house, reminded me of Edgar Allan Poe's cottage at Fordham, New York, where he lived so simply with his beloved "Annabel Lee." And in Jack's little "Phudd's

Bottom" home, he, too, had his Annabel Lee, in the person
of Phyllis—sensitive, sympathetic, intellectual, moving about
in her quaint dresses that accentuated an exquisitely delicate
charm, and permeating the entire atmosphere with tenderness,
genuine love and understanding. Here they worked together,
read books together, planted a beautiful garden and were
extremely happy.

When I first met him that day in San Francisco, he had
been traveling and lecturing alone for several years and I
marveled at the way in which he adjusted himself to hard,
practical, commercial cities. However, just then he was very
happy to be with his charming brother Llewelyn, whom he
loved dearly.

Llewelyn presented a strange contrast to Jack, although
anyone would have instantly recognized them as brothers.
Llewelyn was like a beautiful and trusting child; he had
wonder-loving eyes, and his head was covered with curls that
always looked blond to me although actually they were half
blond and half gray. He was much more the realist than his
brother John, for he wrote such books as *Black Laughter*,
Ebony and Ivory, *A Pagan's Pilgrimage*, *Apples Be Ripe*,
Skin for Skin, *Earth Memories*, and his last, *Love and Death*,
one of the most remarkable books I ever read. In this he
describes all the sensations and thoughts of a dying man who
had a rare zest for every second of life, and yet who fully
realized he was doomed. It is full of love, beauty and tragedy.
Llewelyn's outstanding quality was his intense love of life;
yet, suffering from tuberculosis, he knew he could not live
long.

John was an old soul who possibly had lived for centuries.

I felt sometimes that his spirit was familiar with much that was evil, and that no order of black magic existed that had not been open to him. Despite this feeling that he might have lived through all the forms of evil and acquired certain mystic knowledge, he had evolved through evil to good; his heart was kind toward people and he loved the simple folk. He told me once that on his long walks through the countryside surrounding any city where he happened to be lecturing, he enjoyed talking with the farmers; each one, he said, had his own individual philosophy based on certain truths he had gathered up for himself. It was from these people that he learned about the beauty of simplicity and the tranquility of the soul. And so, after passing through a whole cycle of experience, it was to the simple peasant or uneducated farmer that he went for inspiration.

But to appreciate John Cowper Powys one must read his books or hear him on the lecture platform, where his brilliant mind ran the gamut of sensibilities. To hear him lecture was an experience. I recall one particular evening when his subject was Shakespeare; one felt Shakespeare materializing before the audience as Powys brought out and elucidated certain attributes of the man himself. Jack possessed a fluidity of spirit that enveloped his subject so completely, that, for the time being, he became the person on whom he lectured.

A few days later, we visited the home of George Douglas and his wife, at Burlingame, where many artists, writers, editors, newspaper men and all sorts of interesting people made up an exciting and exhilarating evening. George Douglas, a great storyteller, editor, writer and most distinguished man of culture, became one of Dreiser's closest and dearest friends through the years that followed.

Before leaving San Francisco, we went to the home of Henry von Sabern and his wife Mary, where we met Gustav Frenssen. Having recently read his *Jorn Uhl* and *Hilligenlei,* I thought he looked as sensitive and poetic as his books. Von Sabern gave a large dinner party at his home, where George Sterling read a few of his own poems, shedding tears over the beauty of some of the phrases.

Mary von Sabern was a dancer of distinction. A student of Sanskrit, she was familiar with ancient forms of art, which she interpreted in her dances. Her pet snake "Alice" was about eight feet in length and roamed freely about the house. When I, like most people, displayed fear, Mary said: "Now, Helen, you will lose your fear of this snake, and all snakes, if you will only touch it and look into its eyes. Most people think a snake is cold, slimy and repulsive, but you will see. Put your hand on it."

She brought Alice over to me and I reached out, timidly touching the snake. To my surprise, it felt like a beautiful shell. I then looked straight into its eyes. I will never forget the delicate, fluttering sensitivity of those eyes as they looked up at me. In that look I felt the plight of all snakedom in being feared and hated throughout the world.

"You see, Alice," I thought to myself, "it pays to be a vamp even in the reptile realm, for with a single look, see what you did to one person, for all the snakes in the world."

On leaving San Francisco, we motored north to Vancouver, stopping on the way to visit my mother in Portland. When

Theodore and my mother met for the first time, he spoke to me about the quiet strength he saw in her, and my mother felt at once familiar contrasting elements in Theodore's nature which were not unlike those of her own mother: the quick energy, strength, humanitarian warmth, bohemian vivacity—temperamental traits I had adored in my grandmother and now found in him.

He was fascinated with the countryside and wandered off on short excursions, finally going as far as Seattle, while I visited with my mother. When he returned, he told me he had been experiencing a strong desire to write an "entirely different kind of novel, a philosophical novel," and someday he would do it.

We returned to California by way of Yosemite Park. At that time the roads were poor and we were compelled to drive up 22 percent grades over rough one-way roads. Soon we were home again in our little white cottage with the green shutters and awnings supported by spears. (We once heard a little boy say in passing: "Mmmm! Them's the real spears, them are.") We kept little window boxes with Japanese lilies that many people inquired about because they were always in bloom. People were always asking where we got them and how we kept them blooming—questions that pleased Teddie, for he then knew that the pink, yellow and blue artificial lilies were a great success.

By now, my struggle to pursue a separate career was becoming more and more difficult. I had worked up to the point where I was being considered for fairly important roles; in fact, one was a leading role in a Douglas Fairbanks picture. With these increasing opportunities came increasing social contacts in the movie world. It was impossible to avoid them. Then, too, I was young, and the desire for excitement was strong within me, even though I knew in my heart that compared to my life with Dreiser, everything else was thin and colorless.

So one day, when a certain casting director chided me for my foolishness in refusing invitations to parties and otherwise holding myself aloof from social contacts, I wondered if he might not be right.

"If you want to be in pictures, why don't you play the game?" he asked. "Why hide yourself away where nobody can find you? You have the face, the form and the temperament to get somewhere in pictures if you'd only cultivate the right people."

What could I say? I knew it was all true, but I was under a spell. I walked around, dressed up, went to work and really took an energetic part in things, but the major part of my heart and mind was at home. What was Teddie doing now? Was he lonely? Did he miss me? What was he writing? Was he able to work today? I really should be there doing something for him. Still, he wanted me to continue with my movie work. He had said so over and over. And if I did it for no other reason than to please him, I must go on with it. But how could I be wholly interested in a field where so much lack of artistic understanding prevailed? My mind was now revolving in a world of dreams, of which the outward boundaries were Teddie himself. Yet, he had told me many times that he did not want me to devote myself entirely to his work.

The more I contemplated the casting director's admonition, the more I became convinced that I should try it.

It was not long after this that I received an invitation to a large party given by the director of the picture on which I was working. To refuse this invitation would have attracted the attention of everyone on the lot, so I accepted.

The party turned out to be a gala affair—with an elaborate dinner, musicians, dancing, singing, etc. The particular director involved, having become interested in me during the picture engagement, paid considerable attention to me at the party. Being extremely successful in his work, he could not conceive of a young ambitious girl not welcoming the attention of a man of his caliber, and failure to secure any satisfactory information as to my home life merely increased his interest.

The evening passed quickly and it was five o'clock in the morning when I drove up to our house, to be greeted by Teddie's unrestrained anger and jealousy. He was beside himself and threatened to teach me a lesson, which he did by leaving the house and remaining away for two days. That, for me, was the end of any such experiment in social life outside our own limited circle. It was too late. While Teddie thought he preferred me to create a life of my own, I think it was about the last thing he really wanted.

Over all this was the ever-present shadow of inevitable change. But why worry about change until it comes? I asked myself. Live and love. I did not know in those days what restraint in love meant, as in art, adding beauty to beauty, and Teddie was no one to teach me the charm of such restraint. He only knew how to live to the fullest, love to the fullest, and change or move on. I was determined to be different, and even then, I was reaching for something beyond my grasp.

We were now much better off financially than we had been. I had sold several lots in the Montrose section, which I had purchased out of my earnings in the movies, for a cash profit of $1,000 each. This astonished Teddie and made him feel that I was something of a financial wizard. Although this was a common occurrence for many people at the time, it was a thrill to have it happen to us.

Before we realized it, the summer of 1922 had almost passed. Teddie was becoming noticeably restless and wanted to return to New York in order to secure a new contract for his latest novel. Instead of *The Bulwark* as originally contracted for, the novel was to be *An American Tragedy*. He had already finished twenty chapters and wanted to explain personally to Horace Liveright why he had switched to *An American Tragedy*, a book for which he had great expectations.

Also, he wanted to travel through New York state, to visit the actual scene where the murder of Grace Brown by Chester Gillette, the case on which the novel was based, had been perpetrated.

The decision was final; there was no other way. We would have to discard our little home and move eastward. I knew that New York meant change, and I was afraid of change; yet I realized that Dreiser belonged to the world, not to me alone. As for my picture career, I knew I should stay in California and Teddie agreed on the wisdom of this. But the movies had no real hold on me. I longed to develop spiritually, mentally and artistically. Where, I thought, could I do this better than at the side of so great a man as Dreiser? Not for a moment did I hesitate, and I had no regrets then or afterward, with the exception of grieving for the little house for a while—the little Dutch kitchen in which he wrote so many days, the flower garden, the thrill of hanging a picture together.

Every day for a month before we left I said goodbye to all these little things, until the time arrived in October when we actually pulled out of Los Angeles, bringing to a close three of the happiest years of my life.

7

Having leased the little house for a year and placed it for sale, we found ourselves on the way to New York. My mind was ready to meet the required change; my heart was not. But Los Angeles lacked mental stimuli at that time, and one missed the advantages of contacts—interesting and challenging—to be found in New York. True, we had lived three wonderful years together, but we both felt a change was needed. New York did not mean to me what it did to Dreiser. My personality was in the forming stage and I found myself protesting against the commercial hardness of the big city, which cut into my vulnerable self. I longed to escape for periods of time to regenerate. These problems probably weighed too heavily, but I decided I would do my best to meet them as they presented themselves.

Dreiser was facing New York in a different mood. Having been cut off from that metropolis for three years—willingly and agreeably nevertheless—he had found much that was becoming too congenial for his contradictory and restless nature. The sun shone too much—there were too many people from Iowa. He needed again to feel the sharper conflict of life which had always been stimulating to his mind and his work. The struggles, for instance, that were reflected in the faces of people in a large city. The combat!

It was obvious from his attitude and consideration of everything relating to us that he wanted me to believe in him —"our dream" as he called it, and I was willing to follow and try. While I could not imagine his going back altogether to his old life, yet I felt he would to a degree, still holding on to me mentally and spiritually for he knew no substitute then for our life together and did not wish to give up the wonderful thing we had found. But the urge to continue searching was there, and this was his compulsion through life.

Upon our arrival in New York we went to the Latham Hotel on Twenty-eighth Street near Fifth Avenue. The first thing Dreiser did was to order a rocking chair sent up to his room, and as we listened to the chimes of Madison Square Garden, we tried to forget everything but our main objective —his writing of *An American Tragedy*.

Our first problem was to secure a studio for him in which he could work quietly, and after looking around for about two weeks, he decided on the parlor floor of Number 16 St. Luke's Place. The next step was to get his furniture out of storage and arrange everything as he wanted it. The new quarters consisted of a large front studio adjoining a combination sitting room and bedroom with folding doors between. The neighborhood turned out to be anything but quiet at night, although the days were better.

For my own living quarters, I located a small apartment in West Fiftieth Street where I could continue with my vocal studies, which I had started when I was very young. The singing teacher of my choice was an interesting woman, half gypsy, possessing a powerful strength and hypnotic eye. Having studied the methods of Marchesi and other famous teachers, she knew something of pure bel canto which she was able to impart to her pupils. I worked with her for six months, during which time she did as much toward helping me gain a perspective on my emotional life as she did for my voice. I had told her nothing about Dreiser, but it did not take her long to realize she was encountering a powerful influence reflected in me. One day I would sing very freely, happily expressing myself. Another day I would come in hardly able to stand, hazy and confused. This exhaustion emanated from Theodore, his mood about me or his temporary abandonment of me, or so I imagined, which seemed to rob me of my strength. One afternoon in the middle of a lesson, she paused in her instructions to tell me that no human being in the world should be allowed to hold direct influence over another. She then asked: "Don't you consider it more important to be able to sway thousands rather than one man somewhere?"

"Yes," I said, "I suppose so." But, I thought, she did not know Theodore. She did not know that to touch him was to touch life itself in a very large sense. And I am sure she never realized how much she helped me through this period of adjustment, or how I welcomed her help, although I fell far short of controlling the emotional pull of Theodore which absorbed so much of my energy.

But there were influences at work in Dreiser's life as well. In circulating and meeting people, he had become involved in several light attachments which eventually narrowed down to one serious emotional entanglement, and a real triangle developed. We were both deeply troubled as it progressed, yet avoided discussing it. I doubled my efforts to concentrate on my singing, for I was trying now with all my will to make a life of my own, and even considered breaking with him permanently in order to survive.

However, he kept in close touch with me. We dined together often, and sometimes I could not resist following him to what we then called "home." Possibly the next day the other woman would be there with him, and it seemed almost more than I could bear. But time went on and I did not die.

Once I thought I would test myself. I stayed away from him for three weeks and would not answer my telephone. It rang again and again at night and I knew it was Dreiser calling. Later he told me that he had walked in my neighborhood just to be near me. But after the three weeks were over, there was the inevitable coming together again with more force than ever. I felt as though I had been taking a strong drug for a few years and life without it was torture. I craved to see him so much of the time, and when I did see him I was plagued with memories and doubts. And so our relationship fluctuated back and forth like the waves of the sea—moments of closeness when we realized an exquisite beauty that seemed to sweep everything unlike itself into nothingness, and other moments of darkness that seemed to span the universe.

One night, when I had not seen Theodore for a while, my phone rang about two o'clock in the morning. Teddie's voice, low and muffled, came over the wire: "Come right down. I need you."

I was terribly frightened and sprang out of bed and into my clothes as quickly as possible.

When I arrived at his studio, I found him lying on his day-bed apparently unconscious. I was terrified. He lay there as if the outer shell or personality had dropped from him. He opened his eyes and I felt I was looking at the real Dreiser without personality covering or consciousness, a significance, however, that I did not fully grasp until the next morning. What arrested my attention was the indescribable softness of his gaze as he looked at me in a trusting and admiring way; my hair, my eyes, my mouth, as though he knew it all too well but was looking at me for the first time. I saw such love and tenderness in his expression. Somehow it was this experience that convinced me beyond all written or spoken words that he did care for me deeply, and no matter how cruel he was to me later, I always returned in my memory to this moment.

I did not realize that he wasn't fully conscious when I started asking him questions, because he gave such clear and prompt replies. I thought he was paralyzed in body while his mind was normal.

"How did you ever get home, and where were you?" I asked.

He said he had been at a party at Carl Van Vechten's and had been brought home. Every question that I asked him was answered promptly until the full story was revealed. After going around the corner to a drug store to obtain something to sober him, I got him into his pajamas with difficulty as he was completely paralyzed. He then lapsed into a deep sleep.

The next morning he awakened perfectly normal. He was extremely surprised to see me there, for he did not remember one thing about calling me the night before, which I thought strange. How did he remember the telephone number in such a condition, I asked myself. And when I went through the questions of the night before, and in about the same order, I received precisely the same answers, with no least deviation. I thought about this for days—the revelatory quality of his look that night, his attitude toward me! I was sure that at this moment I had been closer to him than I had ever been to any human being in my life, and no heartache could ever efface that moment when I had looked into his very soul. It was as though some secret had been revealed to give me the courage to carry on.

8

One day in June, Teddie phoned me to say he was taking a trip to upper New York state to gather more data for *An American Tragedy*, and did I wish to go along? If so, we would drive the Maxwell car which we had shipped to New York from Los Angeles. Of course I wanted to go.

We packed our things and were soon on our way through New Jersey, northward along the Delaware River toward Port Jervis, Monticello, Cortland, Utica and Herkimer County, up into the lake section, where the actual crime of Chester Gillette and Grace Brown, on which the story of *An American Tragedy* was based, had taken place in 1906, seventeen years before.

Theodore had already described to me how and why he had finally chosen the Chester Gillette-Grace Brown case for the framework of his story, after pondering for many years over various cases which presented the psychological problem he was most interested in. This problem had been forced on his mind not only by the extreme American enthusiasm for wealth as contrasted with American poverty, but the deter-

71

mination of so many young Americans, boys and girls alike, to obtain wealth quickly by marriage. When he realized the nature of the American literature of that period and what was being offered and consumed by publishers and public, he also became aware of the fact that the most interesting American story of the day concerned not only the boy getting the girl, but more emphatically, the poor boy getting the rich girl. Also, he came to know that it was a natural outgrowth of the crude pioneering conditions of American life up to that time, based on the glorification of wealth which started with the early days of slavery and persisted throughout our history. When Theodore was only twelve, he read serials in the *Family Story Paper*, the *New York Weekly*, *Golden Days* and George L. Monroe's *Seaside Library*, which ran from as early as 1840 to as late as 1910, showing how the poor working girl dreamed of marrying the rich scion of wealth and how, after many trials and tribulations in which he sought to betray her, true love conquered and she became the lawful mistress of a brownstone mansion on Fifth Avenue, New York. These papers made fortunes for such people as Robert Banner, P. F. Collier, Monroe, Street and Smith and others.

Then, of course, followed the Four Hundred: Fish, Knickerbocker, Gould, Astor, Vanderbilt, to name a few. And so on down to 1894, by which time he began to observe a certain kind of crime in the United States. It seemed, as he studied it, to spring from the fact that a young man had an ingrowing ambition to be "somebody" financially or socially, it being a rare American heart that was set on being a great scientist, discoverer, religionist, philosopher or statesman, or benefactor of mankind in any form. And though a man might

72

start out to be a doctor, lawyer, merchant, or inventor, perhaps even a scientist, his private obsession, springing from the national obsession, was that the quick way to be all this was to get money. And the quick way to get money was to marry it.

In St. Louis, for instance, where Dreiser was in 1892, a young dealer in perfume, who had been consoling himself with the love of a girl on a lower social scale than himself, suddenly found that he was becoming successful and that the door of one of the old French families of St. Louis was open to him by marriage. Fearing frustration by the claims of his little working girl, he murdered her by administering through perfumed candy a deadly poison.

But about the time Dreiser began to meditate on this tragedy, he was intrigued by the tragic case of Carlisle Harris, a young medical student, who promised to be an excellent doctor. In this case, Dreiser chanced to know the mother, a fine and loving one utterly devoted to her son's welfare. But she had little money, and the boy's father was dead. And she wanted Carlisle to get up in the world, be famous and marry money. She told Dreiser so. She struggled and saved to give him a New York medical education. Then, as in the preceding case, while an intern in one of the leading New York hospitals, he seduced a poor young girl. No sooner had he done this than Carlisle met an attractive girl of much higher station than his own, one who possessed not only beauty, but wealth. And with her as an objective and a star, he naturally wearied of the poor girl. By that time he had satisfied his passion for "Miss Poor" and now there was only "Miss Rich" —his true American ideal. The way he finally sought to rid himself of his poor sweetheart was (to vary the St. Louis man's formula slightly) by supplying her with a dozen pellets, presumably intended to bring about a miscarriage. Four of them contained a deadly poison, the others not. The poor girl, wanting to escape illegal motherhood, took no more than four of the pellets before she encountered one of the poisoned ones and died. But the remaining pills were discovered in her room, and among them, three containing the deadly poison. And so the jury sentenced Carlisle Harris to be executed.

This particular type of tragedy, it seemed to Dreiser, was becoming more common. After that, there was scarcely a year in which some part of the country was not presenting the American public with this typical American tragedy.

Then in 1906 came the Chester Gillette-Grace Brown case. The locality was Cortland, South Otselic, Big Moose Lake, Utica and Amsterdam, all in New York.

There were other cases in which Dreiser was intensely interested. There was the Harry New case. He was the alleged illegitimate son of former Senator Harry New of Indiana, at that time Postmaster General of the United States. According to the papers of the day, the boy had been cast off and neglected by his father, and left to shift as best he might. While in this state, not knowing anything of his distinguished parentage, or expecting anything from that source, he became involved with a poor girl. Soon, New was surprised to learn about his father and that he intended to do something for him —give him money to help him rise, etc. But just at that time, the girl became pregnant and New found himself facing a poverty marriage which would ruin all his opportunities, as he thought. So he killed the poor little girl on a lonely highway near Los Angeles. In this case the Postmaster General was powerful enough to extricate the boy from his predicament. At any rate he was not hanged.

Then came Avis Linnell of Hyannis, Massachusetts, and her preacher lover, Richardson—a pathetic case that Dreiser planned to write as *An American Tragedy* and of which he did write six chapters, before he decided to change to the Chester Gillette case. For here was a young preacher who had a particularly small church in Hyannis, Cape Cod. He himself had come up from nothing, learned little, if anything, accumulated no money, and was still struggling along on a small salary with a small flock of parishioners. He was good-looking, socially agreeable, a fair orator, while Avis was a most charming and emotionally attractive girl, of circumstances and parentage as unnoticed as his own. Result—love, a period of happiness, seduction and a promise of marriage. And then a call to one of the richest, most socially distinguished congregations in Boston. Its vestrymen had for some time been observing Richardson's outward conduct, his magnetic personality, his charm, and had concluded that he would prove an ideal minister for their church. In consequence, after Avis had become pregnant, he was invited to Boston to speak, and later, quickly installed as pastor. No sooner was he installed, than one of the wealthy beauties of his new congregation decided that he was the one for her, that he was now sufficiently distinguished to enter into the realm of wealth to which she belonged. Yet, in the background was Avis, his promise of marriage, and her approaching motherhood. And so, since his new love moved him to visions of social grandeur far beyond his previous dreams, he sought to cast off Avis. She, in love and agonized, demanded at least that he rid her of the child or marry her.

Like the St. Louis perfumer, Carlisle Harris and Chester Gillette, he sought but could not find a medical remedy. Several trials proved futile. Then, exactly like Carlisle Harris, he put poison in some, not all of the pills. With Avis' death came a search for the murderer, and at last Richardson, in his grand new pulpit, was dragged down to a cell and eventual death in the electric chair. Dreiser doubted whether he had ever read of Carlisle Harris and his strategy or of Chester Gillette. He thought, rather, that coincidentally the same idea occurred to both of them.*

There were other cases—fifteen of them—studied carefully by Dreiser before he finally decided to use the Gillette-Brown case for his model. However, his representation of the original story varied from it in many ways—psychologically, emotionally and factually. For instance, in the Gillette-Brown case a tennis racket had been the instrument allegedly used to strike the girl, whereas in Dreiser's story, Roberta is struck by a camera and stunned by a blow from the gunwhale of the overturning boat, thereby establishing the element of accidental death. Also, Clyde did not actually drown Roberta but, overcome by indecision, he allowed her to drown by failing to swim to her rescue, which created a question of his actual guilt. Upon his one shadow of a doubt Dreiser hung his story structure.

After the book was finished, he was charged with having stolen the entire idea from the newspapers. Not only that, he

* From Dreiser's manuscript, *American Tragedies.*

was charged with lack of originality and with copying a tragedy instead of creating one. To which he replied: "No one
creates tragedies—life does that. Writers report them, and
after all, Goethe copied his Faust from Dr. Faustus and so,
by the critic's standard, should have been charged with stealing the old legend of which, throughout Europe, there were a
dozen versions. And what about Shakespeare? He should have
been charged with stealing *Antony and Cleopatra, Julius Caesar* and *The Merchant of Venice,* in fact, every play he ever
wrote, barring none. Ditto, Kipling and his Indian tales."

Later, when these typical crimes were repeated, Dreiser
was charged with promoting murder! During one case in 1931
(the Kane case), when a copy of *An American Tragedy* was
found among the murderer's belongings, Dreiser was deluged
with letters and telegrams asking him to explain this. Was he
guilty of provoking murder?

At that time he happened to be in Harlan County, Kentucky, investigating the mine troubles there and being almost
murdered himself. Yet he received the reporters and told
them that he thought the roots of crime were not in his novel
or the Gillette-Brown case or in any of the various typical
cases studied by him, but in the enduring American obsession
in regard to wealth with its fear of poverty and its determination to achieve wealth by murder if necessary.

Here again I would like to quote from Dreiser's *American
Tragedies*:

> Yet, in connection with this matter of the psychic or mystic
> power of an idea in a book or in life at large to evoke related
> effects, I append the following illustration of the late Stuart P.

Sherman, one-time professor of literature in the University of Illinois, at Urbana, Illinois, and later literary critic on the *New York Herald Tribune*.

I first heard of Sherman from an editorial writer on the *Indianapolis Star*, I forget his name. But previous to his being an editor on the *Star*, as he told me, he had been assistant professor of English under Sherman at Urbana. And not only that, but Sherman had caused him to be discharged. And on account of me and my books! For somewhere back in 1913 or 1914, he said, he had come across several of my books and had become an enthusiastic exponent of the same, discussing their significance in his classes, and urging students to read them, and later, according to him, there were pro-Dreiser freshmen and sophomores, a college newspaper mention of the same, and finally the troubled attention of Professor Sherman. For he was my young editor's superior.

"One day," said this man, "Sherman walked into my lecture room and asked me who this man Dreiser was. What books he had written. Why was I so enthusiastic? And then learning that I had copies of *Sister Carrie, Jennie Gerhardt, The Financier*, etc., he asked for the loan of them—took them away with him. Some weeks later there was trouble for me, for he came back to say that he did not think the books were decent, and more, they did not merit the emphasis I was placing on them. They were vulgar, brutal, immoral, and as such, subversive of all the best tendencies in our literature, and that he personally was going to attack Dreiser on that ground."

Not only that, but he also indicated to his assistant that he would prefer it if no further mention of Dreiser were made, unless it were condemnatory. But since this young editor was not a little courageous and even defiant and continued to discuss my books, he was dropped.

Actually that was the first time I had heard of Sherman or his attitude toward me. But not so long after, there appeared in the New York *Nation*, a four-page analysis and attack on my work— very vigorous and very bitter, for which afterwards the paper officially apologized to me. I retain the letter. It was as the Editor implied, a sort of "witch-burning" procedure on the part of Sherman. For my part the whole thing amused me, since, as I knew, such violence together with the large space devoted to it could only provoke discussion, and probably favorable discussion. In fact, I said to myself, "This man will probably do me more good than my wildest admirers. He is too conservative and too blatant."

And true enough, and to my great advantage, he continued to fulminate against me, about as Luther did against the Catholic Church. I was of the devil, and here and there in the newspapers throughout the country I read excerpts from his critical estimates of me. He outshone my other violent opponents, and finally even seemed to achieve a kind of leadership among them, for before roasting me they seemed to want to see how thoroughly he would roast me. And ultimately, if you will believe it, he attracted sufficient attention to himself, through me, to be called by the *New York Tribune* to take charge of its literary page or department. And from that point on, or almost weekly thereafter, until his death in 1926, I heard from him, and never but once, favorably.

This particular once came somewhere between January and March of 1926, after I had published *An American Tragedy*. At that time, it was generally assumed by my publisher, Liveright, and critics who were favorable to me, that he would produce his critical masterpiece insofar as I was concerned— that is, he would hand out the grand slam of his life.

However, and to my really thorough surprise, he executed a full face-about, a complete back somersault, as one critic phrased it, and landed in my camp. In short, his entire article was devoted to an analysis of the force of the work, and in the main he praised it. Privately I learned that he was really greatly impressed by it, and from then on it was likely he would treat me much more kindly. I decided that I had made a convert, and more than likely, should he continue in this mood, that his espousal of me and mine would ruin him.

Whether that was true or not, I never learned, for suddenly in July or August of that same summer, the whole odd change was rounded off by Sherman departing for his summer vacation somewhere in the Northern New Jersey or Pennsylvania lakes, I believe. And then a very little later, all the New York papers carried the news of his sudden tragic death. But now comes the really curious part of all this, and which, to me at least, seems somehow to have a psychologic unity with his previous attitude and his subsequent change of heart. For the newspapers explained that though married —his wife on the coast at the time, I believe—he had set forth on this summer lake with a young girl who was listed as a friend of his. Out on the lake only a moderate distance from the shore, and in pleasant weather, the boat overturned and both of them were drowned. I can furnish the exact text of one of the reports:

"Apparently after endeavoring to assist the girl, she sank, and he appeared to seek to save himself by reaching the overturned boat, but before he could do so, he sank himself."

My friend, Charles Fort, would and did say, that he felt that psychologically Sherman was impressed in the direct of such a tragic end by the similar end of Roberta Alden whom he so much pitied.

No, I think it was not Dreiser but America that was to blame for *An American Tragedy* and all the other related tragedies. And, as Dreiser said, not only America, but humanity which, finding the conditions America provided for it, proceeded to react in the way he described.

Dreiser was an interpreter of life as it is. With all his novels, the ideas were carried in his mind for years before ever he sat down to work them out. In the case of *The Bulwark*, he conceived the idea for it in 1910, actually starting to work on it in 1914, at which time he wrote only a few chapters. Edgar Lee Masters told me recently that he and

Dreiser walked for hours up and down Michigan Avenue in Chicago in 1912 or 1913 when he told him the story of the novel he intended to write about "the good man," which turned out, more than thirty years later, to be *The Bulwark*. Taking it up again in 1916, he wrote one third of the book. He worked on it in California in 1920 and 1921. But he picked it up and put it down several times in through the twenties and thirties. In 1942 and 1943, he started writing it over from the beginning, and in the winter of '44 and early part of '45, he finished it.

Sister Carrie was written four years after the idea came to him. *The Financier* was forming in his mind from about 1904 to 1911. *The Titan*, written in 1913, was published in 1914. *Jennie Gerhardt* was thought out after he finished writing *Sister Carrie* in 1900. He sketched it out in 1901, started writing it in November, 1909, and finished it in about July of 1910.

The "Genius" lived in his mind from about 1904 to 1915, when it was finally completed and published. However, *The "Genius"* was not as objective a work as his other novels, but grew in and around him out of his experiences. It was a composite of the lives of three men: the artist Everett Shinn by whom he was fascinated, and the physical and nervous form of a young art editor of the Butterick Publications, who had committed suicide, imposed upon the structure of Dreiser himself, that finally produced *The "Genius."* *The Stoic* was nearing its finish the night he died, December 28, 1945.

But as he himself once wrote to Mencken, as late as 1943, in answer to Mencken's inquiry as to the chronology of his works:

I was always starting something and then finding for some reason or other I couldn't go on. I was always getting a small advance from a publisher on some one book and then being ordered to make good. Meanwhile I would have become interested in another. For instance, while writing *The Financier*, I had completed three or four of the studies which were to make *Twelve Men*. Also at least ten of the sketches that were to make *The Color of a Great City*. In 1903, while dreaming of doing *Jennie Gerhardt*, I wrote 32 chapters of what was to be *The "Genius,"* and in 1907 or 1908, tore them up and burned them in order to do *Jennie Gerhardt*. Somewhere in there, as a sideline, I began *Dawn*, and actually wrote a half dozen or more chapters, only to find that at that time it was too soon to be doing it—family reasons. So it was left until much later.

Then came, of course, *Jennie Gerhardt* and *The Financier* and, after my trip to Europe with Grant Richards, *A Traveler at Forty*, because he wanted it done. Then *The Titan*, for reason of which Harpers kicked me out. Then *The "Genius"* and John Lane. They had made me a slight advance but refused to publish the book, as you know. You were in on that. For some reason *Jennie Gerhardt* sold and I made some money, enough (what with articles, stories and such) to go on for quite a little while, even though Horace (Liveright) didn't show up in my life until about 1918. He took over *The "Genius,"* as well as *Twelve Men*, finished at that time, both of which sold. Meanwhile, *The Bulwark* idea had come to me and I did some work on that—now and then. Also, around the same time, *A Hoosier Holiday*, which was due to Franklin Booth's desire for me to go back and see Indiana. You edited that book for me. Also I finished *Plays of the Natural and Supernatural* and *The Hand of the Potter*, which Horace published. Also (in there) having given up *Dawn*, which was to be volume one of *A History of Myself*, I decided to work on *Newspaper Days*, which was to be volume two of my life. Meanwhile, as you know, I decided to remove to Los Angeles and did so. There, between 1919 and 1921, I finished *Newspaper Days* and sent it on to Horace. Without my consent or

with any word to me he changed the title to *A Book about Myself.*
I didn't like that. It interfered with my *Dawn, Newspaper Days,
Literary Apprenticeship, Literary Experiences* series. (*Literary
Apprenticeship* was to be volume three and *Literary Experiences*
was to be volume four.) Later, as you know, I had Horace drop
the title *A Book about Myself* and put in its place *Newspaper Days.*
Between 1922-1930, after I returned to New York, I finished *The
Color of a Great City, Free and Other Stories, An American Trag-
edy, Dawn, A Gallery of Women, Chains, Tragic America, Dreiser
Looks at Russia* and God knows what else.

Riding along between Port Jervis and Monticello, we noticed an attractive little cabin sitting back in the woods, about
a hundred and fifty feet from the road. There was something
about it that arrested our attention and we decided to turn the
car around and examine it.

The cabin was beautifully built, with French windows all
around. As we peeped through the windows, we saw that it
was equipped with artistic rustic furniture, an old-fashioned
wood range, a long natural wood table with benches to match,
and many little things that showed signs of comfort and interest. We thought it must have belonged to some romantic
couple. Inquiring of the nearest neighbor, Teddie secured the
name of the owner with the thought in mind that we might
rent it for a time—perhaps for the two months left of the
summer.

Continuing northward, our next stop was Cortland the
Lycurgus of the *Tragedy*, where, upon our arrival, we drove
around to different sections to get a general impression of the
city as a whole—the best residential section, the factory section and the poor streets of the town.

Next we drove to South Otselic (Biltz in the book), where
Grace Brown (Roberta Alden) had lived. The narrow country road leading to her home was about as Dreiser described
it in the book. I wondered, as we rode along, how a young
girl could have lived so far away from everything in so bleak
a spot at a time when automobiles were scarce and one had to
travel three miles behind a horse to the general store. The
lone house up on the hill under great trees had all of the lorn
feeling that he later put into its description. It might seem
charming to one who had always lived in cities, but for a girl
who had never seen anything it must have been a rather drab
existence to return to after knowing Cortland and the little
gaiety she encountered there. A haunting note prevailed in
this atmosphere that Teddie caught and played on with varia-
tions throughout the book.

We soon reached de Ruyter, Utica and Old Forge (Gun
Lodge) which was an entrance to the lake country. The place
was crowded with horses, carts and automobiles, many of
which had been brought down from the lake country for supplies, packages and mail.

After servicing our car, we started up into the lake country,
through thick woods, over winding roads encircling lakes. Finally we arrived at Big Moose Lake (Big Bittern) and went
to the Glenmore Hotel facing the lake. It was an isolated spot,
very beautiful. One felt the weight of the surrounding woods
stretching for miles in every direction.

The following day, Teddie rented a rowboat from the boat-
house near by to go out on the lake to the actual spot where
the girl had been drowned. As we were hiring the boat, Teddie asked the boatman if he had ever heard of the Gillette

case. The attendant said Yes, he knew all about it; he had been working there in the same capacity at the time. Describing the boy as dark and swarthy, young and good-looking, he even pointed out the actual spot where the murder had taken place, a bend in the lake completely hidden from everything excepting the shore line of trees all around.

It was after we passed this point and found ourselves drifting into a quiet, deathlike stillness, that the mood of the most dramatic note of the *Tragedy* seized us both. Here it was that the girl had met her death, and her unheeded cries had rung out over the waters that closed about her. As we sat there the hypnotic spell of it all frightened me a little. I thought:

"Maybe Teddie will become completely hypnotized by this idea and even repeat it, here and now."

The air was motionless, as though we had been raised to a different level of existence or had become a minute part of the ether itself. It was a little as one feels when, looking over the side of a very tall building, one is tempted to jump. I wished something would break the awful spell of the moment. And just then, the strange call of the bird that Teddie called a "weir weir" in the book sounded on the still air as he flew and alighted on a protruding limb of a dead tree in the distance:

Kit . . Kit . . Kit . . . Ca-a-a-ah . . . !
Kit . . Kit . . Kit . . . Ca-a-a-ah . . . !

Was it the departed soul of Grace Brown hovering near the scene of her untimely death? I thought it might be.

The sensation and mood of this moment never left me and never will. A death moment . . . or as near as one could come to it, perhaps.

9

Soon after our return to New York from Big Moose Lake, we retraced our steps along the same road, this time only as far as the little cabin we had spotted near Monticello. Dreiser had gotten in touch with the owner and found he could rent it for two months.

When we arrived, we ran our car alongside the cabin, making ourselves at home, opening windows, adjusting furniture, unpacking bags. We were elated to discover an attractive red canoe stored in an open loft overhead, along with walking sticks, rifles, and other recreational equipment, some of which indicated possible hunting in the vicinity. We had not as yet discovered the dense wood at the back of the cabin, where, on several dark nights, I saw a wildcat cautiously creeping up to the open window, his eyes like burning torches glaring into the kitchen. He invariably ran away the instant he was observed.

Building a fire in the old-fashioned wood range to prepare our first supper was a delight. To get water, we had to cross the road in front of the cabin to a shaded and protected spring, which added to the novelty and charm of the place. It proved to be such an inspiration that ten years later we built a similar cabin on our country estate in Westchester County, New York.

In a few days Teddie settled down comfortably to his writing, and we felt as though we had lived there for years. At Teddie's invitation, Gertrude, daughter of his sister Emma Nelson, came to spend her vacation with us. She was a true descendant of the Schnepp (Shanab) family and had all the familiar characteristics of that strain; the resemblance being not so much of feature as of temperament, which was made up of a certain bohemian gaiety and vivacious charm blended with a mercurial scale of temperamental shades from light to very dark. One never knew what shade would be in the ascendancy for the day. However, she was very pretty, talented and witty, quick in mind and action and light of foot.

The three of us went around to the neighboring towns to look them over and take in what we could find in a gala spirit, enjoying every moment of it. We all were very happy and contented together, and I developed a real love for Gertrude. Often she and Theodore would go to the spring to fetch water, and one morning as they were returning, Gertie was startled to hear me singing in a clear soprano to high C, with a freedom and abandon she could scarcely believe. Gertie had been quite unaware of my interest in singing, whereas she, with her own full rich mezzo-soprano voice, had engaged in vocal studies for some time. She made Teddie stop and listen, and when they finally entered the house, she was beside herself with exhilaration. Later Gertie and I studied duets together with Elmo Russ, but she never failed to remind me of the effect my singing had on her that morning. Three weeks later, Gertie left, while Teddie and I remained.

I was happy and went around singing a good part of the time. In the evenings we read before the fireplace. I was reading *Wuthering Heights* for the first time and Dreiser had me read parts of it aloud. He had again swung his great writing machine around into place, was proceeding rapidly and I typed parts of the first handwritten draft of his novel for him.

One day, when we had been there for about a month, we decided to go into town for a couple of days and then return to the cabin for another month. While he was packing his overnight bag, he wandered off into the woods, perhaps to take a last look. After he left, I noticed a bundle of letters lying on top of some things he had thrown into the open bag. Ordinarily I would not have touched them, but at that moment I could not overcome the feeling that they concerned me in some way and I should read them. After reading two or three, I replaced the rest, for I had seen enough to know that this was a more serious triangle than I had supposed. I was jealous, fiercely so.

When he returned, I told him that I was not leaving for a "couple" of days, but for good; that I had no desire to return to the cabin, and as I was now convinced that he had no need for me, I would be on my way.

Our drive back to New York was a nightmare. He was nervous and I was torn between conflicting emotions of love, hate, jealousy and sorrow. I left him at his studio, telling him I would take the car back to the garage but after that he need not bother to look me up. He seemed to be deeply affected by my attitude but made no attempt to restrain me. That night I

Above: Esther Schnepp Parks, grandmother of Helen and aunt to Theodore. *Below:* Helen's mother, Ida Viola Parks.

Above: Helen and her sisters in the pony cart given to them by their mother. *Center:* Hazel. *Below:* Helen and Myrtle.

Above: Movie days in Hollywood, 1921. *Below:* Helen and Theodore in Hollywood, 1920.

Above: The Four Horsemen of the Apocalypse. Helen left of Valentino. *Below: The Flame of Youth.* Helen in center.

HELEN DREISER

went to a hotel instead of going back to my apartment. In the morning I returned to his studio to gather up a few of my things, fully intending to break off our relationship completely, but when he came to the door and I saw his face, I realized that I could not leave him in this abrupt manner. There were deep shadows around his eyes indicating a night of suffering and sleeplessness.

"I walked the streets all night long," he said. "Where were you?"

While I knew that I could not live with him under the circumstances, I thought I would have to remain in New York for a while and endeavor to arrive at a plan that would make things easier for both of us. I felt he should not be living entirely alone at this time and suggested he go to live with his sister Mame (Mrs. Austin Brennan), who, with her husband, lived in one of the charming old Rhinelander houses on West Eleventh Street. I knew she would be glad to have him, and to my surprise, he welcomed the suggestion; he seemed to have grown tired of the St. Luke's Place studio.

Mame was a fascinating person whom everyone loved at first sight; she radiated kindness and well being to all those who came in contact with her. All sorts of misfits in some kind of difficulty appealed directly to her for encouragement and spiritual warmth, which they received. She had a lovely face, soft kindly eyes and a fascinating personality. I loved her from the first day I met her, and as the years passed, I spent many an evening with her discussing metaphysical subjects. I often thought she had the enthusiasm and spirited anticipation of a girl in her teens. She was for constructive progress of any kind, and always said "yes" to the hopes and dreams of

89

others. I loved her for this and for her open-mindedness in allowing one to think aloud in her presence. So often, years later, we sat over tea in her little kitchen, having the most wonderful time just talking the hours away.

At that time Teddie's room in Mame's home consisted of a large front room adjoining her apartment on the ground floor, with a fireplace and his own private entrance. But the little one room and kitchen apartment which I occupied on a top floor in West Fiftieth Street soon became the "home" to which Teddie returned every night. If he left town to run down to Washington or elsewhere, he always wired me just what time to expect him.

I did part of his editing, typing revisions, etc., but I was not strong enough physically to sit the entire day at a typewriter and then be with him in the evening. But being so very tired, I felt I was losing ground and knew I must get away from the situation which seemed to be taking all my strength.

When I explained this to Teddie, he agreed with me that it might be the wise thing to do. However, as the time drew near for me to leave, he said he doubted whether he could go through with it, and I had to muster all the strength I could for I still loved him as much as ever. He said he would try it for ten days, and if he could not go on working, he would come out to the west coast and finish his book there.

The night before I left, we went to the Pennsylvania Hotel where we had enjoyed our first breakfast together. We talked very little, just wanting to be together. I could hardly imagine a separation. We were so much in love, and yet there we were actually parting,—I with the thought of never returning, and he, perhaps, thinking the same. I do not know.

It was March of 1924 when the train pulled out of Pennsylvania Station. I was confused and bewildered, and, although my eyes were filled with tears, I could see Teddie standing on the platform waving goodbye as he watched the train until it passed beyond his vision. We were both torn by the uncertainty of the future—the long road ahead before we met again, if ever.

10

As the train sped westward, taking me three thousand miles away, I thought of Teddie leaving the station and returning to his desk. How sad it was—how difficult! And yet, even at this time, certain facts were obvious. I could not go on drifting as I had. At least that is the way it appeared to me then. Whether he needed me—and how much he needed me—to sustain him in his world struggle remained to be seen. If not at all, then I should know and face that fact, too. I was spiritually exhausted and ill. It seemed to me that the most beautiful dream of my life had ended with no hope of its being revived.

But as we approached the Rocky Mountains and started to plow through them, I was reminded of the vastness of Teddie's spirit, for he was as roughhewn and broad as these. And strangely enough, I felt a little easier as soon as I saw them and felt the great expanse of the western landscape again. I needed sunshine and rest. I needed to set foot on California soil. Perhaps, I thought, this one thing alone would bring with it a sense of peace, for it was there that I had acquired a new consciousness of life.

As the train neared Portland, Oregon, where I planned to visit my mother and sister before going on to California, the porter came forward to help me with my bags, saying: "Ah hope that you ah feelin' bettah, Miss."

I looked at him in amazement.

"You is been cryin' ever since we pulled out of Chicago. Ah hope that nothin' terrible is wrong."

"Oh, no," I said, smiling. "I have been ill and I am tired, that is all."

My mother and Myrtle, devoted as always, welcomed me as most children are welcomed when they have strayed too far from home. My mother was happy to have her child back, for that is all I had ever been to her. Myrtle was happy for she had her pal again. But I was not myself, as they knew me. I was exhausted in body and spirit. While I have never been physically robust, I have always had excellent health with an unusual amount of energy. When I am spiritually inspired, a strength flows into me which at times seems able to move mountains. But then I was depressed and, therefore, had nothing to give. I told my mother that all I wanted to do was to rest.

One day my sister took me for a drive along the Columbia River Highway, but my depression was so increased by the beauty of it that I cried bitterly. I did not care to see anything beautiful. Teddie had been so closely associated with beauty in my mind that I could not bear it. I told her to take me home and just leave me alone. I would be all right sometime. I would go back to California. Maybe there I would become spiritually whole again. And so, after several weeks, I arose one day and told my mother that I would be leaving in a few days for California. Reluctantly she let me go.

It was Easter morning when I alighted from the train at Los Angeles, and immediately I was conscious of a satisfaction I had not known since departing two years before. Here I was back on the actual ground on which we had tramped together so much.

New York was far across the continent and I was glad. What had it given me that I missed? Nothing much but lonely hours. To be sure, Teddie came *home* to *me*, but so often fatigued from his eternal search for grist for his mill—or an escape from his mill.

I went to the Christie Hotel in Hollywood. Later on I moved from the hotel to a little house on Sycamore Street, with a family in which there were three daughters. The day I called in answer to an ad in the paper, a lovely little girl about fourteen years of age, who was watering the lawn, smiled at me so warmly I decided to live there if I could. It seemed to me that this beautiful smile was just the thing I needed from life. Perhaps through it I would again feel the response to beauty which I thought I had lost. But when I returned later and talked to her mother, I was somewhat disillusioned. She was a coarse-grained midwestern woman with a set expression about her mouth and a harsh voice. I was inclined to change my mind about living there, but when the beautiful little child with the slender arms and warm smile entered the room, I decided to take a chance. So I engaged the front room looking out on a pretty garden, rented a piano and soon felt at home.

On investigation, I found that our real estate holdings could be sold at this time with considerable profit, and these negotiations kept me busy for a while. Gradually my nervous tension lessened and with the money derived from a few property sales, I renewed my vocal studies.

Arthur J. Hubbard, a distinguished teacher from Boston, was conducting a summer master class in Los Angeles. When I learned that he had been the teacher of Roland Hayes, the great Negro singer, as well as Arthur and Charles Hackett, I had a desire to work with him and went to him for an audition. He was pretty well booked up, giving as many as eighteen lessons a day, but agreed to take me on, which elevated my spirits considerably. From then on, my time was fully occupied. I attended concerts in the city and at Hollywood Bowl. I read books on music, singing and the opera and learned some new German, French and Italian songs. Eventually I made a few friends, but most of my time was spent in study for I was fully aware of this wonderful opportunity.

The three girls of the household of which I had become a part were most friendly and often came into my room to talk about their respective love interests; at least the two older girls did. Little Eleanor, with the beautiful smile, noticed the same handwriting on the letter she brought me every day, and was even a little sad on a day when there was no letter. When the family purchased a larger home in another part of the city, I moved with them, for I was now studying in earnest and liked the atmosphere of their home. I had no desire to look ahead or face decisions. I knew that I loved Teddie, but he laid such heavy hands on beauty. I still felt the ache of it, and some of this feeling, I am sure, crept into my letters to him.

Letters from Theodore were arriving almost daily, most of them sad and brooding. He was lonely, he said; could not see the value of anything, not even work; he asked too much of life, more than I could or would give him. By that he meant, as I knew, his complete freedom in which he would indulge to the fullest, at the same time expecting my undivided devotion to him. A woman might be willing to give this to a man with whom she was deeply in love, but if the object of one's affection was absent a large part of the time, what was one to do? Turn to someone else? That would probably be the human thing to do. But where would it lead? To separation, as I saw it, no matter how we faced it. For I doubted my ability to live as he commanded. I wanted to do what I could for him, but how could I live the suspended existence that he demanded of a woman? In such a way of life, I did not have the joy of living or the joy of dying.

Then for a few days, I would be rather happy in myself because I was not with him and was free after a fashion. As even I could see, I was beginning to look better. My eyes lost a lusterless expression they had borrowed for a time and began to sparkle as they had before.

Again a letter was received in which he said that he had pictures of me, going here and there—dancing around and having a good time. How sad I felt when I read this kind of letter, for I was then existing on a dream—a golden dream that had vanished. And while I appeared to be free, I knew that in reality I was chained to him in spirit. I belonged to him, and the thought of a substitute never occurred to me.

Then I would picture him ill or depressed so that he could not work, and this disturbed and troubled me, for I knew that working on his book was the one thing he needed most. Perhaps I should be with him—good or bad—life or death. There were nights when I lay awake with a gnawing torment in every nerve, yearning to be in his arms again, and almost invariably after such a night, a letter would arrive telling me of similar longings on his part. Attuned chemisms, one highly responsive to the other, is the only explanation I know of this thought transference, which happened over and over again between us. Here is one of the letters I received at that time:

August 4, 1924

DEAREST:

You are all of that to me. I spent such a troubled Saturday and Sunday thinking of you. Do you brood about me so much? And don't you know that it is easy for you to trouble me so that I get nothing done at all? Last night at nine I sat down and started an account of you from my Gallery. And I loved doing it, but at once found it hard to select from all the wealth of material. It will not be easy to make a sketch of what should be a book.

And today comes a letter asking me to write you a love letter—"a few little love-words" you used to say, as though I ever thought anything else but love words in my heart of you. But, honey, I have never been able to picture to you what I really feel or how I think about you. You and my thoughts of you are like filtered star dust at times; or they are like faint and heartbreaking echoes of old songs; or they are like winds that stir in the evening; or like birds that flash and are gone. They flutter about me like bright and sad things that I feel or hear rather than see. You are really ten thousand or a million beautiful things—memories of incidents, places, colors, tones, ambitions, desires—and each one is you in a different form—and hovering about like bright beautiful realities that are yet invisible and sad.

A few little love words. You say your heart has called to me at

97

Aug 4 – 1924

Dearest:

You are all of that to me. I spent
such a horrible Saturday & Sunday thinking
of you. Do you brood about me so much?
And don't you know that it is easy for you
to trouble me so that I get nothing done at
all? Last night at nine I sat down
& started an account of you from my
Gallery. And I loved doing it. But at
once found it hard to select from all this
wealth of material. It will not be
easy to make a sketch of what should be
a book.

Facsimile of first page of letter of August 4, 1924.

times but in vain. It never has. You are never out of my heart. I may have said harsh things and seemingly meant them—even to myself at moments. I may have seemed cruel and to you have been cruel but I have tortured myself more in so doing because within me you have always been—safe and centered in my very heart—and when I have hurt you I have felt so sad afterwards—ah—so very sad.

A few little love words.

I wish I could take my Babu into some still garden and let her forget the world. I wish I could stop time and life and just dream a dream with you in a garden—itself a dream like ourselves. I wish all your ambitions could seem to come true while all the time you were merely dreaming them close to me—held safe against a time when they should dissolve and you would awake to be still happy —because of me. I wish you could really know that my thoughts are not a few but many love words—and not little.

I think you are the dearest spirit—the most perfect poetry in terms of flesh and mind. I have always thought so. At your worst and your best you seem to dream gay or sad dreams, but to me always lovely ones because always—always—I really love you. Your mind must tell you that. As I write this it would seem as if you must sense it—coming direct to you. It must come to you in some form, I know. And it will always be so, I know.

You mustn't be angry or sad. You must think of ways that will not only make your life but mine come true in the way that each would have it for the other. What less than that would be worth while.

You wanted a love letter.

But I have not written it more for you than for myself. I wish I could take you in my arms and keep you still and happy—this night and always—not to grieve any more about anything.

I am coming out in September if you wish. I started divorce proceedings some time ago as I wrote you. I am going to Detroit to-morrow or Wednesday to try to do an article for Hearst's in order to help get the money together that I will have to have. I am to make a study of Ty Cobb—the baseball star—psychoanalyze him. I will write you from there—a few more love words to my Babu.

All my love
TOADY

Revived recollections were painful. But I felt closer to him, separated as we were, when nothing of the physical obstructed my approach to him, whereas when we were together, visible barriers presented themselves to the eye and heart, which I was not always able to brush aside as insignificant.

By this time I had taken a smart apartment on Wilshire Boulevard in one of the new apartment hotels, as Teddie had written that he would be out in September and I wanted a place of my own. Having made a considerable amount of money in real estate, I felt I could well afford a better place, although, with the exception of the apartment and my singing lessons, I lived simply, preparing my own food in the modern white kitchen and keeping regular hours. Of course, there was every kind of service in these apartments: Filipino boys came in every morning to wash the dishes and put everything in immaculate order. Occasionally in the afternoon I went swimming at Crystal Pier in the Pacific Ocean, and in the evening, I would have coffee in the little neighborhood coffee shop near Westlake Park, where Teddie and I had so enjoyed watching the rowers four years before. I was happier—not depressed any more, for Teddie was coming out soon. He had said so in several letters.

But time passed and his letters became more discouraging. He did not see clearly any opportunity of a change, and he had no idea when he would be able to finish his book. The end always seemed farther and farther away.

Myrtle had motored down to Los Angeles to visit me, and when Mr. Hubbard offered us a room in his house without charge, if I would help him occasionally with a meal, I decided to accept his offer. I thought it might be advantageous to me in my studies for I would have an opportunity to listen in on a few private lessons which he gave at home after leaving his studio.

Almost immediately upon moving into his house, he took a paternal interest in me, thinking I was a lone child in the world who needed guidance and one who reminded him, so he said, of his five-year-old grandchild in Boston. Being a rigid disciplinarian, he disapproved of anyone coming in after midnight, and made it known that if anyone violated this rule, he could not sleep the rest of the night as he was extremely nervous. It was not a sacrifice for me, because I was so interested in the vocal work I was pursuing. But for Myrtle, it was impossible. She could never be controlled by anyone, and often she would call up to say she would be home at one o'clock, when I would tiptoe to the door to let her in. One night Mr. Hubbard appeared at the door to meet her, garbed in his white nightshirt and pointed nightcap, holding a lighted candle in his hand. With his long white beard and enormous stature, he looked like Mephistopheles himself descending upon her. Taken with hysterical laughter, Myrtle disgraced me then and there.

Added to this, when a handsome Nordic movie star friend of mine, whom I had known on my first trip to California, called in his luxurious car to escort me to a party, the discipline of the household was again thrown out of balance. When I was presented with a beautiful female Russian wolfhound —Lady by name—Mr. Hubbard did not seem to object to her so much, but in spite of this, I could see that she was a disturbing factor. The season was about over, so I made plans to leave for Portland with Myrtle in her car.

The trip was a pleasant one. We laughed and carried on together like a couple of kids all the way, until I nearly struck a passing car on the side of a mountain where the unpaved roads were especially rough and winding. This checked us sharply. We stopped the car after the near accident and sat looking at each other for fully five minutes without saying a word, after which she decided she would do all the driving through the Siskiyou mountains.

We had the beautiful Lady with us—a thoroughbred Valley Farm specimen of borzoi, all white, spotted with brown over her ears and one hip. Her lines were delicate, reminding one of a finely cut cameo, and though she looked neglected when she first came to us, she rapidly changed into an exquisite animal. Her coat became silky white and smooth, and her fine lines were accentuated as she became more spirited. Later on, Myrtle secured a champion male borzoi for her and soon raised some of the finest wolfhounds I have ever seen.

My mother, as always, was delighted to have us home again. She said it was like old times to see us coming with a strange animal as we so often did when we were children. It was good being back in my own northwest country again. This time, we spent day after day driving around the countryside, taking trips to the beaches and Mount Hood.

The letters from Teddie were not very cheerful. They seemed heavy with difficulty. Progress on the book had slowed up; he was tired and the task seemed beyond his strength.

One day about a month later, I told my mother that I would have to go to New York. It might be possible for me to help him. If so, it was where I belonged. She was opposed to the idea and tried in every way she could to dissuade me from going. But I felt the urge to go so strongly that I could not deny it. I eased her anxiety somewhat by assuring her that I would stay in New York for a short time only, and would then go to Boston to continue my vocal studies with Mr. Hubbard, who was urging me to join his class there.

Myrtle was saddened by the prospect of losing my companionship. I will not soon forget her as she stood in the station, an eager expression on her face as if she were saying: "Can't I go with you?" How could I make any promises when I had no certainty of anything? Surely, I thought, the time would come when I could do something for such a talented soul as she was and proved to be later. The time did come, and I tried to make up for that moment when she stood there, her eyes filled with tears, waving an eager, wistful goodbye.

11

As I adjusted my hat before a mirror, I was pleased with myself. I could see I was fresh and young again. And as I stood in line waiting to leave the train, a young woman leaned forward, touching me on the arm, saying: "You are meeting your sweetheart?"

"Yes," I smiled, "I am."

Then Pennsylvania Station, and as I came up the stairs, two familiar legs visible under a sign that cut off all but this part of him. There he was, the same as ever, in a gray suit, with his usual bright-colored scarf and walking stick.

"Well," he said as he looked me over. "It's Babu, all right," and kissed me.

We went to dinner at Mouquin's, at Sixth Avenue and Twenty-eighth Street, the famous restaurant which had wined and dined the outstanding celebrities of the era. Seated at a side table, we settled down for an intimate chat and visit. We were amused and pleased with each other. Teddie teased me about my phantom love affairs on the Pacific Coast, while I laughed and looked guilty at everything he said. We talked of nothing serious. Ever so often he would look at me as if to reassure himself that I was really there. "Yes, it's Babu all right," and then he would smile. I noticed, however, a hollow look about him, a seeming lack of vitality which worried me, although I said nothing about it.

I took a room at the Albert Hotel downtown to be near him, and we spent as much time together as we could arrange without sacrificing too many of his working hours. He was still living in the home of his sister Mame, and she was delighted that I had returned. Mame had been terribly worried about him, because he seemed so exhausted in mind as well as body. She told me he had been practically living on gin to stimulate himself, and that once he came into her apartment and cried bitterly when he told her he could not finish his book. Also, he had been smoking cigarettes continually. To my knowledge he had not smoked before and never did so afterward.

When I told Teddie I had been thinking of going to Boston to continue my vocal studies, he made no comment. Instead, a week or so after my arrival, he said he would like me to go to Washington with him, as he needed a few days rest and wanted to do some research in the Library of Congress.

During our Washington stay, Teddie took me to many points of interest—the Congressional Library, Washington Cathedral, the Capitol Building, embassy residential section, and the White House grounds. Then down to Mount Vernon and the magnificent home of George Washington overlooking the Potomac. On returning to Washington, we lingered about the Washington Monument and Lincoln Memorial—a great inspiration to any real American. As we stood looking at the sad strong face of Lincoln, I could feel the deep reverence with which Teddie regarded this Great Emancipator.

At the end of a week we were back in New York where, not more than fifteen or twenty minutes after we stepped off the train, I was witness to a most disturbing incident. We were getting out of a taxicab in front of Dreiser's studio when a woman dashed toward him, making a sharp and accusing statement. Taking my arm, he pushed past her to the door of the house, unlocked it and told me to wait inside; he would be back shortly. I heard them talking outside, his voice low and firm, hers troubled and insistent. Shortly afterward he entered the room and locked the door behind him without comment.

One day when Teddie and I were having an early luncheon, he said: "Why don't you go over to Flatbush in Brooklyn, and rent a small apartment?" Flatbush—! Of all places, I thought. But I did not hesitate; in fact, I went over the same afternoon —a very cold day, with the wind cutting around every corner. Before dark, I had found an apartment on Bedford Avenue, in a rather attractive neighborhood near Prospect Park. The apartment consisted of a fairly good-sized living room, kitchen, bath and rather spacious bedroom. The rent was sixty dollars a month, and while the building was modest, it was modern and altogether pleasing. When I went back to Manhattan and described the little apartment, Teddie said: "Yes, go over and take it on a year's lease."

After drawing up a lease to run from January 1, 1924, to January 1, 1925, I sent for a few of his things in storage, and when Teddie came over a few days later to see the apartment, he was agreeably surprised to find how homelike and comfortable it was. After looking at the apartment, we walked about the neighborhood and through a part of Prospect Park. We had our first dinner in Brooklyn at an interesting Italian restaurant.

My Boston trip skyrocketed into thin air, but I was more than compensated by the happiness this change evoked in him. During the following year, we enjoyed exploring almost every foot of the shore line and each neighborhood of Brooklyn as Dreiser was wont to do no matter where he lived.

Now that we were back together again we both felt like celebrating, and since it was New Year's Eve, we accepted an invitation to a night club from his friend Ed Smith. The party turned out to be the merriest I ever attended. Ed Smith had arranged everything the way he liked it, and he was a past master when it came to playing host.

Before starting out for the party we went to Mame's, where we exchanged greetings with several members of Teddie's family, including his nieces, Vera and Gertrude, both beautiful girls who danced happily about the front room with him. Mame was beside herself with joy to witness Teddie's contagious lightheartedness, and whispered to me that she thought from then on he was going to be all right. I even remember the gown I wore that night: a lovely pink creation which I had had designed in California for just such an occasion. An airy tulle scarf about the shoulders added to the ethereal quality of the ensemble, and I was happy, as I always was, when Teddie approved it with one glance. "Stunning," he said.

We left for the party in as high spirits as any couple on that New Year's Eve, and our spirits did not flag once through the whole night as we danced till dawn. Teddie had told me he was a very poor dancer, but during this one night he learned to dance in a graceful rhythmic way. What pleased me the most was the way *men* all over the room were drawn to him. He would make some intimate friendly remark to them to which they responded in a boyishly affectionate manner. Several young men called to me as we danced by: "Don't let him get away. Hang on to him. He's O.K."

Teddie had a genius for work, but when he played, he played with his whole heart.

Teddie had drawn his second wind and was taking hold of his work with renewed vitality. He reminded me of a man attempting to land a huge whale, and after succeeding in getting a good portion of it on the shore was struggling to maneuver the rest of it single-handed. I reread the manuscript three times, typed revisions, did my own housework, and once or twice a week we entertained friends.

But I never think of that period in our lives without recalling one man whose brilliant intellect and warm, sympathetic understanding were a constant source of inspiration to us. He was J. G. Robin.* Born in Russia, he was a man of powerful stocky build, with blue eyes and ruddy complexion. After a fabulous career in the banking business, during which time he built up a fortune of approximately fourteen millions, he was defeated by a much more powerful financier of his day and was sent to prison on some technicality of the law. As Dreiser told me: "He was doing no more than many other

* J. G. Robin was the subject for the portrait "X" in "Vanity, Vanity, Saith the Preacher," from *Twelve Men.*

financiers at that time, that is, financing one bank out of another, thereby developing a chain of banks." After this crushing blow, Robin turned to the study of law, and before many years he was being consulted as a legal expert by lawyers.

But law was only one of his interests. Under the pen name of Odin Gregory he was the author of two plays, *Jesus* and *Caius Gracchus* which were acclaimed by many critics as brilliant examples of classical writing. In his last years he turned his attention to the development of disinfectant, and a short time before he died, there were negotiations afoot to sell the process for the princely sum of four hundred thousand dollars. I have heard him talk brilliantly on science, politics, finance, art and literature, even medicine. When Dreiser was ill, he would drop everything to rush to our apartment and, regardless of Dreiser's objections, insist on giving him a massage or administering some remedy which invariably helped. He had the tenderness of a woman, but there was something Mongolian about him, probably springing from his Tartar blood, and often as he sat philosophizing with the pure wisdom of a young Confucius, I thought of China and things old and rich and wise.

Robin considered Dreiser a most impractical man in connection with his business dealings and was always giving him advice as to possible traps and snags he should guard against. Dreiser did not always take kindly to this, and their discussions would often become more than a little heated. Sometimes they would quarrel and not see each other for months. Then they would come together again and go on as before. Nothing pleased him more than to be going with us to dinner. If it were midsummer, we might go over to an East Side res-

taurant, where, at times, we had the entire top floor to ourselves. If so, he would take off his coat, turn up his sleeves
and settle down, not so much for food as for real conversation.
He often said that Dreiser crystallized his thoughts. It was at
Robin's insistence that Dreiser rented an office in the Guardian
Life Building, near Union Square, in order to work without
interruption. Robin had an office in the same building in association with Arthur Carter Hume, the lawyer, and these two
men gave Dreiser invaluable assistance on points of law involved in the *Tragedy*.

The friendship between Dreiser and Robin persisted over
many years, through periods of confusion and despair, wealth
and poverty for Robin, and when he died at the age of fifty-
four, Dreiser lost a real friend. At the end he lay in his bronze
casket in The Little Church around the Corner, a small hand-
ful of friends gathered about him—the few who really loved
him with the love and friendship he so truly inspired.

Teddie was now deeply engrossed in his great task. He was
like a sculptor working on a figure which had grown so large
that he seemed to be throwing his clay high to the top with a
mighty hand. He modeled, chiseled, formed and reformed
until one could see and feel the whole structure coming to life.
There was so much mass material and so much modeling to
be done before it was acceptable to him—writing, rewriting,
revising, four, five or six times. I was now doing his first draft
as well as copying revisions.

Occasionally Dreiser got some relief when he went to Ho-
boken to meet with Henry Mencken, Ernest Boyd, John Dos
Passos and others, where they sat for hours discussing every-

thing under the sun while consuming beer after beer. As he said, their conversations consisted mostly of "hisses and baahs!" No less and no more.

Excitement was growing in connection with the book. Liveright was putting on pressure to get it in their hands and there was a marked tenseness in the air whenever the book was mentioned. As publication had been announced, the public was waiting patiently for it, but there was considerable work yet to be done. One chapter was lost en route to the publisher, which tightened up the guard on succeeding chapters.

In the midst of all this excitement, we went down one weekend to Philadelphia to visit Wharton Esherick, the distinguished artist who created masterpieces in wood and stone. Teddie had met him when I was on the West Coast, and in one of his letters he described the lovely Esherick place at Paoli, where Wharton, his wife Letty and their two children lived an idyllic life in the beautiful rolling hills near Philadelphia. He had awakened one morning quite early, and looking out on the lawn had seen the tiny nude figure of little Ruth weaving her way through the beautiful garden. Esherick's abstract figures, carved from woods imported from all over the world, reflect an imaginative power and originality of expression that mark him as one of the really great American sculptors. He is equally well known for the beautiful furniture he builds, pieces of superb craftsmanship and striking originality of design. His studio, which he designed and built himself, is a starkly functional building of wood and stone situated on a hill, its windows commanding a glorious view of the beautiful Chester Valley. His charming house and garden lie below it. After a visit to the Eshericks at Paoli, one invariably went home with a refreshed conception of the creative life.

But this particular weekend was spent in a different way. It was late in the summer and Dreiser was persuaded by Esherick to join him and some friends for a sail on Barnegat Bay. I stayed behind with Letty and the children. The day was sizzling, and the men were exposed to the broiling sun for hours. As a result, Teddie's sensitive skin was burned almost to a crisp before the damage was discovered. When I joined them toward evening, I found him in a desperate condition. He could not lie down and was forced to sit up all night. Not being able to leave until early morning, he suffered intensely. His skin was like leather and his eyes were bloodshot. He lay in agony for ten days under the care of a doctor who informed me that he came very close to losing his life.

This, of course, retarded progress on the book, but as soon as he was up again, he resumed his work with a feverish passion. On and on he wrote. The Liveright Publishing Company, waiting for every chapter, was setting the book up as it came along. Louise Campbell of Philadelphia, who had been doing some editing on the manuscript from the beginning, came over to work on revisions in the galley proofs. Liveright had received one report from a reader who did not praise the book too highly. Then he turned it over to his closest literary adviser, Thomas Smith, who raved over the book, telling him that he had a sure hit. Liveright trusted Tom Smith and was elated to get his report, but he was not satisfied with the title. As he said: "How in the world can Dreiser call a book *An American Tragedy*? No, Dreiser must change the title!" Well —to ask Dreiser to change a title which he had chosen for the specific reason that it *was* a typical American tragedy was to ask him to mutilate his book, and he would have none of it. Liveright or no Liveright, the title would be *An American Tragedy.*

One day in November, the twenty-fifth to be exact, he penned the last word. There was a rewrite on the last chapter, several revisions and then—finis.

It was now December 1, 1925. We had taken the apartment in Brooklyn almost a year before. What had happened in that year? For one thing, I had lived through the most complicated emotional experience of my entire life. But I will always know that I learned more in that one year than I ever learned in any five years up to that time. For I was enveloped in an emotional triangle, in which Dreiser's creative mood cared for nothing but its expression and accomplishment, over which no one had any control. While I had no contact whatsoever with the other woman, I felt her every mood and vibration as they registered in Teddie. It seemed there was a living, seething current flowing back and forth, touching us all with its penetrating force. Even Dreiser, with his great strength, was battered by it.

The grilling task was over. Dreiser had tried many times to find relief of some sort, but he could not escape. The story tracked him everywhere he went. He could only return to his desk as helplessly as a man under sentence.

"The dark days of Brooklyn," he once wrote. And so they were. Dark days for all of us.

12

An American Tragedy was finished. All Dreiser wanted to do was to get away from any contact with the book. He did not even care to speculate as to how it might be received. He had always had trouble with his books, he said, and why should the fate of this one be any different? Anyway, he was too tired to think about it.

So we gave up the apartment in Brooklyn, took out the Maxwell car and started for Florida in search of something different. On our way we passed through Baltimore, Maryland, where Henry L. Mencken lived with his sister in their Hollins Street home, and Teddie decided to see if he were in town. I waited in the car while he inquired at the door. Mencken was there and welcomed him in. After a few minutes, when he discovered from Teddie's conversation that I was waiting outside, he rushed out, graciously insisting that I come in. A glowing fire was burning in the fireplace of his charming writing room and Mencken made cocktails. As I sat watching their warm and affectionate reunion, I realized how deep the bond of friendship had become through the years. They had many interests in common, although their social views were at opposite poles.

Dreiser has written so engagingly of his first meeting with Mencken, I will quote it here:

It was sometime during the spring or summer of 1908, and my second year of editorial control of the Butterick Publications, that there came to me a doctor by the name of Leonard K. Hirshberg, who explained that besides being a physician of some practice in Baltimore, he was a graduate of Johns Hopkins and interested in interpreting to the lay public if possible, the more recent advances in medical knowledge. There had been recent developments as there always are. Some phases of these he proposed to describe in articles of various lengths.

And then it was that he announced that, being a medical man and better equipped technically in that line than as a writer, he had joined with a newspaper man or editorial writer then connected with the Baltimore Sun, Henry L. Mencken. The name being entirely unfamiliar to me at the time, he proceeded to describe him as a young, refreshing and delightful fellow of a very vigorous and untechnical literary skill, who, in combination with himself, would most certainly be able to furnish me with articles of exceptional luminosity and vigor. Liking two or three of the subjects discussed I suggested that between them they prepare one and submit it. In case it proved satisfactory, I would buy it and possibly some of the others.

In less than three weeks thereafter I received a discussion of some current medical development which seemed to me as refresh ing and colorful a bit of semi-scientific exposition as I had read in years. While setting forth all the developments which had been indicated to me, it bristled with gay phraseology and a largely suppressed though still peeping mirth. I was so pleased that I immediately wrote Hirshberg that the material was satisfactory and that I would be willing to contract with him and his friend for one of the other subjects he had mentioned.

And then some weeks later in connection with that or some other matter, whether to discuss it more fully or merely to deliver it or to make the acquaintance of the man who was interested in this new literary combination, there appeared in my office a taut, ruddy, blue-eyed, snub-nosed youth of twenty-eight or -nine whose brisk gait and ingratiating smile proved to be at once enormously intriguing and amusing. I had, for some reason not connected with his basic mentality you may be sure, the sense of a small town roisterer or a college sophomore of the crudest and yet most disturbing charm and impishness, who, for some reason, had strayed into the field of letters. More than anything else he reminded me of a spoiled and petted and possibly over-financed brewer's or wholesale grocer's son who was out for a lark.

With the sang-froid of a Caesar or a Napoleon he made himself comfortable in a large and impressive chair which was designed primarily to reduce the over-confidence of the average beginner. And from that particular and unintended vantage point he beamed on me with the confidence of a smirking fox about to devour a chicken. So I was the editor of the Butterick Publications. He had been told about me. However, in spite of *Sister Carrie*, I doubt if he had ever heard of me before this.

After studying him in the almost arch-episcopal setting which the chair provided, I began to laugh. "Well, well," I said, "if it isn't Annheuser's own brightest boy out to see the town." And with that unfailing readiness for any nonsensical flight that has always characterized him, he proceeded to insist that this was true. Certainly he *was* Baltimore's richest brewer's son and the yellow shoes and bright tie he was wearing were characteristic of the jack-dandies and rowdy-dows of his native town. Why not? What else did I expect! His father brewed the best beer in the world.

All thought of the original purpose of the conference was at

116

once dismissed and instead we proceeded to palaver and yoo hoo anent the more general phases and ridiculosities of life with the result that an understanding based on a mutual liking was established, and from then on I counted him among those whom I most prized temperamentally as well as intellectually. And to this day despite various disagreements that mood has never varied.*

Dreiser and Mencken talked at length that afternoon about their great fight in 1916 against John S. Sumner and the New York Society for the Suppression of Vice, when the latter had forced J. Jefferson Jones of the John Lane Publishing Company to withdraw copies of The "Genius," just published, from bookstores throughout the country, thereby cutting off Dreiser's income. So infuriated had Dreiser become over this misfortune to his latest book that he soon rallied to the first line of defense of the freedom of all writers—such men as Mencken, Harold Hersey, John Cowper Powys and others of great prominence in the United States and England. The war against suppression raged on into 1917 and 1918 with Dreiser and Mencken leading it, but The "Genius" remained in the John Lane Company's stockrooms until 1923 when it was finally reissued by Horace Liveright.

As we were leaving Mencken's home that afternoon, Dreiser turned to me saying: "It doesn't matter what he ever says about me or does to me, he is a great guy and a great friend and I will always love him."

He had demonstrated the truth of this declaration by presenting to Mencken in 1914 the entire handwritten manuscript of Sister Carrie, which Mencken subsequently presented to the New York Public Library. I recalled Dreiser's words years

* Manuscript by Theodore Dreiser at the University of Pennsylvania.

later when a message arrived in California from Mencken which read: "He was my captain in a war that will never cease."

As we continued toward South Carolina and Georgia, the roads became worse and several times we were held up because of washouts. The rains had been heavy, and some of the small towns in Georgia were in mud six or eight inches deep. We had the sensation of floating in it. Once we came to a stream and thinking we could ford it, we started across; but to our astonishment and great concern, it widened suddenly so that we could not possibly follow the road. The water being up to the level of the running board, our motor stalled and we were completely bewildered. Suddenly, from nowhere, a Ford started across the water toward us from the other side, stopping as it came alongside us. The two men riding in the car asked us what was wrong. After explaining our predicament, one of the men said in a most friendly way: "Now you stay right quiet. We'll get you out of this in no time." They then proceeded to climb across the hood of our car onto the running board, where they raised the hood to dry the motor in some miraculous way. In a few moments, one of the men said: "Now you just let me drive this car. I know where the road is and I'll get you out. Just sit tight." Then, upon turning my driver's seat over to him, another miracle happened. The motor actually started and we found ourselves moving across what to us looked like a lake. The expert driver felt his way surely and carefully, and soon we were safely on dry land. Once reaching the edge of the state of Florida, we found the roads dry, the skies clear and our driving troubles over.

A hundred miles or so inside the Florida border, we ran

into a maelstrom of cars and people. It was the height of the real estate boom, and one couldn't walk or drive a step without being approached by a salesman urging an investment of a few dollars which would reap a fabulous profit in no time at all. They approached people in banks, hotels, railroad stations, everywhere, taking them out in large busses and providing luncheons on the spot in which they were most interested; then, while the victim was feeling better after a hearty luncheon, they sold him a lot—at least in 75 percent of the cases. Real estate was in everyone's mind and if it was not, mass psychology soon put it there. Even Dreiser spent four thousand dollars for a lot which a few years later was washed out to sea in a tropical storm.

There were no good accommodations to be had short of forty dollars a day. Hundreds of miles were dotted with million-dollar hotels, all of which, we were told, cost a vast sum to build, and, therefore, the rates were normal, based on the great and unparalleled future of Florida. The entire state from border to border was to be a grand long row of luxurious hotels with Venetian swimming pools, floating ballrooms, and canary bathrooms!

Not being able to afford forty dollars a day, we were forced like many others to spend a few nights in bare portable shacks, scattered along the roadway, which rented for three dollars a night. We searched the entire east coast of Florida from north to south before we found one simple hotel at Fort Lauderdale, the former home of ex-Senator Watson of Indiana, about which there was an air of something other than luxury.

However, when we stole away from the real estate crowd,

we found tropical gardens with the most amazing array of strange fruits and plants. And journeying up the picturesque Indian River, lined with thick vegetation, berries, palms, drooping tropical plants of every description and tall trees gracefully draped with moss, we saw alligators basking in the sun along the water's edge. Around a bend in the river, we came upon a most luxurious and expensive yacht which had been abandoned and was rotting away. Later we learned that it belonged to Harry Thaw of the famous Evelyn Nesbitt-Stanford White-Harry Thaw case.

In the dusk of evening we often watched the pelicans vigorously diving for food. We went in bathing at dawn and in the evening, often running to dodge coconuts falling from the tall leaning palms. Teddie always said that the whole state of Florida was a voluptuous garden.

Within a few weeks, in which we had succeeded in forgetting the heavy working hours of Brooklyn, we were receiving news from New York, definitely verifying the fact that the book was an instantaneous success. At first Teddie could hardly believe what he read. He had never before received such unanimous approval and he was skeptical. But it was impossible to discount the enthusiastic reviews and the congratulatory letters and telegrams that steadily poured in on him.

"Well," he said, "it looks as if I've hit the mark this time. I think I'll go back home and collect some of the spoils."

Above: Paul Dresser. *Below:* Theodore Dreiser.

This the Sterling that I knew.
the one and of whom Life could
wring tears of both ecstasy & pity
Dreiser

George Sterling.

Above: Llewelyn and John Cowper Powys. *Below:* Dreiser with the bust of John Cowper Powys, Hollywood, 1942.

Rabindranath Tagore.

13

On our return to New York, we rented a suite in the Pasadena Hotel, west of Broadway on Sixty-third Street. The hotel was old-fashioned but quiet; however, we soon realized that from then on things were destined to be anything but quiet. Almost before we had time to unpack, we were plunged into a whirl-pool of excitement and confusion due to the enormous success of the *Tragedy*. Horace Liveright, in a high state of exhilaration, anticipated extensive success. There were conferences and more conferences; talk of a sale to the movies, play productions abroad as well as on Broadway. Patrick Kearney, a young playwright, author of *A Man's Man*, appeared on the scene with a strong desire to dramatize the book; Dreiser and Liveright settled on him as the one most likely to preserve the theme and content of the book in play form.

Finally the sale of the motion picture rights reached a point far beyond the talking stage. It was Jesse Lasky, of Paramount Famous Players, who was interested and the sum being considered seemed a large one to Theodore, for although there had been motion picture proposals before in connection with his books, this was the first time a cash offer had matured. He was like a wide-eyed child talking in terms of big figures, with his usual reservation of skepticism however, as to its consummation. But the strong, confident, adamant man who walked into the Ritz dining room to discuss terms with Lasky, Liveright and others over a luncheon table was hardly the surprised childlike man who had left the hotel suite with some doubt as to the outcome. Nevertheless, he could drive a hard bargain when holding a good hand.

It was not many hours before Theodore returned saying: "Well, I just threw a cup of coffee in Liveright's face!"

"And that's how the interview ended?" I gasped.

"Yes, that's it. To hell with him! He'll never call me a liar in public! He is making plenty of money on the book and now he has the play rights. Ten percent is all he'll get from me on the sale of the movie rights, and that's final."

The story was that the original contract for the book between Dreiser and Liveright provided for a 10 percent commission to be paid to Liveright in the event of a sale of the motion picture rights. A subsequent agreement was made the day Dreiser signed a contract for the play rights, to the effect that should the motion picture rights be sold before the play was produced, Liveright would receive 10 percent of a sum up to $30,000, but no commission on anything over $30,000.

On the way over to the luncheon, however, Liveright asked Dreiser what he was going to ask for the motion picture rights. When Dreiser said he would ask $100,000 Liveright was amazed. He told Dreiser he would never get it, to which Dreiser replied: "It will be that or nothing." Liveright then asked if Dreiser would give him all over $60,000 in the event that he was able to sell the rights for that large a sum, since he had brought about the meeting between Dreiser and the movie magnates. Upon Dreiser's refusing to do this, Liveright then asked him if he would take care of him. To this, Dreiser agreed. At the luncheon when Dreiser insisted on the price of $100,000, Liveright excused himself and left the table. When he returned, a final agreement had been reached between Lasky and Dreiser for $90,000. Liveright immediately put in his claim for all over $60,000.

"You will get your ten percent," said Dreiser.

"But you said you'd take care of me in spite of the new clause," exclaimed Liveright.

"I said I'd take care of you up to our original agreement, and I don't even have to do that," Dreiser countered.

"You're a liar," Liveright lashed out.

It was then that Dreiser hurled the cup of coffee at Liveright and brought the luncheon to a speedy termination, ending all negotiations for the time being.

Dreiser was determined in his attitude but slightly disappointed that the deal had not gone through immediately. It was the way he wanted everything to happen—suddenly, clearly and dramatically, and knowing how hard and long he had worked on the book, I could understand his attitude.

But a few days later the deal was closed and he had his $90,000. And now the man who in 1920 had held fast to a poverty complex found himself in possession of what to him was a fortune. The first thing to do was to find out about investing it profitably. He knew nothing about sound investments but he intended to learn. He would take no one's advice; he had always been self-reliant and would continue to be so. And so, for a time, he came and went to and from the bank, with bond statements and financial reports, even stocks, in his pockets. He delved into the matter with his customary thoroughness, and it was not long before he was quite well informed on the stock market, for Dreiser was a man who could put his mind to anything and emerge knowing a great deal about the subject. It was the same with the selection of a theme for a book he planned to write. A case in point is his book *The Financier*. Although he had no first-hand knowledge of finance, he wrote a book conceded to be a masterpiece in its field. And when a prominent financier from Philadelphia came over to New York for the specific purpose of meeting a man so well advised on the subject, Dreiser told him he knew nothing about finance.

"How then did you write such a book as *The Financier*?" the man queried in astonishment.

"Well," said Dreiser in amusement, "I read up on the subject, as I always do when writing a book."

That was his way, and it helped to make his books realistic. He also had the gift of reducing a complicated problem to its common denominator so that it appeared simple and clear to the reader. This was the same conception of writing held by Abraham Lincoln. When he was criticized by Secretary of State Seward for the simplicity of his style in a foreign State document, Lincoln said: "Well, you understand it, I understand it, and I dare say they will understand it when it reaches its destination." It was this same clarity of expression that made Dreiser comment on Lincoln's ability as a writer.

Dreiser was fundamentally interested in human beings,

human emotions and the motivations behind them, and as the years went by I learned more about his creative mood and method. I learned, for instance, to weigh the value of and, I might say, the necessity for his association with the various women in his life.

One day in March the telephone rang, and when I heard a woman's voice asking for Dreiser, I instinctively knew that it was the woman whose presence I had felt during those dark days of Brooklyn. These were the first words ever exchanged between us. She asked me to tell him she was leaving for California and would be at Pennsylvania Station at a given time. Would I tell him?

Yes, I would be glad to tell him, I replied.

Probably something in my voice made her hesitate. And then . . . did I know who she was? Yes, I did, and wished her all good luck on her trip.

Then she said: "You are Helen, aren't you?"

"Yes," I said, "I am."

"Well, you know, Helen, you are the only one I was ever afraid of. . . . You know," she continued, "*I* was one of the important contacts in his life. . . . yes, I was. I was as important as *Sidonie** and *Aglaia.** He won't forget me, I know."

It would be difficult to record what I felt at that moment. Here I was speaking with a woman who had made known to others that she hated me. And yet what did *I* feel? Warmth —the understanding that one woman instinctively feels for another who has suffered through the same source—regret

---

* "This Madness" by Theodore Dreiser, published in Hearst's International *Cosmopolitan*, February to August, 1929. Original manuscript at the University of Pennsylvania.

for the human misunderstanding that I knew was involved on both sides. And at the same time, I wondered if she was not really better off in her freedom.

"You have him *always*," she continued, "he comes *home* to you."

"Yes, I know that," I said, "and I appreciate it, but there is a kind of responsibility involved in it, too, isn't there, and many disappointments?"

"Yes, I know you have suffered a great deal, but, you know, when you came back from the West there was a definite change in him, a psychic strength I felt I could not beat. Before that, nothing he did seemed to worry me greatly, but he was entirely different after you arrived."

"And don't you think he needed that strength, working under such terrific pressure?"

"Yes, I suppose so, but it weakened me," she said, simply and honestly.

I felt as though I wanted to put my arms around her, but I could do nothing more than wish her a pleasant journey, saddened by the realization of the incommunicability of human relationships. I never forgot that strange telephone conversation between us, after so many strenuous months of intermingling emotions and moods.

I learned that Dreiser had liked the stress and strain of this particular creative period so much that he attempted again and again to repeat it. He tried to place himself between opposing forces in order to gather reactions of a stimulating quality and character, and at the same time to safeguard himself against being weakened or destroyed by the indispensability of any one person.

14

As summer approached, we decided to take a trip to Europe. Before leaving, however, we gave a party for a few of our friends at a New York night club, to celebrate the success of *An American Tragedy*. About thirty people were invited. It was the first party we had ever given together and it proved to be quite successful.

On June 22, 1926, we set sail on the *S. S. Frederick VIII*, bound for Scandinavia. There were many interesting passengers aboard, and as Dreiser was soon discovered, we met a number of them, among whom was Otis Skinner, the actor, on his way to a *Hamlet* festival in Denmark. There were Scandinavian movies, dancing, singing, and, as usual, much flirting. We had perfect weather all the way over, and the food, presided over by a Danish chef, was excellent.

After seven days of sailing, we caught our first sight of land—the Hebrides. Standing at the rail, we were enchanted by the scene: blue water lapping dark blue-gray headlands, sea birds, fishing boats, white lighthouses emerging from the mist, and a sense of the desolate life of the hills of north-western Scotland. Teddie said he would never forget the Hebrides. He commented on the flying madness that was taking hold of the world, which would make them habitable for summer cottages and hotels. Then the Orkneys on the left —a sea storm with thunder and lightning—a fascinating sunrise at 3 A.M., and everyone on deck as we neared our destination.

Finally we entered the North Sea and the Norwegian coast loomed in the distance. The harbor of Oslo (Christiansand) came into view where the waters were crowded with small rowboats filled with men and women, boys and girls, who circled around the boat waving their hats and hands and singing a welcome to all on board. They seemed like graceful seagulls as they moved about in the sunny waters. As Teddie said, the village suggested an old German one with its church steeple, factory and scores of small boats.

The sensation of approaching a foreign shore for the first time in one's life is unique. To be separated from one's own land by a vast body of water creates a feeling of freedom and detachment from the native soil on which one has moved, lived and breathed from birth. I was thrilled at everything I saw.

In Oslo, we found the two principal hotels filled to capacity, but we did obtain accommodations at the Norge, after submitting to interviews and pictures for the newspapers. As soon as we had adjusted ourselves to our new quarters, we lost no time in exploring the city. The stores were small and quaint, the houses faded and rather neglected in appearance. We noticed the absence of drug stores with soda fountains, and the new buildings one is so accustomed to in America. Instead, there were small shops attended by large stout Norwegian women, numerous rooming houses, flowers in many windows, a car line but no streetcars in sight, cobblestone streets and many horses. The Norwegian eye seemed blue and wind-blown, as though it had been forever squinting before sun, wind or rain; Norwegian hair was pale blond or red; odd Zorn-like figures of men, women and children, with red weatherbeaten complexions. Teddie said the quaint little stores and houses reminded him of Warsaw, Indiana, in about 1884. There were vegetable markets but little color, a canal full of motorboats, a Shell Oil station, and finally a rather smart shopping street. As we walked around the town, I could not help but think of the "Christiania" of Knut Hamsun, in his book *Hunger* which I had just finished. His mood dominated my first impressions and came back to me in a dozen little turns in the streets or in some weird little doorway or deserted shop. His book *The Growth of the Soil* is considered the greater book, but *Hunger* had taken hold of me by its sustained feverish vividness and a certain stark beauty which I could not put out of my mind.

Dreiser would have called on Hamsun to express his admiration for his work, but rumor had it that he had the habit of disappearing into the impenetrability of his vast acres when faced with the prospect of entertaining visitors from abroad.

We visited the graves of Ibsen and Bjornson, and museums, containing the old Viking ships, which were a revelation to

me. I had thought the Vikings were the heroes and great men
of the Northland. Probably they were, but it seems that their
kingship depended mostly on plunder. I looked up the word
Viking which means Vik (inlet) ings (men)—Inlet-men
who, like the robber barons and pirates of old, went out in
great numbers to rob their victims and then lost themselves in
the maze of hundreds of fjords which they knew as well as
our Indians knew their mountains, valleys and streams of
early America.

The atmosphere had a depressing effect upon Teddie; he
missed the bright colors he was accustomed to in America.
We hired a car and drove up the hill to Holmenkollen, where
we took pictures of quaint little homes roofed with sod, one
being supported by giant whale ribs. We came to a lake surrounded by silent pines and thickly bedded moss on which
we stretched out. Two Norwegian girls were singing in the
distance and a blind man was playing a concertina to the
young folks. Later we found a little restaurant in the pines
where we had an excellent fish dinner with Spanish wine, and
Teddie mellowed into one of his best moods. Norway now
seemed more colorful, warm and friendly.

It was late, but still light, and as we started walking down
the hill to the car, I could hear the silent song that Teddie
was singing as we walked—the song of tranquil pine woods,
of little blue and red petals blown by soft breezes across the
traveler's path, of birds and cool shadows and fresh water
trickling through the deeply embedded rocks, of dreams of
rest and sleep here in the woods, of strong animal-bodied
girls and boys, of woodchucks and badgers and squirrels and

ferrets that peep and pry, under a sky without stars but all
burnished silver the whole night through.

Before leaving Norway, we headed north to Trondhjem,
and embarked on a trip into the land of the Midnight Sun.
Returning to Trondhjem, we set out on an expedition, heading
south along the rugged coast of Norway on a nine-day trip
through the fjords. Instead of taking one of the liners, which
made few stops, we traveled in small boats carrying mail and
provisions to the little villages. We cruised for miles through
deep and narrow waterways bordered on both sides by high
mountainous slopes, so steep and dangerous that one would
think only a mountain goat could venture there. Yet we saw
an occasional hut on high inaccessible spots halfway to the
summit, and now and then we noticed a man ascending or
descending. Bare rocks, granite and sparse grass; one sharp
turn after another in which one had the illusion of heading
straight into the mountain ahead, when suddenly the fjord
would take a sharp turn and a narrow opening would appear.
This went on for miles and miles. Then a small Norwegian
village, not much more than a boat dock and a few houses,
and friendly, eager, smiling faces to greet the boat carrying
mail and provisions so welcome to them in their meager surroundings. Among the many stops we made were Soholt and
Merok on the Geiranger Fjord; Olden on the Nord Fjord.
Traveling was slow. Mountains 6,000 feet high were sighted.
Thundering falls were seen and heard. One side trip by taxi
was to Graakallen, a summit 1,800 feet high overlooking a
bay. Teddie, impressed by the majesty of the scene, said his

soul needed mountains and seas for company, and he never experienced loneliness in the presence of a great view.

In the little villages which we visited there were no radios, no blasting noises, and I remember Teddie saying: "This in itself should be sufficient to convince the average American that the country is all wrong. What! No loud speakers going? No 'Yes Sir That's My Baby'? Why, good God, the country must be a total loss!"

After arriving at Brigsdal, we started out on foot to climb the glacier, a long trek upward over blue ice studded by enormous rocks between which we saw flowers blooming— bluebells and pink trumpets. On our way down, we came across a tiny bleating lamb which had fallen far below us between rocks. Teddie was much moved by the hopeless plight of the small creature and immediately upon our arrival at the bottom notified the authorities in charge, who assured him they would rescue it at once. We left by car for Vasenden along the fjord, on a thrilling road cut along the sides of towering cliffs. We passed through a terrifying gorge—an overpowering Götterdämmerung country where the cut ran through mountains 8,000 feet high on either side; a deserted witches' canyon if there ever was one, which might have once been inhabited by gnomes, ogres, witches, giants and the like, who had since departed, leaving the deserted grass-roofed huts to their fate. Overhanging rocks protruded halfway across the road as we sped anxiously beneath veritable walls of granite. We both sighed with relief when we finally emerged from this weirdest of lands and were able to laugh at our fears.

We stopped at many places on our way back to Oslo, from

where we journeyed to Stockholm, Sweden. Immediately upon our arrival, we skirted the waterfronts, canals and inlets. I began to realize what traveling with a man of Dreiser's caliber meant: vigorous and rigorous program every hour of every day. Early in the morning he was ready to go. "You wanted to travel—to see Europe. Well, come on, up with you now," and we would start off to see all there was of interest. Of course I needed little coaxing to go along at any early hour, for I was eager to see, learn and experience all that I could.

We were delighted with the panorama of Stockholm— grouped sails of ships, crowded market places, lovely old medieval houses facing rippling sea water, boats passing through open drawbridges—all blended together to suggest the paintings of Ruysdael, as Teddie remarked.

We spent an afternoon at Dreiser's publisher, Norstedt and Soner, and another day, Thorsten Laurin, one of the publishers, took us to the home of the Swedish sculptor, Carl Millis, whom he admired deeply. We returned to our hotel only to start out again to Djingarden (Beergarden) Skansen to see examples of old Swedish life. Teddie was impressed by the intelligence of reproducing old Swedish houses, barns, farms, implements, costumes—all relating to the very earliest social and economic life of the country and the charm of having a folk play in the open air theater showing the manners and customs of the period against a setting of an old Swedish church, Lapp huts, etc.

We wound up our brief stay in Stockholm by visiting a Nordiske Museum, where we saw a statue by Millis of Gustav Wasa (Wansa), the founder of Stockholm. We studied old manuscripts, documents and letters signed by Gustavus Adolphus, Napoleon, Frederick the Great, and other notables; also, the original silver-backed Gothic text—or a part of it— of the four testaments from the Fifth Century, A.D. Teddie was delighted.

In Copenhagen, Denmark, we stayed at the Palads Hotel, facing a large square. On our first morning there, we saw a steady stream of thousands of cyclists, ten or fifteen abreast, peddling along to business. There were attractive girls and boys, each with a neat little basket or small box, probably containing lunch, hanging from the handle bars. No autos, no carriages, just cyclists, practically noiseless, all moving in one direction. The city, being flat, made this bicycle traffic most practical—but how enchanting!

After having breakfast at the sidewalk café connected with the hotel, some very charming Danish people, whom we had met on the boat, called on us with a lovely bouquet of flowers and an invitation to go to the Glyptotek—a distinguished art museum filled with Greek, Roman, Egyptian and modern sculpture collected by Carl Jacobsen, founder and builder, and presented to the city of Copenhagen. His modernity was expressed by originals of Rodin, Folqurre, Sinding, Thorwaldsen, Corpeaux, Gullienne, Barrias as well as examples of English and American sculpture. Painting was represented by Cézanne, Picasso, Matisse, Renoir, Degas, Donnier, Manet, Corot and many others. There was also an excellent collection of crypt or burial art.

One afternoon we called on Georg Brandes, famous critic, who at that time was eighty-four years old. He spoke English, French, German, Italian, Latin and probably other languages.

In his day he had been a friend of Ibsen, Strindberg, Clemenceau, Gerhart Hauptmann and Sudermann. He had met Shaw, Wells, Anatole France, Pierre Loti. I recall he decried the growing trend toward nationalism in Europe. When he was a boy, he said, Danish, Norwegian and Swedish were all one tongue, whereas since that time they had been pulled apart by nationalism to the point where they scarcely ever read each other's books. He did not believe in religion or too much conservatism, and said he thought there was no such thing as democracy. We were amused by his account of how he came to know of Dreiser and his work. When he had been in the United States in 1914, he had asked someone: "Is there no such thing as sex in America, in its literature, at any rate?" For answer he had been referred to the books of one Theodore Dreiser.

The next day some Danish friends called to take us to Kronborg Castle at Elsinore, of *Hamlet* Ghost fame. The castle, surrounded by a moat, contained a church, dungeons and trees growing out of some of the lower windows and cellar apertures. Teddie remarked: "If the ghost walked today he would be followed by a company of Cook's tourists, photographed, filmed, radioed and megaphoned. Front seats would sell for fifty dollars each."

When we visited Frederiksborg Slot, the marvels of its rooms and architecture (Christian IV) impressed us. Teddie thought The Knights Hall the most magnificent room he had ever seen. I came across a large portrait and bust of my great-aunt Johanne Luise Heiberg, celebrated Danish actress (1812-1890). As I learned, she had begun her career very early as a dancer and was soon enrolled as a student at the

Royal Theatre School of Ballet; later, when she showed rare talent, she was promoted to dramatic actress. Her popularity and success grew until she had cut out for herself a permanent niche in the hall of fame. She married Johan Ludwig Heiberg, Danish writer, poet and playwright, on July 31, 1831, when she was nineteen and he thirty-nine. He was the son of Peter Andreas Heiberg and the Baroness Gyllembourg Ehrensvärd. Johanne herself wrote many short plays, melodies and songs, and her autobiography in two volumes, covering a period from 1812 to 1888, was published in Danish in 1904.

Later in the Christianborg Slot, we visited the Konighige Hof (Royal) Theatre where she had been the star. There were old playbills, old books containing pictures of her costumes, a glass case holding many of her intimate personal belongings such as small vanity cases, a pearl-handled cane, fans, etc. There were royal stalls for horses in the next wing, marble floors, crowns on the stall posts, everything that went to make up a Royal Theatre. There were other relatives, the Allerups and Aalborgs of Denmark, many of whom were army officers and lawyers, who could have told me much that was interesting, but Teddie was anxious to keep to our travel schedule so we prepared to leave. As we sailed away from artistic Copenhagen, we stood on the deck watching the last spire and tower fading to a mere scratch—less than a pencil mark above the distant waves. Teddie remarked that the native Danes were then gathering at their delightful open air tables to have "koldretter."

When we first touched German soil, especially in the smaller towns, I felt a strange harmony come over Teddie.

But after we were in that country for a while, and had reached Berlin, his reactions were different. Over coffee one evening in an outdoor café, he suddenly exclaimed: "Can one indict an entire people?" Then, without waiting for an answer, he went on: "Yes, I think one can indict the temperaments of some nations. Can these temperaments be changed? I wonder. I think nations are products of soil and light, and I wonder can soil and light be changed? While I like the Germans, or at least some of their qualities, I think others could be greatly improved. The Prussians are too drastic. They should mix and mingle with the milder Germans. The landscape is dark and, after a fashion, sad. The Germans should move to brighter lands. They think too much about abstruse and esoteric problems—life, death, the destiny of man—too little of their immediate surroundings."

In Potsdam we saw the new Imperial Palace, but we did not trouble to enter. I am sure the warlike statues prevented us. Teddie said they should all be taken down. "Artistic atrocities" he called them. "What is the matter with the German soul that it can endure—let alone rejoice—in such things!"

Next came Prague, Czechoslovakia, where Teddie spent three days with President Masaryk. Then Vienna, Salzburg, Paris, and finally London. Otto Kyllmann of Constable and Company, Dreiser's London publishers, insisted upon our staying at the charming old Garland Hotel, where Whistler and many other distinguished artists and writers had lived. I regret that on the day Dreiser had lunch with George Bernard Shaw, I was unable to accompany him because of illness, but he told me about it on his return to the hotel. At one point in their conversation, he rather facetiously brought up the subject of Shaw's vegetarianism. In order to demonstrate the efficacy of such a diet, Shaw jumped up from the table and, placing two chairs at a little distance apart, raised himself between them, holding his legs out horizontally some distance from the floor. Dreiser had to admit it was quite a feat for a man of his years, but as to the vegetarian diet being responsible, he was not too sure.

Everywhere we went, the people we met included distinguished writers, painters, sculptors, statesmen and publishers. But by the time October had rolled around, we were getting a little tired of traveling. We had gone through eight countries and had taken in about all the new impressions we could possibly assimilate. We were glad to be sailing from Southampton, October 15, 1926, on the *S. S. Columbus*, for New York City and home.

15

New York harbor—and as we viewed the skyline Teddie leaned his elbows on the deck rail, and a covetous smile spread over his countenance as though he were secretly taking it all into his heart. Then I felt a nervous wave of restlessness pass through him as he thought of all the personalities waiting to see him, some of whom were women, all mentally and emotionally tugging at him. As he expressed it: "the eager wirelessing of certain people" which he found a strain on him at times, when he actually suffered physically. Then again, he would become more calm as he contemplated "my city," as he always called it.

We returned to our suite at the Pasadena Hotel, and Dreiser rented an office for himself in the Manufacturers Trust Building on Columbus Circle. It soon became apparent, however, that a larger and more suitable place in which to live was absolutely necessary to cope with our increasing social and professional obligations. My mind turned at once to the duplex apartments in the Rodin Studios, at 200 West Fifty-seventh Street. I had been there several times to teas and parties and always left wishing we could have such an apartment.

The day I called, I was shown number 13, on the thirteenth and fourteenth floors. A large reception hall led to the main studio, which was an enormous room with a huge north window overlooking Fifty-seventh Street. A high ceiling extended over the entire two floors. On the lower floor, back of the studio, there was an attractive dining room with folding glass doors and a kitchen adjoining. A long narrow hall led to a bathroom and maid's room. The stairs to the upper floor led to another reception hall, with its own private entrance from the elevator. There were two large bedrooms with bathroom between. The whole arrangement seemed ideal, but what captured my heart completely were the bookcases extending from ceiling to floor and covered with glass doors which could be locked. I knew what these would mean to Dreiser. Here was a place where we could intelligently handle our more complicated life.

But when I went back and told Dreiser about the place, he refused to consider it. "Too expensive," he said. Liveright and others were urging him to take a better place to live and work in, and while he was willing to cooperate, he was not ready to take such a leap as this. However, he agreed to look at it, and when he entered the studio and saw the bookcases, I felt his heart melt. "Yes," he said, "the bookcases are wonderful, and I have never in my life had adequate room for my books. But I will never take it. The rent is too high."

With that the subject was dropped, but only for the time being, because a few days later negotiations were started on a deal that promised to be financially remunerative in a fairly big way. Noticing that I showed no enthusiasm for this added good fortune, he asked me why. I told him frankly that he wouldn't do anything interesting with even a small part of the money in any case. And then I hit upon an idea.

"If the deal goes through," I asked, "will you take the apartment in the Rodin Studios?"

He hesitated, expressing his customary doubt as to the successful outcome of pending negotiations. Finally he agreed, and having complete confidence in his ascending star, I replied: "Wonderful! Then the apartment is as good as ours!"

He immediately wavered: "Yes, the deal and providing you can get them to accept five hundred a year less."

"I'll try," I said. Whereupon, fully believing that apartment 13, Rodin Studios, was destined to be the future home of Theodore Dreiser, I called on the manager and secured the necessary reduction. The deal went through; the lease was signed by December 1, 1926, and I started to work at once with the decorators. The weeks that followed were a mad orgy of planning, designing and shopping, interviews with decorators, painters, electricians, furniture and moving men. Eventually, out of the litter of crates and boxes, my dream home took shape, and in February it was ready for occupancy.

It was a beautiful apartment. There was an elegance and warmth about it that impressed itself on all who came there. I never saw women look more beautiful than they did against the background of the natural wood walls, under the soft glow of the indirect lighting. At last, I thought, Dreiser had the setting he could so brilliantly and graciously fill.

But no way of life ever remained undisturbed for any

length of time in connection with Dreiser and myself. This time it was my own emotional security that was invaded. For there had appeared on my horizon a young, introspective, philosophic musical genius, whom I shall call Jason.

I first met him at a distinguished musical gathering where we had been invited to hear him play. Before taking his seat at the piano, he bowed stiffly to the audience, making one think of a schoolboy who, finding it embarrassing to have to bow at all, did so exactly as he had been told. As he sat down, a hush spread over the hundred or more sophisticated New Yorkers, who sensed his quiet mood and concentrated poise. But when his long, white fingers touched the keys, and then fairly flew as he played some powerful passage from Sibelius, Scriabin, Bach, Debussy, Chopin, or Liszt, he had the power of transporting his audience to another element. When he finished, Dreiser along with the other real music lovers, gathered around him demanding encore after encore. Afterward, during their conversation, Dreiser gave him much encouragement, and invited him to call at the studio.

It was not many days before Jason called. He said he did not have the proper place in which to practice, and, after seeing our Steinway concert grand piano, asked Dreiser if he could come there to play. Without pausing to consider, Teddie told him he could use the piano any time that he, himself, was not actually writing in the studio.

In a very few days, he came in the afternoon to play. The maid let him in at the front door and he went directly to the piano in the studio. I was in my own room on the fourteenth floor finishing some new dining room curtains at the time and the studio was very quiet. Suddenly I heard the most heavenly

142

music pouring forth on the still air. Quietly tiptoeing to the door which led to the balcony overlooking the studio, I saw him below at the piano. The gentleness of the lighter tones as they poured forth found their way to my innermost being. It was as if a nebula of light, in which he dreamed and projected his thought forms, had spread over the entire atmosphere. I quietly returned to my room where I could listen in seclusion. I wondered how I could ever live again without music, as I had been doing much too long. For the first time, I felt the full extent of what music meant to me, and how it might cure all of my spiritual ills. I was so inspired, I wrote a poem to him:

HEAVENLY INFANT

You stand—
Fragile, pale—
You bow—
Stiffly—
As a child,
Or some automaton, aloof,
Or robot, weird.

And then—

Your hands run over the keyboard,
And with your touch,
The heavens open,
And
Showers of filtered stardust
Rain upon the keys
As you caress them lightly,
With supernal tenderness.

A strange unearthly presence
Moves like magic

Through your form—
Your fingers
Pulsing steel wires
Surcharged
By mighty Zeus
You are as one to whom
Some sacred portal
Has been opened—
And only you admitted.

And then—

You stand—
Fragile, pale—
Spent.
You bow—
Stiffly—
As a child,
Or some automaton, aloof,
Or robot, weird.

Oh child!
Eternal spring—
Bubbling forth
Its dancing madness—
Up from the rocky bed
Of its immortal secrets.

For some days I listened and was satisfied, experiencing a sense of gratitude to life that here at last was a way to have music near me. And then suddenly I felt a different call. Perhaps as he was playing, a part of his loneliness escaped into the notes that so easily found their way to me. I wondered, as I listened, what I would do if I found myself physically drawn to him. Then one day he looked at me with such a wistful and childlike expression that I thought I would die if I could not respond in some way. He seemed to know this, and from then on his playing took on a different character. Not so moody or melancholy, but more powerful, poignant and appealing.

Teddie, being involved in a new love interest, Camilla,* at the time, I found myself alone day after day and many evenings. But Teddie had the idea that I was all right. Did I not have a beautiful home and a famous man who, after all, came home to me? That in itself must compensate for a lot, or so he thought. However, I was young, attractive, pulsating with an energy that only health and youth can radiate. I was torn in several directions, but my devotion to Teddie had been the pull with the most strength. He needed me, I felt. I had many proofs of it. Surely, I reasoned with myself, Dreiser would understand. He had always written so sympathetically and comprehendingly of the storms which lay hold of youth. Undoubtedly he would say: "All right, go ahead and live out this emotion. You'll get over it. I know you care for me. You have proven that." I could almost hear him saying these words. And so, before becoming too involved with Jason, I decided to tell Teddie all about it.

Dreiser was then away on one of his walking tours which had taken him into southern Pennsylvania. Knowing his itinerary, I wired him at a small village that I would arrive in the evening. When I reached his hotel, he had just gotten in from his day's walk and was tired. I sat on the edge of his bed and he talked about things that had happened to him on the way. He told me about people stopping their cars and

* "This Madness." *Camilla* sketch unpublished.

offering him a lift, and how he always had to explain that he was walking for his health. I listened, waiting for an opportunity to break in with the subject uppermost in my mind. Finally it came.

"Teddie," I began, "if I met someone I liked pretty well, do you think it would be all right for me to have a close friendship with him?"

"You can be friends with whomsoever you choose," he said impatiently.

"That's not the point," I said. "I am asking you if, in view of the way you live, you would understand my forming a constructive emotional attachment to help me live through the time you leave me so much alone."

"Do as you please!" he replied, becoming more impatient. "But when you do, I'm out!"

"But Teddie, I don't care about anyone that much. If it came to a choice, there would be no choice. I have never forced you to make that decision. You live your loves through, and I thought that if anything ever came up that was important to me, you would see it in the same light."

"I'm out of it, definitely out! And I don't want to talk any more about it!"

"But that's so unjust," I pleaded. "You've always talked about freedom, written about it, preached about it. What does freedom amount to if it cannot stand one test?"

By now his tense expression frightened me. "I don't want to discuss this," he shouted. "I've told you what I think, and that's the end of it!"

"But, Teddie, how can you say that, and live as you do?"

"How do I live? You don't know anything about it. And I

don't want to hear anything about that!" And then, suddenly: "Who is it? Out with it! Just what are you trying to put over?"

I was so intimidated by his anger, as well as disappointed in his reaction, that I was speechless and on the verge of tears. I could not have said any more, regardless of what he said or did. He had closed the door to frankness and understanding in my face, and I felt the sting of it for hours into the night. There was no use; if I went on with it there would always be a cloud of deceit surrounding us. I thought, as I lay there, it would have to be a complete break with Jason, but it was asking a lot. His temperament had suddenly become important to me, and I knew if I gave him up, it would mean more loneliness. And yet, as I contemplated the problem, I knew I could only choose Dreiser.

The next day I joined him in his walking tour. We left about seven o'clock in the morning. He was then in the habit of covering about twenty-five miles a day and I agreed to go along as far as I could and take a bus the rest of the way.

As we started out over the country, past farms, villages, green hills and lovely valleys, I tried to shake off my emotional problems. At least, I could say nothing more about them. But somehow as we walked mile after mile through the beautiful, ever changing landscape, everything but the scene that accompanied us faded out. There was no decision to make about Jason, and there was really no Jason. Suddenly everything seemed to be solved and Teddie and I were back again in California. If only we could stay like this, and there would never be any more lonely nights. If only . . .

The next morning, after completing a full seventeen-mile walk the day before, I took the train back to New York. And

---

as I rode homeward, my thoughts kept returning to the adamant attitude that Teddie had taken on the night of my arrival.
I thought of my grandmother—a strong tempestuous woman
with an unbounded capacity for living—and tried to picture
her against the background of New York life. How would she
have functioned? Placed in my position, what outlet would
she have found for her warm, loving, maternal nature?

When I reached the studio, I called Mame and asked her
to come and stay with me for a few days. When she arrived, I
told her the whole story. She listened attentively and sympathetically, and her mere presence helped me. A few days later
I called Jason on the phone and told him, as simply as I could,
that everything in connection with our newly born friendship
was impossible and that it was over, explaining to him that
there seemed to be no such understanding, as I had thought,
between Dreiser and myself. To my surprise, these words,
which I found so difficult to say, were received in silence, an
ominous silence, however, that I mistrusted. I left the telephone feeling frustrated and bewildered.

Then Dreiser returned, and the force of his presence
brought with it something that invariably created a change
in me toward everything and everyone. I found myself viewing the problem with more strength.

In a couple of days, returning to the studio in the late afternoon, I found Dreiser writing furiously on the typewriter;
something I could not understand, as he seldom used the typewriter. His face was dark with rage, and as he looked up, he
fairly hissed these words at me: "I'm copying a letter. It's
from Jason, and it finishes you, I can tell you that!"

After a day of suspense, he let me read the letter. As I

readily saw, it was written with the desire to blast me out of
my home for good. No one could miss the obvious intent.
Even Dreiser in his blind rage and indignation saw that, and
I knew he saw it. I was so hurt and humiliated that I could
not speak, but little did I think that Dreiser would take a thing
as he was taking this. And yet why? What atavistic male law
had I transgressed? Had I not been left day after day, week
after week, alone? What had I to fear? Nothing really; but
the wrath of Dreiser made me fear him nevertheless. I was
numb and melancholy. For days, he came in and went out
without speaking a word. Finally one day he told me that
while he had no sympathy for me, he thought much less of
Jason. "Imagine, you wasting your affections on a man like
that!" And in this, I must say, we were by now in complete
accord.

I wondered if I could go on with Theodore in his present
mood. Still, I was glad to try and went about my household
duties quietly and thoughtfully. But he had no intention of
letting me off easily. An impregnable door was closed
against me. If I thought I had been neglected and lonely in
times past, I was to learn what spiritual isolation meant. True,
he showed no indication that he wanted me to actually leave
him, but he seemed to be trying to kill me by degrees with
neglect and indifference. Day after day he spent most of his
time away from the apartment. If he came in during the late
afternoon, it was merely to dress for dinner and an evening
out.

And yet, I never gave up in my attempt to draw close to
him again. While he was shaving or dressing, I would try to
talk with him. This usually led to abusively cruel words on

his part, with a final sarcastic remark as he went out slamming the door behind him. Sometimes after he was gone, I would throw myself on the bed and cry for hours until physical exhaustion finally brought sleep. At other times, I would lie awake listening for the familiar turn of his key in the lock, which brought some relief in the realization that he was home again.

Dreiser had always been the sum and substance of my affection. He was all I had—the only one I could go to with every joy and sorrow, and when I had displeased him in some way, it was always to him I had to return. But now I had no one. Another man was out of the question. I would have to find something else if I was to continue to live. But what? I had chosen a man to worship in life. He was my religion. I had forgiven him everything. For months I seemed to drift in utter darkness. What in the world was I to do?

Then one day I came across a book, an introduction to Oriental philosophy by L. Adams Beck. After reading it, my curiosity was stirred. Immediately, I secured all of the books I could find that dealt with this subject.

Up to now I had learned one thing from life: To cling to human values was hopeless. I was drydocked. I had to learn to navigate all over again. To devote oneself to man only, and worse, to one man, was wrong. I must find a broader interpretation of life—something more secure. And now at last, in this oldest philosophy known to man, was something promising—something worth the effort of search and study.

16

In turning to the study of Oriental philosophy, I was seeking something through which I could gain equanimity and self-control. I wanted to live with some measure of poise and grace in a complex society, where no one apparently was satisfied or happy. Everywhere I turned I encountered discontent, restlessness, the pursuit of anything that promised a thrill, a change, an adventure. Not because people were lacking in material needs of any kind; rather, they were suffering from satiation, too much of everything—too much luxury, too much love, too much material comfort, but no spiritual ease. I heard story after story, which clearly traced the trend of dissatisfaction in the entire country.

First I grasped at the ideas in this old philosophy as an escape from emotional turmoil. Then, as I began to get an idea of its penetrating insight into life, I gave the subject more serious study. While I went about the daily tasks connected with our widening social life with my usual interest and attention, I was embarking slowly but surely on a journey into remote regions out of range of the material world of which I seemingly was a part. This experience through which I eventually passed covered a period of about two years before I reached a realization I did not think possible—a spiritual summit from which I naturally had to descend, but the memory of which will remain with me to the last day of my existence.

Since our studio apartment occupied the thirteenth and fourteenth floors of the Rodin Studios, we had direct access to the roof. It was here that I went to practice nostril breathing, high breathing, low breathing, and complete Yogi breathing, in the early morning and again in the evening. I found, to my astonishment, that it was opening the way for me in my study of singing and my voice reached a new depth.

After several months of these exercises, I had the distinct sensation of an expanding consciousness, as though my mind was opening to a deeper understanding and wider perception of life. The minute I sensed this change in myself, I eagerly anticipated the continuation of these studies, and although I longed for a guru to take me through them, I knew that true yogins, not believing in the crossing of water, rarely left their native country of India. Swami Vivikenanda, whose books I was reading at the time, had come to America long ago and had delivered a series of lectures at the World's Fair in Chicago, but he was long since dead. However, I did meet several of the swamis connected with the Vedanta Society, located in our building. They came up to visit us at times, when I consulted them on philosophical points interesting to me. Encouraging me to go on studying, they advised me that I would never regret the effort made to gain a realization of detachment, seldom achieved by people of the Western world where concentration and meditation are not taught in the schools.

Of course, I already understood the natural way of living through the physical self—the well-being and care of the body, the instrument through which spirit manifests itself, the body being the temple of spirit as taught in hatha-yoga; but I did not know the far-reaching value of deep breathing.

Later I studied the development of the latent powers in man—gaining control of the mental faculties by the will; attaining mastery of the sensory self, leading to the acquisition of the more subtle perceptions; turning the mind inward as well as outward, in order that hidden knowledge may be unfolded; and substituting hunger for abnormal appetites. To me, the discovery of the science of yoga—over four thousand years old—was like finding the root language from which all philosophical languages stem.

I studied the law of karma and the law of causation—inevitable cause and sequence. I learned that causation does not exist beyond the range of our minds and our senses, as there is no mental association of things in the region beyond the senses and no causation without the association of ideas. It is only when being or existence is molded into name and form that it obeys the law of causation.

I learned that to acquire freedom, we must go beyond the limitations of this life. Until we can give up the thirst for life, the strong and compelling attachment to our transient, conditioned existence, there is no hope of catching even a glimpse of that infinite freedom beyond. As transmutation of personality takes place in the silkworm when it gives up its former physical life and changes into a butterfly, so does one achieve freedom after giving up one's attachment to life with its myriads of possessions. For unhappiness comes through attachment. With the sense of possession comes selfishness and selfishness brings on misery. This sense of possession holds for love as well as for material things for it is the desire to possess that mars love, often leading to its complete destruction. After all, we never really own anything. We are but stewards of all we have and that for a very short time.

There are two ways to achieve detachment from possessions. One is the negative way—immediate and total renunciation of life as we know it. The other is the positive way which comes about gradually by knowing the nature of things, until at last the mind lets all go and becomes completely detached. In other words, making use of the bondages themselves to break those very bondages.

I became saturated with these fascinating thoughts, for I felt that I was on the right road to the discovery of the cause of my trouble. There was no more weeping or brooding. I was now only too glad to be left alone. Teddie soon noticed a difference in my behavior and often came to the door of my room to ask: "What are you so engrossed in? What are you studying?"

"Some yoga books I came in contact with. They are intensely interesting, and I feel I have found something that is making a change in my outlook on life."

He seemed amazed. And yet, later, when he noticed how my interest grew instead of lessened, he would occasionally smile as though he doubted the possibility of one finding anything that could make one an iota happier in this world, and out he would go on his "round of life." As I went deeper into yoga, I felt I was being washed leagues away from Teddie and the immediate world about him, leaving old shores for new. But as I became more involved in this study the importance of life as I saw it around me diminished steadily. It was a strange experience.

To be sure, there were teas, parties, gatherings of all kinds that I not only took an active part in but managed and directed. And there were many charming and vitally interesting people forming a part of these social functions, but instead of giving less attention to them, I found myself giving more with less effort; not being so emotionally involved and accessible as I had been formerly, I had a freer hand and could move unimpeded through disturbances of any kind with ease. I received credit for being sociable, gracious, diplomatic and hospitable to everyone. Some of these qualities I probably had, but my new sense of detachment equipped me to handle myself in a much more effective manner in connection with all problems, and I was determined to continue in the direction I had chosen.

There was the discussion of the Atman, which has neither form nor limit, and being beyond time, space and causation, must therefore be infinite. If the spirit (breath) be infinite, then there can be only one spirit, and the idea of various spirits—you having one, I another, and so forth—is not real. The idea of involution and evolution, matter and form rising out of ether and dissolving again into it; the exhaling and inhaling (repulsion and attraction) of the cosmos through eons

and eons of time, cycle upon cycle, had a definite appeal for
me.

I learned that the essentials of Buddhism are the same as
those of Hinduism, and the much discussed nirvana of the
Buddhists is the same as the Hindu idea of self-realization or
yoga (union with God), the losing of the personal egotistic
self in the larger self of God. The idea that nirvana is annihilation was well answered in the words of the Buddhist high
priest in Ceylon to Edwin Arnold: "How could nirvana be
annihilation when our Lord attained nirvana while he existed, and being already Buddha, moved about in the sight of
men?"

Buddha is considered one of the great avatars. In India,
his teaching became ultimately another high road in the realm
of inquiry, and it remains today as the everlasting path of the
Hindu race. But beneath the surface of the different movements, the one grand note that encircles and throbs through
them all is the note that was struck by Sri Krishna, the central
name in both Indian history and religion. He is to the Hindus
what Christ is to Christians, though in a more complex way. To
some he is simply the human ideal, but to the majority of
Indians he is the greatest of the avatars. According to the
Hindu conception, God has revealed Himself in human form,
many times. Krishna's injunction is perfect yoga or communion with Him who is the author of all.

I found that aggressiveness is not a part and parcel of the
Hindu religion. This religion is non-violent. A Hindu sannya-
sin is a being apart, yet in close personal relation. The indi-
vidualism of the Hindu is directly opposite to the individual-
ism of the western world—the latter being a process of

isolation, whereas the former is a losing of one's self in the whole.

I determined never to hold to anything again, never to attach any real importance to material possessions. Enjoy things, yes, but always with a consciousness of detachment, so that if all were swept away, I would be content just to be. I had a distinct sense of breaking through some kind of veneer that had been superimposed on reality. I had a wonderful sense of inner joy and exaltation, which made me long to stand perfectly still and not do anything but realize being. It was like gazing into a clear pool that reflected only the beauty and truth of existence, without the blurring shadows of man's misinterpretation.

I looked deeply into this vision, knowing in my heart and mind that my view of life would never be the same again.

While I knew that I would falter, stray and err over and over, I also knew that I would return again and again in my mind's eye to this wonderful experience, from which I derived an inner peace that has really never left me.

17

The summer of 1927 brought a pleasant surprise: my mother was coming to New York to visit me. So eager was I to see her again that I boarded a train for Chicago to meet her part way. After our affectionate greeting, she said she had a present for me, and as we walked over to the baggage car, a Russian wolfhound, disheveled and extremely nervous, bounded to the ground in one leap. For years I had wanted a fine dog, and now here, as I saw in an instant, was a dog that fulfilled my every desire, and although he was dirty from the train, quite young and undeveloped, his beauty could not be concealed. He was an offspring of Lady, the lovely wolfhound given to me in Hollywood several years before, and Far Niente Baree, a male champion owned by Myrtle. His name, my mother informed me, was Nicholas Romanoff; he was the finest specimen in my sister's kennel of wolfhounds, not so much because of the blue ribbon he had won in the puppy class but because of what she termed his "angelic disposition."

I was a little concerned with the problem of taking care of such a large dog in a New York apartment, but I knew I would find a way. However, when I walked into the studio with a Russian wolfhound in tow, Dreiser was shocked. A dog was something he could very well do without. But later when Nick was paraded before him, freshly bathed and groomed, a look of admiration came into his eyes and he admitted he had never seen a more beautiful animal.

Of course, I had my difficulties at first. Nick had always lived in a kennel, and now he had to be taught to walk upstairs to the roof which made it necessary to restrain him from leaping up the stairs four at a time. But he was an apt pupil, and eventually developed into a sophisticated New Yorker. Well he knew his Manhattan, riding in taxis and sport cars here, there and everywhere. Many times in the evening, he and I walked from Fifty-seventh Street to Washington Square and back. It meant nothing to Nick to walk in on an exclusive Park Avenue party at one or two A.M., where he would capture the heart of everyone present with his suave and naturally friendly but reserved manner, as he made his way around the drawing room by himself, greeting each guest in turn quite as though he had known nothing less than a grand salon all his life. His poise and breathtaking beauty seemed to be his carte blanche everywhere. In fact, he got to be quite a character about the city and was photographed and written about by social columnists. He was a familiar figure in the Carnegie Hall drug store across the street from us, where he delighted the soda fountain boys by standing upright with front feet on the counter while they fed him bits of chicken.

Our maid, Pearl, and Nick became fast friends and, I am sure, loved each other very much. When Nick would pester Pearl to take him out for a walk, she could be heard saying:

159

"You jus' wanna be in the street all the time. Regular old sport. In the street. In the street. That's all you know." And Nick would look as if he understood and agreed with everything she said.

As the months grew into years, Teddie learned to love Nick deeply. As O. O. McIntyre, the famous columnist once wrote, "Dreiser's wolfhound, Nick, has taken on something of the melancholy mood of Dreiser." However, before this love and understanding had taken place, they had one physical encounter which might have proved fatal to one or the other. It was one day after arriving home from a journey in the country, and Nick had thrown himself on the floor to sleep. During my absence, a lady came in for a short visit and Teddie wanted to show Nick off to her. When he did not respond immediately to the order to "get up," Teddie repeated his command rather sharply. Whereupon Nick, not accustomed to being spoken to in such a manner and somewhat startled, made a lunge at him. Infuriated, Teddie took Nick by the collar and led him back to the bathroom, picking up a leather whip on the way. Pearl tearfully told me when I returned that Dreiser had struck him with the whip over and over again. I said nothing to him about it at the time, as I could see he was deeply disturbed by the entire episode. Later, he told me that Nick had lunged at him between blows, but finally realizing that he was master of the situation, had displayed his characteristic wisdom by the penitent gesture of placing his head close to his knee, indicating he no longer wished to resist him. Immediately, as Teddie related the story, he dropped the whip and told Nick to follow him, whereupon, keeping his head close to his knee, he walked behind him along the hall back to the studio to be exhibited to and approved by the lady caller.

For three days thereafter, the dog lay quietly and inertly in the darkest corner he could find, displaying a melancholy depression well within the understanding of Dreiser. But so affected was he by Nick's unusual behavior that he finally told me he had learned his lesson; it was evident that a dog of such beauty and sensitivity could not endure being beaten, and Teddie assured me that he would never be the one to strike him again.

On the other hand, Nick's attitude changed. Before this unfortunate occurrence, he had considered me his sole mistress to whom he looked for everything, but afterward, he was very conscious of Dreiser's personality, responding to his least attention. He understood that Dreiser was the head of the household, and I felt they both had learned much from the incident.

But that was not the only improvement in the atmosphere surrounding our household at this time. For with my mother's presence there came a change for the better in Teddie's attitude toward me. They had many of the same characteristics. She was so primitive, so understanding of the weaknesses of others, and yet so passively strong. She was inclined to minimize the importance I attached to some of his "foibles" as he always called them, and I felt she understood him as no one else did. However, after hearing the story of Jason, when Teddie made a remark complaining about it, she told him frankly but firmly that he was responsible. Why had he left me alone so much of the time? Why did he allow a young man like that to enter the studio when he was away? What did he expect of a young woman? And Teddie, who had a deep respect for my mother and her quiet unobtrusive ways, was impressed by her firm stand.

That summer, while my mother was with us, we purchased a beautiful piece of rolling, heavily wooded land in Westchester County, bordering one of the Croton chain of lakes near Mount Kisco. There was a little rustic cabin, used for many years as a small hunting lodge, on the crest of a knoll overlooking the lake. We enlarged it into a beautiful log house with wide porches on all sides. The three or four underground springs from which we drew water were converted into a natural swimming pool about 50 by 100 feet long. It was lined with rock and had four sets of steps descending into it. Huge hickory trees encircled it, providing partial shade in the heat of the day. Teddie had a dry stone wall built along the entire road frontage of about 850 feet, which was a year in the building, and Wharton Esherick designed the two front gates carrying the name "Iroki," meaning "Spirit of Color" in Japanese. It was a superbly picturesque country place that we had found, and a source of gratification to both of us as the years passed, for many a happy hour was devoted to the development of its natural beauty.

About this time, we heard that *An American Tragedy* was being banned in Boston, and Teddie left to attend the trial. As he was walking through the train, he was surprised to meet Clarence Darrow.

"Well," said Dreiser, "where are you going?"

"Why, I'm going to the trial of your book in Boston," Darrow replied. "As you know, I think you have written a great novel and I want to do anything I can to defend it."

162

Dreiser was delighted. On the way up they had much to talk about, for Darrow and Dreiser had a parallel philosophy, in that they agreed that no one was really guilty if his conditioning environment was understood. Darrow told Dreiser that after reading *An American Tragedy*, it would be impossible to determine Clyde's guilt on the basis of the book.

"Crime," he said, "is due to causes that are not always clear and distinct and readily understood; to prevent it we must remove the cause. Listen to the story of anyone who has gone to prison, and see if he ever had a chance to go anywhere else."

In October of 1927, Dreiser was invited by the Russian Government to observe at first hand what had been achieved by the Soviets in the ten years during which the U.S.S.R. had been functioning.

In connection with this, a Mr. F. G. Biedenkapp, Executive Secretary of the International Workers Aid, appeared at the studio on October 11. He explained that the International Workers Aid was, after its fashion, a Russian Red Cross. Its plan was to aid workers in all countries and it was rapidly being organized in as many countries as possible—Germany, France, England, America, etc. The conversation ran like this:*

Dreiser: Just how many workers in America do you represent?

Biedenkapp: About 300,000.

Dreiser: And you seek to do what for them?

* From the personal notebook of Theodore Dreiser, covering his trip to Russia, in the University of Pennsylvania.

Biedenkapp: Furnish them relief in distress due to strikes, etc. Furnish them life insurance at a low rate, and legal, medical and other aid in a crisis.

Dreiser: And what does the International Workers Aid want of me?

Biedenkapp. Nothing that will cost you any money. We have been authorized by the Soviet Government at Moscow to extend to you a personal invitation to visit Russia at its expense.

Dreiser: Yes, and what for?

Biedenkapp: To witness for yourself what has been accomplished for Russia by the Soviet Union in the ten years of its existence.

Dreiser: But why me?

Biedenkapp: The Soviet believes you to be the outstanding literary intelligence of America and it would like to convince you, among others, of the meaning and value of its existence.

Dreiser: What others?

Biedenkapp: Well, here is how it is. The Russian Government is planning a decennial celebration of its reign which begins November 3, and ends November 10. It wishes to show its economic and cultural developments. There will be pageants, exhibitions and entertainments. You personally will have an opportunity to meet the leading government and art figures and forces in Russia and learn for yourself how things stand.

Dreiser: In a single week?

Biedenkapp: No. In your case the time is to be extended. You may stay a month or six weeks if you wish. Go where you will, accompanied or unaccompanied by Russian officials and judge for yourself what has been done and what is happening.

Dreiser: And to what end?

Biedenkapp: Well, your opinion in America, should it chance to prove favorable—and we think it would be favorable—would have weight here.

Dreiser: The Russian Government is seeking recognition by the United States Government?

Biedenkapp: It is.

Dreiser: But supposing my opinion should prove unfavorable?

Biedenkapp: We will risk that.

Dreiser: But suppose it should.

Biedenkapp: We, or rather the Soviet Government, reserves the right to argue your conclusions.

Dreiser: And who is to pay for this long stay?

Biedenkapp: The Russian Government.

Dreiser: All of my expenses to and fro?

Biedenkapp: All of your expenses.

Dreiser: And who is to guarantee me this?

Biedenkapp: Well, I will tell you how that is. The majority of those invited—some 1,500 in all—are not going to be reimbursed for anything but their expenses after they cross the Russian frontier. Some few, like yourself, are to be guaranteed all their expenses.

Dreiser: By whom?

Biedenkapp: The Soviet Government.

Dreiser: And how am I to know that?

Biedenkapp: We will bring you official cables from Russia, if you choose.

Dreiser: Well, I so chose. I have important work in hand. Under no circumstances would I trouble to travel to Moscow to see a pageant that endured for a week. My only object would be to see the real, unofficial Russia—the famine district, on the Volga, say—some of the small towns and farms in Siberia and the Ukraine, some of the mines and fisheries. And then the principal engineering and manufacturing feats or features introduced or achieved during the life of this government. If you can bring me letters and cables guaranteeing me my time, expenses and personal freedom I will go, but otherwise not.

Biedenkapp: And how soon could you go?

Dreiser: Why should I need to go soon?

Biedenkapp: The official celebration. The Soviet Government would like to be able to announce that you are coming to that.

Dreiser: But I am not interested in any celebration or convention.

Biedenkapp: But you could meet many distinguished people who speak English and discuss with them their views. You would be entertained and learn maybe (I do not mean to influence you in any way) of some things which you yourself might choose to see. After the celebration you proceed at the Government's expense.

Dreiser: And will you confirm this by letter and cable?

Biedenkapp: Yes.

Dreiser: Well, then, how soon would I have to go?

Biedenkapp: To reach Moscow in time for the celebration, you would have to leave here by the twentieth at the latest.

Dreiser: In nine days?

Biedenkapp: Yes.

Dreiser: Well, bring me your letters and cables at once. Until I see them I will not feel justified in preparing in any way.

Biedenkapp: I will send you a letter from myself in the morning. Today yet, we will begin cabling and show you our replies as quickly as they appear.

Mr. Biedenkapp, a small, dark, self-confident man, bustled out.

As soon as I saw that Dreiser was favorably inclined toward the idea of going to Russia, I wanted very much to go with him. But he explained that in order to be free to travel anywhere, under varying conditions, it would be necessary for him to go alone. Besides, building was in progress at Mount Kisco, and someone must supervise it.

"Well," I said, not entirely convinced, "I can at least meet you in Paris or London when you return, and you can bring me a pair of red Russian boots, if you will."

"God!" he exclaimed. "I am to travel six or seven thousand miles to find a pair of red Russian boots. That's what the revolution was for, so that I could go and find red boots. Well, anyhow, if they have them, I will."

Mr. Biedenkapp left for Russia, but delegated Mr. Ed Royce to carry out arrangements with Theodore. Soon cables came from Russia confirming the invitation extended to Dreiser by Biedenkapp, and guaranteeing all obligations undertaken by the International Workers Aid in connection with the entire venture. One cable arrived from Maxim Litvinov, then Assistant Commissar of Foreign Affairs, saying that Dreiser was to come to Russia as a guest of the government. Another was from Olga Davidovna Kameneva (Trotsky's sister). At that time she was head of the Soviet Society for Cultural Relations. A few days later a Mr. Ian Gileadi, of the foreign department of the Amalgamated Bank in New York, arrived with a number of introductions to Moscow personages: Sergei Eisenstein, leading Soviet movie director; Vsevolod Meierhold, one of the principal theatrical directors; Olga Davidovna Kameneva; Sergei Dinamov, Russian critic whom Theodore already knew; May O'Calaghan, translator and cultural relations expert; Ivan Koshkin, head of the state academy for the arts; Shura Gavrilova, who conducted a salon for celebrities; Ivy Litvinova, wife of Maxim Litvinov; Jacob Doletsky, director of Tass; Karl Radek, journalist, connected with Tass; Bill Haywood, ex-American labor leader; Sergei Stanislavsky, Director of the Moscow Art Theatre, and a number of others. Dreiser was assured these names would prove of the greatest value and that he was personally to present all the introductions. Following this, when a delegation of ten reporters called on Dreiser, he gave his views and his reaction to this opportunity.

A farewell dinner was given at Sam Schwartz's, in Greenwich Village, where a large company was gathered. Among the guests were Ernest Boyd, T. R. Smith, Hans Stengel, W. E. Woodward, Joe Freeman, Diego Rivera who was sailing on the same boat with Dreiser, Joseph Wood Krutch, Floyd Dell, Carl Brandt, Ernestine Evans and Lester Sharp. There were speeches by Floyd Dell, Diego Rivera, Ed Royce, Joseph Freeman, Ernest Boyd, Mrs. Woodward and a reply by Dreiser. However, at that time, it was one of the most difficult things in the world for Dreiser to stand on his feet to say anything; he actually suffered physically, and this night I suffered with him, as he seemed so nervously affected. It wasn't until after he returned from Russia and felt the pressing need to speak of what he had seen that he was able to overcome this, eventually becoming an excellent public speaker.

After the dinner we all went down to the ship, where Teddie's attractive stateroom was filled with flowers and gifts, among which were a lucky Roumanian handkerchief from Konrad Bercovici and a shark spine cane from Hans Stengel. As we arrived a charming girl appeared in a smart kidskin coat. Her name was Esther McCoy—tall, slender, refined and intellectual. I liked her at once and the attraction she had for me then has endured through the years.

Many newspaper men and two squads of photographers were present, and there was endless kidding until eleven o'clock, when the "all ashore" bell rang and Teddie found himself alone at last. We all trailed off to the dock, where we stood watching and waving as the ship pulled away.

The first word I received from Dreiser was a cablegram from Berlin saying that in addition to being homesick, he was ill and not sure he would be able to continue his journey into Russia. In Berlin he was seized with one of his chronic bronchial attacks. The two physicians he consulted took X-ray pictures of his respiratory tract and advised strongly against proceeding to Russia, especially in the wintertime. They wanted him to go into a sanitarium for treatment.

"Gentlemen," he said, "this is all very interesting, but it comes on me too quickly. First let me tell you I am *not* going into a sanitarium, and I *am* going into Russia. My condition may be very bad, but I do not happen to be afraid of death."

"Oh, but we do not predict death. Do not misunderstand us. It is not as bad as that. But you are very ill. Your condition is dangerous. Perhaps you would like us to give you the address of another physician."

"No," replied Dreiser, "I will not go to any physician but one whom I select for myself." The X-ray pictures were brought to him to see for himself.

"But I cannot see for myself," he insisted. "I cannot read those things with your skill. But I will do one thing. If you will each write me a letter explaining what is wrong with me, I will take the letters, with a copy of the X-ray, to another physician and if he agrees with you, I will let you know. If not, this particular case is terminated." Both agreed, and the letters were dictated.

Through Sinclair Lewis, he consulted another physician who became quite serious when the letters and X-ray photos were presented. He took several tests in his office and at the Augusta Maria Hospital, after which he, likewise, warned Teddie of the danger of a winter in Russia and tried to persuade him to return to the United States. Teddie did not argue with him, but made all his plans to go on to Russia. Before leaving, however, he visited Frank Harris, Gerhart Hauptmann and several other people in Berlin.

On November 2 he took off for Moscow. A number of people were at the station to wish him well. There were flowers and messages. Finally, as he wrote me, he settled down in his compartment on his way to Russia to see for himself if any of the dozens of contradictions about the country could be straightened out in his own mind—the diametrically opposed opinions he had been reading, which reflected every conceivable phase of this vast country extending over a sixth of the earth's surface.

The strain of such a trip at that time of the year, coupled with the discomforts of travel which he later described in his book, kept me worried during his entire absence. I was powerless as far as alleviating his material dangers and discomforts was concerned, but I could help by giving him psychic support, and to that end I concentrated my every thought on his well being. This telepathic current between us was as real

as any tangible means of communication, and through it I
was able to follow his "spiritual temperature." In fact, a
friend of mine, who came to see me often during this time,
remarked one day: "You're closer to Dreiser at five thousand
miles than when he is in New York."

From my experience in traveling with Teddie in the past,
I knew how thoroughly he would cover the field of his investi-
gations, and his personal notes written for his own information during these travels verify this fact.* He went about
Russia trying to grasp the full social significance of every
plan in action from the Russian point of view as against his
own conception of government, economics, individual and
collective psychology, and the problem of the individual
which he never lost sight of.

During his travels in Russia, and after leaving that country,
when his thoughts were becoming clarified and crystallized in
connection with all he had seen and personally encountered,
Dreiser ferreted out a great deal of what he thought was true
and constructive in the massive Russian social experiment. He
also found many phases of procedure which he heartily dis-
agreed with, often expressing his disagreement in arguments
with heads of departments, directors and officials throughout
Russia. However, this had always been Dreiser's way of drawing people out. While he realized the part capital had played
in the growth and development of the United States, he deeply
and violently disapproved of the evils of capitalism—the ex-
ploitation practiced by its exponents. He had watched and
studied it closely since his early youth and had written extensively on the subject. Having himself been a child of poor
* *Ibid.*

parents, he knew what the pangs of poverty were, and had passed through innumerable hardships along the way when he was struggling desperately to launch himself as a reporter, journalist, editor and writer, without financial security or backing of any kind. He knew the United States, I dare say, as well as anyone ever did, and he loved his native land with his whole heart.

However, he was convinced of the need for reform—social, monetary, political, economic and educational. He not only longed for these changes to take place, but he worked for them. He was never too busy to cooperate in every way with any liberal movement promising to achieve a better world. And once in Russia, he was just as discerning in his search for what he thought was progressive as he had ever been in his own country.

After spending some time in Moscow and Leningrad, where he met and talked with other visiting Americans—Professor H. W. L. Dana of the New School for Social Research in New York, Walter Duranty, Scott Nearing, Dorothy Thompson, Anna Louise Strong, and many others—he started on his trip south into the Ukraine, the Donetz Basin, the Black Sea country, and east of the Caucasus. He was accompanied by a secretary, Ruth E. Kennell, a native American supplied by the Russian Government; Dr. Devodovsky, a Russian woman doctor; and Mr. Dinamov, an interpreter. He visited Nijni Novgorod, Kiev, Stalin, Rostov, Kharkov, Kislovodsk, Baku, Tiflis, Daghestan, Azerbaijan, Tashkent, Samarkand, Batum, Novorossisk, Feodosiya, Yalta, Sebastopol, Simseropol, Odessa and many small places in between.

"He questioned local officials and knocked at the doors of

private homes. When Mrs. Kennell announced that here was an 'American delegate,' all doors would be opened. On one occasion he descended into a mine by a wet, dripping elevator to ask the coal-diggers what they thought of the present regime in comparison with that of the Czar. On another, trailed by the villagers, he sought the local priest, who remained cautiously noncommittal on perceiving the official secretary. He visited orthopedic institutes, museums of agronomy, monasteries, children's colonies, collective farms, workers' dwellings."*

He approved of the divorce of religion from the state. He had nothing but praise for the new schools, hospitals, libraries, workers' clubs, sanitariums, kindergartens, manual training and art schools for the people that he had seen all over the country, and for giving "the collective mentality of Russia, freedom to expand." But he was repelled by the distressingly shabby condition of the hundreds of stray children scattered all over the country, who so often became stowaways on boats on which he traveled, and he was irritated by the constant espionage and native suspicion, so common to the Russian, which one had to endure every moment while there.

It was after he left Russia and bade farewell to his traveling companions that Ruth Kennell, in completing the typing of Dreiser's notes, which she forwarded to him, wrote: "Your mission in coming to Russia was to win me back to my native land"—America.†

* Robert H. Elias, *Theodore Dreiser: Apostle of Nature* (New York: Alfred A. Knopf, Inc., 1948).
† Dreiser notes on Russia.

18

On December 30, I sailed for Europe on the *Mauretania*, after having received a cablegram from Teddie to the effect that he would cross the Black Sea at Odessa and would like to have me meet him in Constantinople. I cabled him to get in touch with me at the Regina Hotel in Paris, but when I arrived was disappointed to find no word from him.

Almost immediately, I received a call from Rada Bercovici, daughter of Konrad, who had asked her to get in touch with me upon my arrival in Paris. I liked her immediately. After a very interesting visit, she promised to take me over the following day to a French quarter in Paris, comparable to that of the East Side in New York, and not having seen previously anything but the familiar European atmosphere, I welcomed this opportunity.

When Rada came to the hotel the next day, nothing would do but for me to change my much too English hat for a tam, which she said would be more appropriate and would attract less attention. It was a most interesting excursion. There were rows and rows of booths, one after another, where entire families camped indefinitely in charge of the sale of every imaginable article, old and new. Sordid displays of discarded and bedraggled finery were strewn about everywhere. Rada greeted and conversed with a few of the people she knew by sight as we passed on pleasantly from one to another.

From there we went over to the Sorbonne neighborhood for lunch and a long chat. I liked her point of view. It was broad, understanding, wise, although she was a mere child. As I looked into her deep black eyes, they seemed to hold all the mysteries of her race from the beginning of its time. A true daughter of Israel, hers was a blood crossed with a Roumanian gypsy strain that gave her a colorful temperament along with the ancient wisdom and instinct of the Oriental. I was very glad I had met her. The following day, I took the train for Constantinople, without having received any word from Teddie.

The trip from Paris to Constantinople, being my first venture toward the East, provoked intense interest in me. The train, of course, was a typical continental type with private separated compartments, wholly unlike our open American cars.

As we passed through Switzerland, northern Italy, Yugoslavia, Bulgaria, Greece and into Turkey, I was completely captivated by the dissimilarity of the countries as we crossed one border after another. The changing scenes—national costumes, a few of which were still to be seen along the road here and there; the lovely tall thin cypresses in Italy, dark and firm, standing out against the clear sky; by contrast, the queer tall reed-like trees topped with clusters of brush; the knotted sticks of trees surrounding bare patches of ground;

the flatness of the earth in Yugoslavia; and, as we neared Turkey, the old women moving along through the countryside herding cattle, doing their chores in long black dresses, their faces actually veiled. Here were the remnants and the end of the old sultanic regime.

I heard no English spoken until the end of the second day, when I heard a man's voice ring out in the dining car: *"No . . . haven't you any roquefort?"*

I was happy to hear the familiar American accent, and looking across I saw a large, young, red-headed, florid-faced American. Afterwards, when we became acquainted, I learned that he was a rug buyer for one of the largest retail establishments in New York.

When the train pulled into Constantinople, I was met by a guide from the principal European hotel. I had engaged him through the Cook Travel Agency in Paris. Registering at the hotel, I found no word from Teddie, and when I went up to my room I was not a little disturbed. What did it mean? Was he ill in Russia? Anything could have happened in all the time since I last heard from him.

The following morning I prepared to go to the American Consulate, to demand entrance into Russia, if need be. My guide was waiting for me bright and early in the hotel lobby. Noting my anxiety, he suggested we go to the post office first to look through the cablegram copies kept on file there. At the post office, we were led to a room where we were presented with a great stack of thin cablegram carbons which we went through carefully and patiently. Finally, after a considerable search, we found a copy of one signed by Teddie, addressed to the wrong hotel, which accounted for its not having been delivered. In it he said he could not get across the Black Sea for two weeks and would have to leave Russia over the Polish border; that I should return to Paris and meet him at the Terminus Hotel. I was greatly relieved and even happy, although I had been looking forward to seeing Constantinople with him.

I learned that the train for Paris would not leave for two days. Only two days to see Constantinople! My guide, who had lived in the United States for eight years, agreed to take me to see as much as possible in this limited time.

First we visited the older section of the city, now called Istanbul, with its narrow winding streets, markets in basements and houses with latticed porches. We saw Moslemites falling on their knees in the street anywhere, regardless of what they were doing, four or five times a day, to pray to Allah as was their custom every time they heard the call of the Mulla.

Later we went to the palace of one of the late Sultans, commanding a most impressive view of the Golden Horn of Constantinople, where the Bosporus joins the Sea of Marmora. There were sunken dancing gardens with enclosed pools that could be viewed from the elaborate private dining room of the sultan; secret listening balconies for spies here and there, when it had been important for the sultan to have conversations overheard; Roman or Turkish baths, filled with steam. In another section of the palace were amazing collections of jewels and diamonded swords of all descriptions.

The second day I spent most of my time visiting various mosques of the city and that evening, I received a call from my American acquaintance of the train, asking me to have dinner with him. Welcoming an opportunity to see something of the night life of Constantinople, I accepted. We went to an attractive café which turned out to be colorful, strange and exciting. The place was spotted with interesting Russian women in exile. A little later we were joined by a Turkish friend of my acquaintance, a wealthy rug merchant of the city who wore a fez and looked Oriental. It was a fascinating evening and I felt quite daring sitting between two strangers in a Turkish café, surrounded by exiled white Russians, and miles away from home.

Back at the Terminus Hotel in Paris, I took a room for myself as Teddie had not as yet registered. The following day he arrived; I was walking down the corridor of the hotel when I saw him coming toward me. In the first rush of joy and excitement over our meeting, I was oblivious to everything except the fact that he was actually there. But it didn't take very long for me to realize that he was exhausted and weary. The trip had been a hard one, for he had been ill two or three times en route. Now he wanted to rest.

We spent a few days in Paris, and one evening we went to see an amusing performance of *Chanticleer*, but Teddie was definitely bored with anything suggesting superficiality. He was too close to scenes of misery which he had never touched before at such a steady level. Russia, at that date, was a far cry from optimistic America, and it was during these first few weeks that I felt that deep feelings had registered in him. Later, in the face of greater comfort and in the light of distance, he became considerably more hopeful and enthusiastic about Russia's social experiment.

179

This transition was extremely interesting to me. In the first place, Dreiser was a man who had written volumes on the sufferings of humanity, much in the vein of the best of the Russian writers. His Moravian temperament, inherited from his mother's side of the family, gave his writings their Slavonic fluidity. His Teutonic strength, force and unrelenting passion for facts came to him from his father's Germanic strain. Thus, latent in his nature was all the sympathy in the world for the Russian temperament, and yet, with all of this, he was still an American, embodying in himself American standards and tendencies instilled in him from childhood. They formed an integral part of his make-up, even though he was continually quarreling with them.

When he saw humanity, as he had seen it in Russia, emerging through struggle from an unbelievably low state, he was grateful and happy to know that it was emerging, but in these first weeks after leaving Russia, he was so close to his first impressions that he was deeply depressed. He was thinking of how little the Russians had in comparison with the average American, and yet, how happy and grateful they were to have it.

Naturally the French lightness bored and irritated him. He suggested going down to the Riviera for a few days where he could get some much needed sunshine, so we went to the Cap Martin Hotel at Mentone.

Teddie felt better in the sunshine, but pictures of Russian scenes were ever passing before his eyes: the people he had seen rejoicing as they carried home a simple old-fashioned brass bed which America had outgrown many years before, or an old and very simple stove; the peasant family he had visited, who welcomed him with plain bread and tea and threw a piece of black bread to the cat which pounced on it growling as if it had before it the choicest piece of meat; and how it was explained to him that the cat was very lucky to be alive after the famine in Russia which had taken all the cats and dogs in the country.

He told me many stories of human suffering and privation, but they were always tinged with hope, courage and a genuine exuberance of spirit; for now, as Dreiser said, they were experiencing a new birth. And he had touched it, had really felt it over and over again as he traveled through the country, and rejoiced in it, for he truly loved this people. And with this experience, there was simultaneously born in him a deep desire for them to grow, succeed and be happy.

From Mentone, we went to Monte Carlo, Nice and Cannes, taking some unforgettable walks beside the sea.

Then on January 27, we departed for London and the Mayfair Hotel. The more sober city of London presented less of a contrast than the lightness of Paris, and consequently, had a much better effect on Teddie. A number of people called on him. He visited Ramsay MacDonald; also, Winston Churchill, with whom he discussed Russia's social and military importance which, according to Dreiser, Churchill minimized. He said Dreiser was all wrong, and that he would give Russia seven years—then it would be all over. Dreiser declared that Russia was a great military power and would succeed in its social program. He criticized the condition of the mill workers in England and described how he had walked all through that section, interviewing the workers personally. Churchill said that England was prepared to contribute half of the country's income to the betterment of labor.

Dreiser replied: "You may be prepared to do so, but you won't."

From Dreiser's description of the visit, I gathered that Churchill was not too pleased with him. But Dreiser was pleased a few years later, when Churchill finally declared that Russia was "the foremost military power in the world."*

Otto Kyllmann, of Constable & Company, Publishers, arranged a trip to Bath through the poetic English countryside. We stayed at the Bath Hotel, Pulteney, where there were paintings by Watteau, Titian and Velazquez. With Mr. Kyllmann and his wife we went to see Wells Cathedral.

Our next trip was to Glastonbury where, under the shadow of giant arches rising out of the soft green grass, you, in your imagination, construct your own cathedral. There were no flags, no hymnbooks, no epitaphs; just the consecrated earth out of which the bones of the church rise to give testimony to time and life.

We stopped at the famous George Inn for tea. There, before a crackling wood fire, we had delicious English tea and scones while listening to Kyllmann relate his personal vision of the Holy Grail. Half German and half English, he was equally sympathetic toward the passing generation and the fast-moving tempo of the new generation in England.

Returning to London, we visited Cambridge and then called on George Moore who was in his eighties. He was delightful. Scheduled for a serious operation on the following day, he was

* *New York Herald Tribune*, February 22, 1928.

---

actually gay about it, and after an enjoyable visit, he presented us with his translation of Longus' *Daphnis and Chloe*.

Before leaving England Teddie reluctantly consented to go to a London tailor and have some clothes made. He ordered a dress suit, dress coat, four suits, tweed overcoat, shirts, and several other items, which he was later to appreciate back in the States.

We sailed from Southampton on February 11, 1928, aboard the *S.S. Hamburg*, and on the voyage home, Teddie worked out a preliminary order for his forthcoming articles on Russia, which were later to be a part of his book. Some he worked out in full. It was during the copying of these articles that I gained a better understanding of what Teddie had been striving for all his life—the establishment of equity for all the peoples of the world. He felt that in the Russian experiment he had seen the first practical steps toward this goal.

19

Home in New York we were almost bowled over by Nick's exuberant welcome. We had left him in charge of our trustworthy maid, Pearl, who kept him in her home in Harlem. He had been with us only a short time before we left, but his leaps of joy over our return convinced us he had definitely decided we belonged to him.

We soon resumed our informal Thursday evening receptions, which we had initiated before going abroad. Interesting people of all descriptions attended these evenings and met not only their own artistic and intellectual affinities but their opposites as well. There were writers from all over the world, distinguished scientists, composers, Metropolitan Opera singers, dancers, producers, actors and actresses, poets, Hindu swamis, art and literary critics, columnists, explorers, educators, publishers, an occasional political figure and people who admired the great and near-great.

The huge studio, with its wood-paneled walls and soft indirect lighting, was a perfect setting for such gatherings. Through the north window light streamed from an electric sign nearby, looking remarkably like moonbeams. The log fire in the white Gothic fireplace created a warm, gracious and homelike air that made people feel at ease. On entering, one felt that here was a room in which thoughts lived and moved. Often as I looked around at the many animated guests, I thought of the times when Dreiser was alone, his massive bulk leaning forward at his square piano desk, under this same window with all of New York growing up skyscraper fashion around him as he worked at his writings.

Occasionally we gave a special party. One evening we invited about two hundred guests to witness a series of symbolic dances by a group of native Nigerians. They had been in this country for only a few months, and the difficult task of gathering these natives together, arranging the order of their dance interpretations and instructing them in the matter of the barest etiquette, that is, conducting themselves in an orderly manner in and out of the studio, was undertaken by Caroline Dudley of New York, who had always been interested in the strange and primeval.

After becoming acquainted with the grotesque yet artistic dances of these people, Miss Dudley conceived the idea of arranging an African program, gauged to startle as well as delight onlookers of discrimination and daring. A part of the studio was roped off to leave sufficient room for the dancers, and as they came down the stairway from another room in the building, they presented a startling sight. Some of them were practically bare except for bands of beads and scraps of feathers. Others were dressed in weird costumes of every conceivable color. One wore a full, long, sweeping gown topped by a large alligator headdress. A few of the natives squatted in a row, beating upon their primitive skin-covered drums, while others whirled in sweeping dervish-like gyrations. Underneath their over-zealous impassioned gestures, one felt a ceremonial significance which imbued their dances with a charm difficult to describe. In their bizarre sword dance, swords were vigorously and dexterously swung about and occasionally banged on the floor, which, accompanied by the overpowering broken rhythm of the drums, left a lasting impression on all of the delighted guests. Even Otto Kahn, who was present that evening, was thrilled and amazed at the daring and originality of Dreiser.

Quite often we attended large parties given by Horace Liveright at his publishing house. The entire place was thrown open to the guests—writers, artists, columnists, caricaturists, actresses and all sorts of people. Tom Smith, his editor, always shared the honors of host to all present and the evenings were invariably gay and entertaining.

Just about this time, Dreiser was giving a great deal of his time and attention to plans for bringing over the Russian ballet which he had seen at the Bolshoi Opera House in Moscow. So impressed had he been by this group's pantomimic interpretations that he decided to arrange for its importation to this country if he possibly could. William Reswick, a representative of the Associated Press in Moscow, suggested interesting Otto Kahn in the project, and Dreiser did so, after he had secured the consent of the Russian Government to allow the American tour.

But Dreiser, regardless of his artistic powers and capabilities, was not an impresario. He soon discovered that the promotion of such an ambitious program was consuming most of his time and energy; he was keeping and making appointments from nine o'clock in the morning till twelve o'clock midnight in an effort to interest people in the venture, and in addition was finding it necessary to set up an organization to handle the business details. Frank Crowninshield tried to persuade him to turn the whole thing over to an organization like the Opera Association. "I'm afraid, Dreiser," he said one day, "you don't know what you're letting yourself in for. The point is, you're an author, not a businessman or a promoter."

However, Dreiser went on gathering funds and support. Then almost before he knew it, the midsummer vacation season came along and with it the usual exodus of Manhattanites from the city. Faced with the fact that it would now be impossible to reach most of the people likely to be interested, and by this time having almost exhausted his own vitality, he decided, though with great reluctance, to give up the entire plan, refunding all the contributions of those who had championed his artistic dream.

It was at times like this that our lovely place in the country, still in the process of development, proved to be a haven of peace and rest. Here we could touch the healing earth, walk in the dense woods surrounding the lake, plant flowers, draw water from the well, and bathe in the fresh spring water pool. As soon as we entered the gates of Iroki, its magic began to work, and after four or five weeks there everything seemed to become whole again.

Wharton Esherick, who had been helping Teddie construct a small, thatched-roof, log cabin among the trees, had arrived to finish the work, and it was John Cowper Powys who spent the first night in it. It was interesting to note that while our

187

duplex apartment at the Rodin Studios in New York and our large, newly built home at Iroki had meant very little if anything to Jack, the small peasant cabin with its primitive fireplace and thatched roof, sheltered by tall hickory trees, had appealed to him; and, one evening when twilight began to settle over Iroki, Jack asked Dreiser if he might not be the first one to sleep in the cabin. So, later in the evening, we all walked down to the cabin where Jack went through one of his mystic ceremonials that he so often performed when alone, in contact with some very old and venerable tree before which he stood in deep reverence.

On this rare occasion, he went to the stone fireplace, where he stood his old gnarled and twisted walking cane, and as he backed away, he declaimed a few mystic words of incantation. We all wondered if he had endowed the little cabin with a supernatural influence, and I am sure Teddie thought so, for he insisted on sleeping there himself the night after Powys left.

A few days later, a lovely white dove appeared at Iroki— a little wildling with no home but this one of its choice. The way it followed Teddie around everywhere he went made us all remark that it must be the reincarnation of some beautiful woman. One day we caught the dove and put it in a tree house we had built, but it would not remain inside, preferring to perch all night on the limb of a tree as it had done so many nights before.

Dreiser was becoming more and more engrossed in matters pertaining to scientific research and development. This was no new interest, for in the past he had had considerable

contact with scientists, among them Jacques Loeb of the
Rockefeller Institute whose friendship he valued highly and
whose books he looked upon as masterpieces in their field. His
reference library* was filled with scientific books of all classi-
fications, many of which were inscribed to him by their authors. Therefore, when an invitation was extended to him
from the Marine Biological Laboratory at Woods Hole, Massachusetts, to spend some time there and observe at first hand
the diverse scientific experiments to be performed by scientists from all over the world during the summer session, he
was very happy to accept.

We set out from our country place on July 2, 1928, and
after driving two hundred and fifty miles, were pleased to
find an attractive apartment had been reserved for us in a
lovely wooded residential section of Woods Hole by the sea.
I am sure I never saw Dreiser more intensely absorbed or in
a more receptive state of mind than he was at this time. On
the other hand, as I soon learned from everyone connected
with the laboratory, the scientists themselves welcomed his
presence at their experiments. They said he stimulated their
imaginations in a way that a technical scientist might not, because he was not limited by any of the accepted scientific
rules. In fact, many experiments were timed so that he could
be present and there were many exciting discussions in and
out of the laboratory.

I remember one discussion that lasted for three hours during a walk along the beach, when Dr. Calvin Bridges, Professor of Genetics, endeavored to explain to Dreiser, who invariably asked the "why" of the mysteries of life, that science

* Now at the University of Pennsylvania.

was not concerned with the "why" of anything. There was no legitimate "why." Only the "how." He said that all knowledge pointed in one direction, going past all known points and moving on in the direction last seen, like a ship sailing due west and returning to the same point—no beginning, no end. Dreiser asked him about the science of genetics and why they used the fruit fly in their studies. Dr. Bridges explained that they used the fruit fly because it bred so fast and gave them the opportunity of observing the genes and chromosomes of many generations over a short period. Under further questioning by Dreiser regarding the hereditary changes taking place over a period of time, he said there was a gradual variation in the characteristics in the course of many generations, but there was an occasional mutant, a sudden variation, differing from its parents.

In another discussion, one of the scientists expressed the opinion that even if life is purely mechanistic, it is encouraging to think that all substance is within a human and not brought to bear from without; that in the chemical changes always taking place, the human is probably evolving into something different. He went on to say that everything in science, as well as philosophy and theology, seems to be bringing all analyses down to the individual, and this made me think of the way Henri Barbusse put it: "It is a flowing out and upward instead of a downward movement. We go from a given point upward or outward, in a reflex or return motion, instead of a reaching out to the ultimate and trying to bring it to us. We flow to it, analyzing as we go."

Among the other scientists we met were Dr. F. Lilly, a Professor of Zoology from Chicago, and his family; Dr. and

Mrs. Loeb, brother of Jacques Loeb; Dr. and Mrs. L. V. Heilbrunn, Professor of Zoology, University of Pennsylvania; Dr. Robert Chambers; Dr. Michaelis and family who had been in Japan for some years; and a Dr. Sen from India. We dined with Mrs. Murray Crane at her beautiful home on Penzance Point where there were still more distinguished scientists, all working at Woods Hole during the summer months.

For relaxation there were occasional beach parties, usually presided over by Dr. Bridges, who had a talent for organizing artistic parties where appetizing food was ingeniously prepared over attractive fires. After dark, there was singing of songs and telling of tales in the firelight to the accompaniment of the lapping of waves along the sandy shore.

On one of these parties, we went over from Penzance Point in the laboratory motor boat to the Elizabeth Islands with a group of doctors and their wives. After a moonlight swim in the sea, we sat around the fire while Dr. Sen, the young and very charming Hindu scientist from India, rhythmically and musically chanted from the Vedas. His classic features and black wavy hair presented an unforgettable picture in the glow of the firelight.

Suddenly Dr. Heilbrunn called our attention to the fog that was rolling in, advising us to return as quickly as possible. Hurriedly gathering our things together, we piled into the boat, but before reaching the mainland, we were enveloped in a dense fog. We tried desperately to get into the harbor, and finally made Penzance Point. The cars were started immediately to speed back to Woods Hole, but the car that was carrying Dr. and Mrs. Heilbrunn, Teddie and myself stalled after a few miles, refusing to start. As it was very late, and no houses were to be seen anywhere, we decided to walk. When we had walked about a mile, a flooding rain burst upon us and before reaching Woods Hole, we were walking in water up to our ankles. Perhaps because we laughed and joked about it all the way back, not one of us caught cold.

Before leaving Woods Hole, we gave a tea for our scientist friends at the Tower Hotel in Falmouth Heights, to express as best we could our appreciation for an inspiring and enlightening experience. All were destined to go in different directions—some to points very near and some to the other side of the globe. But we had met that summer, exchanging thoughts and impressions, and had enjoyed some precious moments together which would never be forgotten.

20

In celebration of the advent of 1929, we dined with some friends at Luchow's, the famous old German restaurant on Fourteenth Street. It was one of the few oases in New York at that time where the gourmet who longed for a harmonious atmosphere could relax to the strains of classical music and be assured of agreeable service. Dreiser was always happy in this restaurant where he usually ran into friends of long association.

Later in the evening we went to the *New Masses* Ball, an unusual affair that attracted interesting people from all walks of life—artists, writers, poets, journalists, politicians, socialists, radicals, educators, musicians, playwrights and other people from in and around Greenwich Village. I had never attended before and naturally I was curious. It turned out to be a costume jubilee of no small proportion. During the evening many of the guests came to our box, one of a double tier encircling the dance floor, to exchange a word with Dreiser, and there were interesting bits of conversation during intervals between dancing, which lasted until dawn. Although we were not in fancy dress costume, I wore a dress of soft white woolen homespun material fashioned after the Russian Cossack coat. It was beautifully embroidered down the front, on the sleeves and high collar in the traditional Russian design. A striking white Russian hat completed the ensemble, and of all the outfits I ever had, I loved this one the best.

During the evening as I was dancing, a very tall and handsome young man, towering like a giraffe above the heads of a large group watching the dancers glide by, attracted my attention. When the dance was finished, he came over to ask me for the next dance. He was graceful, gay and extremely humorous. Intrigued by his personality, I wondered as we danced who he could be. He was probably wondering the same about me, for he finally said: "How in the world did I ever meet anyone like you in this awful place?"

"What's awful about it?" I replied. "I think it's delightful. Everyone is here."

"Are they?" he asked.

"Why yes, of course. Everyone comes to this annual ball."

"Do they?" he mocked. "Well, I'm dumfounded to find anyone here."

"But you are here, aren't you?" I challenged.

"Yes, but if anyone told me I would be here in this same place ten years from now, I would say he was a liar. I'm here because I don't have any other place of interest to go."

"Well, I don't agree with you, and I'm a little disappointed to hear you talk that way. It's a remarkable thing to be here with so many strange and interesting personalities, all having such a good time."

"I like your point of view," he said. "At least it's different. I know that you don't have to be here tonight."

"Of course I don't have to be here," I replied. "I love being here. Come on over, I want you to meet some people."

With this, I took him over to our box where Dreiser and the others were. He introduced himself as the Reverend McKarl Nielsen, Unitarian minister. Everyone seemed charmed by his courtesy, refinement and distinguished manner.

Dreiser said:

"So you're a minister. What do you find to preach about these days?"

Nielsen, taken aback, mumbled something about "loving one's enemies."

Dreiser chuckled and replied: "Well, that's the easiest thing in the world. It's getting along with one's friends that's difficult."

In the following months we became better acquainted with Nielsen. I lunched with him several times and once accompanied him to the races. One evening we went with him to hear the singing of a Negro choir in a church uptown, and I learned that he was very fond of good music as well as sports of all kinds. The head of a small parish in Flushing, New York, he was devoting his entire time and energy to the pursuit of his chosen profession. His reading had been extensive, for he was familiar with all the philosophies and systems of thought, the great books of the world, as well as current literature, and occasionally he built his sermon upon the structure of a book he thought worthy of consideration, one of them, as he told me, being Dreiser's book The "Genius."

One day he called on the phone, inviting me to go with him to a wrestling match. Having a previous engagement, I suggested he might like to take Myrtle, who was visiting me at the time.

"Certainly," he said, "if she wishes to go."

Myrtle, having become a little bored with New York, welcomed the idea, and from what I heard afterwards, the evening was very stimulating, for they had cheered enthusiastically with the rest of the throng at each decisive hold. Myrtle reported that Nielsen was an admirable companion and that she would like to see more of him.

"All right," I said, "sometime I will take you over to his little church in Flushing, so you can see another phase of his personality."

The following Easter Sunday I drove Myrtle and my friend Lucile over to Flushing to attend the morning service. It was a beautiful morning and we were all happy to be together. When we arrived at the door, we were captivated by the simple charm of the little brown steepled church, partly covered with ivy and literally smothered in flowers. The church was soon filled to capacity. When the Reverend Nielsen walked down the aisle in his long black robe, took his place at the lectern and began to speak about the meaning of Easter and the resurrection of Christ, I felt an electric wave sweep over my two companions. During a pause in the service, Myrtle whispered to me:

"Why didn't you tell me more about him? I'm ashamed of the way I rooted for the wrestlers that night. What must he think of me?" I told her not to worry; that he understood perfectly.

When he had finished his moving sermon, which could not fail to leave its imprint on any listener, about fifteen little children came down the aisle to the pulpit where they lined up, shyly waiting to receive a yellow lily from the Reverend Nielsen.

It was one of the most spiritually invading services I ever attended, and many times in later years, when I entered a large church and was perhaps disappointed by the limited religious point of view of the minister, I returned in thought to the charming little church in Flushing which had contained, for the time being, a spiritual giant.

The first months of 1929 caught us up in the current of social activity that flows so relentlessly through a New York winter season: plays, opera, concerts, lectures and art exhibitions, as well as teas and parties at home. In addition, I was having my portrait painted.

I first met Ralph Fabri, Hungarian artist, through my friend Maria Samson, with whom I was studying singing. Maria, a very fine artist herself, had a profound regard for Fabri and was eager for him to do a portrait of me. I hesitated at first, but seeing that the idea appealed so strongly to Maria and Teddie, I agreed to sit for the portrait. After talking the matter over, Dreiser and Fabri decided that Nick, being so much a part of me, should be included in the painting. This complicated the matter a little, for I wondered how I would ever get Nick to pose for any length of time. But I was not aware of Fabri's sharp powers of observation. When at work, his almond-shaped eyes, set in a purely Mongolian physiognomy, darted here and there, and what looked to be a mere glance really included measurement, texture, anatomy, mood and composition. While his exterior manner was soothing and considerate, his inner mind's eyes was examining, introspective and abstract.

Nick and I went for a considerable number of sittings, and yet at the end of two months the portrait did not satisfy Fabri. It had not "begun to live" as he said. Then one day he told me he would like to stop working on it for a while. He rolled the canvas up and stored it in his studio. Several months later, he called me, saying: "I can finish the picture now if you will come to pose again."

So Nick and I resumed our sittings at his studio. Each time he was through working on it, he carefully turned the canvas to the wall, as I was not to see it until completed. At the end of six or seven sittings, Fabri said: "You can now look at the portrait. It is finished."

I walked slowly around in front of the large canvas wondering just what I would see and not expecting too much, but as I looked at the painting, I was amazed. My spirit, as I knew it to be, was revealed on the canvas as though he had reached in and exposed my innermost self. And then I saw the almost-living portrait of Nick lying close at my feet. The background, although it was only a small corner of our studio, somehow reflected the atmosphere of the entire room. When I questioned him as to how he had brought the painting to life in this way, he said:

"My approach to the work was literal at first. I wanted to paint a large but otherwise regular likeness of an attractive woman. After a while, this literal academic approach changed into an emotional one which liberated my hands, my eyes, my artistic mind to the point where I was able to discard the literalness and create a portrait of the spirit and the intense forces that were at work in you, as seen by my own inner eye. Everything in that portrait; you, Nick, the davenport, the book cases, the flowing garment, the color and design, are all one and the same. The lines criss-crossing and segmenting the portrait are the vibrations I see in life. I think everything is a vibration. Art, creative art, is probably a four-dimensional vibration, and things oscillate in circles or parabolic lines, and those vibratory lines have designs, just like everything else in the universe."

I studied the painting for some time, and thought of the great difference in the technique of artists. There was the portrait* Wayman Adams had made of Dreiser about a year before, completed in two sittings. The first one lasted an entire day, and by noon of the following day, it was finished. It still remains my most valuable treasure.

During the season, a dinner was given for John Cowper Powys by Will Durant at Romany Marie's on Washington Square. Leonard Abbot, Will Durant, Dreiser, Powys and several others spoke. Teddie was in good form that evening, as he was talking about someone he not only admired but loved. As he was speaking, I caught many extraordinary striking expressions on Jack's face as he was listening. When it was Jack's turn to speak, he said of Dreiser:

"It was as if a monolith from Stonehenge arose to speak when Dreiser got up. That *monolith* there!" he said with a low bow in his direction—a sort of scoop of his entire body toward Dreiser which brought emphasis to his words.

* Frontispiece.

I had often thought of Teddie as a rock of Gibraltar. Nothing moved him really. He stood like a sphinx, and human emotions washed against him like waves against a stony shore. A kindly, sympathetic and understanding sphinx, however, composed of contrasting elements—kindness and cruelty, warmth and coldness, courtesy and brusqueness, generosity and frugality, constructiveness and a certain destructiveness, naïveté and shrewdness, chastity and lust. I was beginning to realize that genius was like the sun. One could be warmed, nourished, sustained and strengthened by it or horribly burned, even destroyed by the same force, for it was often totally unconscious of its effect on others. It simply *was*.

November, 1929, was a month of drama. Suddenly without warning, the stock market crashed, leaving suicides and chaos in its wake. It was as though a fast-moving express train had been brought to an unexpected and abrupt halt with all the brake force applied at once. People were confused and hysterical. Some of our friends who had been operating on margin alone were wiped out completely. Even Dreiser was hit hard for he, too, had been persuaded by shrewd manipulators to invest in certain stocks and bonds which were "sure to rise to unknown heights." Instead, many of them became worthless. Fortunately for us, he had not had his money long enough to invest it all, and he had been wise enough to purchase our thirty-five-acre country estate.

It was clear that a modified standard of living faced the entire country; and yet, while everyone sensed this inevitable change, little did they realize the depths to which the country would sink in the years to follow.

21

When Count Michael Károlyi, former Premier of Hungary and once considered the only democratic hope of that country, came to America in January of 1930, we held a reception for him. Morris Ernst brought him to the studio after his first lecture at Carnegie Hall, and we liked him immediately. His intense revolutionary quality was exciting as it came and went like the tide, and his sense of humor was refreshing.

The story of Károlyi's life was a colorful one. He had cast his lot with the common people as far back as 1902, when instead of taking the seat in the upper house to which he was entitled by birth, he allied himself with the Liberal party. In 1909 he made his real entry into politics when he became President of the OMGE, the Agricultural Society of Hungary. He was bitterly opposed to Germany and all its aims, and during the first World War he visited this country and addressed thousands of Americans of Hungarian ancestry, exhorting them to adhere to the principles of democracy. In October, 1918, following the collapse of Austria-Hungary, he was appointed Premier of Hungary. The bloodless revolution which followed swept the Emperor off his throne, and when the Communists, under Bela Kun, took over, Károlyi was forced to resign and flee the country with his wife and children. There was worldwide discussion pro and con regarding the wisdom of his action, and many people blamed Károlyi for the debacle. The real truth is a matter for the historians to decide.

During his stay in this country, we had several very interesting talks with him in which he told us absorbing stories of his personal life in Hungary.

Not long after the Károlyi reception, Dreiser had a desire to review the United States from east to west, to see how the country was reacting to the changing economic conditions. On March 20, he left New York for Tucson, Arizona, via St. Louis, Missouri. I was to join him later in Galveston, Texas, where we were to set out on the long automobile tour. During his absence I leased our country place, and on May 3, my car was lowered into the hold of a Mallory Line steamer.

When the ship docked at Galveston, I could see the familiar figure of Dreiser in the distance—blue Norfolk coat, white trousers, Panama hat and cane. He spotted us on the upper deck, and as soon as the car was unloaded, we were on our way to Houston.

Teddie related his experiences in Arizona. He had borrowed a car from a doctor in an effort to learn to drive so he could sleep out of doors in the desert for his health, which was obviously much improved. He had experienced one accident, however, when, to avoid hitting another car which was bobbing around on the loosely graveled road, he suddenly swerved his car into a huge bank, striking his knee against the ignition key. He had suffered considerable pain and discomfort, but at last he had succeeded in learning to drive and would soon purchase a new roadster. In different cities along the way, he had given interviews to newspapers regarding the economic situation in the country.

The next day we left on what turned out to be a 10,000-mile trip through Texas, New Mexico, Arizona, California, Oregon, Idaho, Wyoming, Montana, South Dakota, Minnesota, Wisconsin, Illinois, Michigan, a part of Canada, Pennsylvania, New Jersey and New York.

We had many amusing experiences with Nick, but he was never refused admission to any of the best hotels across the country. At the Mark Hopkins, in San Francisco, for instance, Dreiser went in first explaining that he had a very special dog with him.

"What kind of dog?" the clerk asked.

"A Russian wolfhound, and a perfect gentleman, too."

"Oh, yes sir, in that case, it is all right." And in walked Nick in his dignified manner.

From San Francisco, we went to San Quentin to see Tom Mooney, who was serving a term for alleged participation in a bombing incident connected with the Preparedness Day parade in San Francisco on July 22, 1916. Although he had been proven innocent, having established an alibi as to his whereabouts at the time, he was still, for reasons presumed to be political, a prisoner.

We waited for a few moments in a reception room until Mooney walked in, self-possessed, vigorously alert and radiating a kind of youthful energy. He was immaculately dressed in a white uniform and had the manner of one who enjoyed many privileges and a large share of freedom. People from all over the world came to see him from time to time, and this distinction evidently placed him in good standing with the prison authorities.

After a few words of cordial greeting had been exchanged, he left us, proceeding as the strict prison formality dictated, to the visiting room where he and Dreiser were to have their conversation. We sat on one side of a screened grating and he sat facing us on the opposite side. Mooney was extremely well informed on every detail of his case, having made a thorough study of it during his long confinement. He was familiar with all the legal aspects, and it was plain from his conversation that he was well prepared to defend himself in any court if and when the time arrived. He was intensely eager to be released, he said, so that he could work for the cause of labor.

Dreiser asked Mooney if he had ever given any thought to the possibility that there might be a difference in his status if he were released from prison. As Dreiser pointed out, in San Quentin he was an international figure in close contact with world liberals who respected him. Devoted friends and followers shuttled back and forth from San Francisco to do anything they could for him. Would he have any such influence after attaining his freedom, Dreiser asked? Mooney listened attentively and seemed to be mulling over in his mind the import of Dreiser's words when suddenly he broke down and wept. All at once he looked like a child pleading for the support he felt he needed. After a few moments, he managed to pull himself together, saying that his one determined aim in life was to walk out of prison, not only a free man, but a cleared one. Dreiser said he would do all he could to help him achieve his goal.*

How prophetic Dreiser's words were! For from the day that Tom Mooney walked out of prison a free man, on January 7, 1939, pardoned by Governor Olson, his position of wide influence in the world of just causes began to shrink. By March 6, 1942, he was not only ignored but dead.

Reaching Oregon was a high spot in the tour for me, for it meant seeing my mother and sister again. We stayed with them for almost two weeks, and I was elated to discover that my sister had developed a beautiful lyric soprano voice. We spent hours singing together and found we were able to contribute much to each other. From her I gained a better conception of singing in the natural free-flowing way, and she in turn was grateful for my suggestions as to interpretation and diction. At any rate, my spirits soared, for I loved singing, and now I felt we might one day arrange a concert tour; we would take mother with us and travel over the country. It was something to dream about, and I was very gay about the idea as we started on our way again through the hills of eastern Oregon.

In Yellowstone Park, we were overwhelmed by the many natural wonders to be seen—gigantic mountain ranges, colorful canyons, falls, geysers, hot springs, well-stocked trout streams and varied species of wild life. We were warned about the danger of a bear attacking a dog in an open car;

* In 1932, Dreiser returned to San Francisco by plane, directly from New York, for the specific purpose of addressing a Tom Mooney mass meeting of some 15,000 people at the Civic Auditorium, under the chairmanship of Leo Gallagher. Lincoln Steffens was also one of the speakers.

whereupon, we immediately put the top up. One night I received a real fright; I had taken Nick out from the camp where we were lodged for the night, when we ran into a big black bear standing erect on his hind feet pawing the contents of a large refuse can. Nick and I were so startled that we ran back to the safety of our camp where we remained.

When we arrived in Montana, we experienced a hazardous and terrifying five- or six-hour struggle through rain-softened "gumbo" up to the wheel hubs, making it necessary to crawl along in the dark about three miles an hour, the gumbo gathering and hardening like clay around the wheels. After about twenty miles of this, Dreiser had lost all trace of patience and had developed a most threatening mood, vehemently announcing:

"To hell with the trip, we are shipping the car and taking the train back to New York in the morning."

It was 4:00 A.M. before we reached the next village, where we floated in on gumbo in front of the town hotel. Exhausted and numb, we entered the lobby, asking if we could bring the dog in. We were cordially greeted by a warm, friendly, talkative and entirely charming man with a trace of Southern accent, who said: "Hell yes, you can bring a mountain lion in he-ah! And do come out for a nice hot brandy before you reti-ah. From this moment on, you are free of gumbo. You leave in the morning on a wide paved highway. Your troubles are over; I promise you."

Well, that turned the tide for us and changed the Theodore Dreiser temperature from fever heat to almost normal, and true enough, the next morning we peacefully departed over an excellent paved highway never to experience rain-soaked gumbo again. We were even able to laugh about our ghastly experience of the night before, thanks to that charming man at the hotel who, with the warm hospitality of a Southerner, had stood on the front veranda of his hotel, feet wide apart, grinning in his infectious way as he waved us a friendly farewell.

In Chicago we stopped to pick up Teddie's brother Rome. For a long time Teddie had been paying for his board and lodging in a mediocre hotel maintained for men only, and this was his first opportunity to investigate the situation. He had always been led to believe that the money he sent was being used to take proper care of Rome, but when we saw him we were shocked by his appearance. He was generally neglected in every way; his clothes were old, his hat weatherbeaten, and his shoes worn out. His shoulders were rounded from habitual poor posture, and we could see he was aging fast.

Rome had left home when he was in his teens, and for many years followed a roving, adventuresome kind of life, connected with railroads, eventually winding up in Chicago. From exhaustion and neglect, his thoughts were disconnected in spots, but he retained many indelible memories of railroad experiences, family affairs and special events, talking interestingly enough about them when stimulated by some reminder. But he had lost the thread that held them together. He persisted in calling Teddie "Paul," possibly because he had been so fond of Paul and remembered his proverbial generosity.

The first thing Dreiser did was to have him fitted with a health belt to improve his posture. Next came a new suit, new hat, new shoes, underwear, handkerchiefs, everything a man needed to feel he belonged to the respectable circle of society. He seemed so happy sitting there in the back seat of our large car as we motored through Detroit, a part of Canada, western New York, Pennsylvania and New Jersey. He became more at ease with us, calling Teddie "Theo" and me "Helen" and talking of "Mother," which made Teddie sad but at the same time glad for her sake that he had been able to rescue the so-called black sheep of her flock.

When we arrived in New York, we were filled with fresh impressions and the conviction that a country possessing such vast natural resources and extensive expanse of rural uncultivated land, capable of supporting three or four times its present population without misery to anyone, also contained boundless potential possibilities and promise for the progress of the entire world. But that progress should be in the hands of the people and shared by them, we thought, instead of being hoarded and marshalled by huge monopolies.

We took Rome to Mame, as she had previously agreed with Theodore to take him into her home and try to take care of him for a monthly allowance. Although she was advancing in years, Mame felt she should make the effort to do it because, as she said, she could not bear the idea of his being out in the world alone any longer. After deciding to accept him, she followed her true pattern of love and charity and he received the benefits of warmth, comfort, good food, and above all *love*, which he so poignantly needed. And how he responded! Later on, when we called at the Brennan home, which at that time was in Astoria, he radiated a happiness that was more than touching. As he sat telling his favorite stories of the "round house," occasional signs of a rare mentality would come through, and as he emphasized certain points by the involuntary movement up and down of his heavy eyebrows, one thought of a distinguished bishop. Rome lived with Mame until he passed away, ten years later, near complete rehabilitation.

22

During the summer, Teddie went back to work on the section
of his autobiography (*Dawn*) covering his youth. He had
done a great deal of work on it years before, but put it aside
after deciding against publishing such a frank revelation of
his early life while certain members of his family were still
living. Now he took it out again to concentrate on its completion, and Louise Campbell, with whom he had been associated
in a literary capacity for a number of years, came over from
Philadelphia to work on it with him.

Occasionally we attended interesting social affairs in and
around New York. One of the most interesting salons we
frequented was that of Madame Alma Clayburgh, a gracious
and versatile hostess who had a genius for blending personalities from the various professional fields. It was here that we
met such prominent personages as Mrs. Sara Delano Roosevelt, the O. O. McIntyres, George Gershwin, Lily Pons, the
Lawrence Tibbetts, Sigmund Spaeth, and scores of other
celebrities.

On December 10 Teddie took me with him to meet Sir
Rabindranath Tagore, the Hindu poet, who was paying a visit

to the United States. When we left the studio that day, Dreiser was in an irritable mood, having just concluded a disturbing interview, and when he had to wait in the lobby of the Elmhurst Apartments on Park Avenue because of some misunderstanding with the attendants about his appointment, he became infuriated. But a few moments later, we were ushered into the drawing room of Tagore's apartment, and he soon entered, chatting, laughing and apologizing for the discourtesy of the attendants. He moved forward with a smooth sweeping motion, and pausing to look at Teddie with his deep brown eyes, exclaimed: "Ah! A Brahman!" Instantly, Dreiser was transformed; the best note in him was sounded and his irritation disappeared into nothingness.

Tagore is probably best known for his beautiful lyrics, but his poetry is only a token of his immense range and variety. Skillful in drama and narrative, he was also a novelist, artist, lecturer, social reformer and educator. When he was awarded the Nobel Prize for Literature in 1913, he utilized the money for the upkeep of his International University, which he established in 1901 near Calcutta. The University, known as Vis Va-Bharati, had grown to be a world center of culture and he considered it one of his greatest achievements.

They conferred on many subjects that day, but as Russia was uppermost in the minds of thinkers at the moment, it was not long before they reached that subject. Tagore spoke ecstatically of his delight in the success of the Soviet Government. He described how he individually and personally handled the caste system with his students in India. He told them, so he said: "You are free to do as you please; to isolate yourselves if you wish."

He went on to explain that by giving them their freedom in this way, in one week they were united to all. He felt that "the mentality of the world must be changed"; that "the man of the future must be educated to believe in the wide brotherhood of mankind." It was his abiding ambition to harmonize the spiritual resources of the East with the scientific learning of the West.

Speaking of Indian children, he said: "They had their kind of Communism, before English rule. Each village had its communal center. Since English rule, illiteracy predominated ninety-five per cent to five per cent literacy." As he sat drawing with his finger on his lap, he continued: "While there were certain patterns that were effective in English rule, it was negative. It did nothing for the individual—did not enable him to draw on his own forces in any way. It was lifeless." The dream of India, according to Tagore, was to enable the Hindu to take care of himself, to draw on and develop his own potentialities, to industrialize the country. Only Communism, as he saw it, could do this. He said, "Russia is a miracle, and as it becomes more sure of success, the object lesson will be world-influencing—no less. All of Asia will be and needs to be influenced by this object lesson."

He went on to speak about his impressions of this country. He considered us the most tyrannical people in the world from the standpoint of the individual; the most aristocratic—arrogantly so. He was irked by his inhospitable reception here.

"I have stayed two weeks over my time limit," he said, "and I have been fined, not to mention the annoyance caused me for the privilege to stay on."

212

I was very much disturbed by these statements. Here was a man almost seventy years of age who had hazarded much to even venture on such a long journey, and instead of America welcoming such a distinguished visitor to its shores, it had reacted in this way.

Tagore said he felt he must leave—that it was no place for him and that no interview was printed as he gave it. Many things appeared in articles over his signature that he had never said and when he took the trouble to contradict them, the contradictions were printed in small type on back pages of the papers.

What answer was there to give to a stranger in our midst— an important stranger at that? Could one say that this kind of behavior did not occur often in this country? What about Count Károlyi, who was excluded for four years before he was permitted a limited visit of six weeks? And what about the great Russian writer, Maxim Gorki, who was held on Ellis Island for questioning when he dared to travel with a female companion, Madame Andreyeva, whom he claimed as his wife? The authorities thought otherwise, and while formal immigration charges were not made against him, he was annoyed and publicly embarrassed to a marked degree, which angered him so much that his visit to this country was cut off and he soon departed.*

So much for American hospitality at times.

The latest phase of what Dreiser once frankly wrote about as *This Madness* brought about a new pattern of behavior

* An article entitled "The Social Lynching of Maxim Gorki and Madam Andreyeva" appeared in the *Independent* magazine, April 26, 1906, while he was still in this country.

that I found difficult to accept. I decided to move out to Iroki and try to make a home there in the large house which had just been completed, if a home anywhere was longer possible. Besides, there was a real necessity for economizing in some way in the face of the depression. The lease on the apartment was to expire in the fall and it would take most of the summer to get settled in our new environment. There was landscaping to supervise, curtains to be made, some painting left to do and many other small items to take care of. I wrote my mother and sister, asking them to come and help me make this necessary adjustment which encompassed many problems for me.

By the middle of June, 1931, they had arrived and we had moved a large part of everything, including paintings, books, literary materials, furniture, dishes, etc., to our new "permanent" home. Some of the furniture was left at the apartment, as Teddie planned to stay on in the studio until the lease expired in October.

Dreiser was at this time cooperating with the International Labor Defense Organization, as well as taking an active part in the social reform program of the American Writers League, of which he later became president.

We were invited to a private preview of the screen version of *An American Tragedy** just produced by the Paramount Publix Corporation (originally the Famous Players Lasky Corporation), the result of which was grossly disappointing to Dreiser. Originally, Sergei Eisenstein had been brought over from Russia by the Famous Players Lasky Corporation, when the story was first purchased in 1926, to prepare a

* Philip Holmes, Sylvia Sidney and Frances Dee had the principal roles.

script and direct the picture.* His script was not used, however, and he had since returned to Russia. Finally, after four years Joseph Von Sternberg had been engaged to direct the picture. Dreiser then flew west with H. S. Kraft to discuss with the producers ways and means of presenting the story, but after seeing the preview in New York, he brought an injunction against the Paramount Corporation in an attempt to stop the picture—a court action which failed.

A partial separation had taken place between Dreiser and myself, and even in the midst of our various activities and interests, we both felt the sting that accompanies any form of separation after long years of constant companionship. One of these moments brought forth the following letter from him, written at the studio:

July 6, 1931

HELEN DEAR:

I wish you would believe that I meant no criticism of you in speaking of the piano and the possible dampness. What brought it up was ————, saying that it was such a beautiful instrument. Besides it seems to me that you are stressing the wrong thing. Last night in this place I lay thinking of us. I can never get over us. I felt and feel so unbelievably sad. And you—feeling as you do, make me so. But I feel that if you would only view it all in a little less conclusive way that you would know that it is not all over. I would not feel as I do if it were. Let us wait—a little while. I am trying to find myself. If I can solve my own problem I can solve yours. And if I can I would come back to you for good—just to go on to the end together. But do not be so tortured. There is more

---

* A copy of Sergei Eisenstein's moving picture script is in the Museum of Modern Art in New York City.

of my spirit with you hourly than you would ever guess. I follow
you in your dreams and know the loveliness of your spirit. Hard
words mean nothing.

The spirit is all.

TOADIE

This statement that the "spirit is all" was not a conclusion
that he reached years later, as some critics point out. Regardless of what he wrote in the meantime or how savagely he
castigated society for its social evils; no matter how he
pointed out that man had made a mess of life as we know it
here on this planet; or how realistic his books were on any
subject he chose to depict—whether his principal character
was a ruthless individualist like Cowperwood, a simple under-
privileged ambitious boy like Clyde Griffiths, a religionist
like Solon Barnes or a temperamental artist like Eugene
Witla, Dreiser was a mystic, first, last and always. He had a
cosmic consciousness—a scientific, searching and direct approach to the study of the natural laws of existence. "Naturalist"? Yes, but a naturalist with an intuition which had its
roots in the cosmic elements of the universe itself. It was this
knowledge that held me to Dreiser during the painfully dis-
tressing thirties that were to follow with all of their conflicting emotions, turmoil and confusion.

His was a dual nature, and there were times when I felt the
opposing force struggling for control within him so power-
fully that I felt he might be torn apart by it. But somehow he
would emerge from the most dangerously threatening situa-
tions to continue his creative work. True, he received some
psychic wounds which persisted for a time, for as John Cow-

per Powys so ably pointed out in his introduction to *Dreiser's Notes on Life*:* "This *force* [in Dreiser] however, was not a *catalytic* power. It did *not* remain integral and intact while it effected startling and significant changes in all with which it came in contact. It evoked such changes; but it also changed."

Dreiser had an indescribable innocence about him which was never touched by anything. More than one woman sensed this quality in him, some to their discomfort while others revered it profoundly.

After the preliminary settling process had taken place at Iroki, things began to acquire a new look. Nick, our borzoi, was deliriously happy in his new-found freedom. We had built a large house on a new site near the swimming pool and lake, our original lodge having burned to the ground during our absence over a year before. Ralph Fabri, the Hungarian artist, contributed much toward making this new house a thing of beauty. After its completion, he erected an adjoining guest house and connected it to the main building with a rustic bridge. He decorated parts of the interior of the main house, as well as reinforced some very unusual stone-columned arches adjoining the large central studio on the ground floor, preparatory to the building of a second-story dining room which was to rest on these columns. Henry Poor, of pottery fame, designed and placed the lighting fixtures; Wharton Esherick, the wrought-iron andirons and several other lovely things of metal and wood. But when the bust of John Cowper Powys was at last placed in a window niche in Dreiser's writ-

* *Dreiser's Notes on Life*, unpublished.

ing studio, Iroki suddenly came to life. Heretofore, it had been just a place to go. Now it became a home—a center from which to function.

Iroki was in perfect order by the time Teddie came out to spend his first weekend since the move had taken place, and as he walked around examining everything, he paused with pleasure when he saw a familiar object in its new setting. He went down to take a plunge in the swimming pool, and seemingly appeared to find Iroki for the first time.

The summer of 1931 drifted away and with its passing went many a troubled hour and heartache for both of us. Occasionally Teddie came to the country for a restful weekend but even though interesting friends were invited to cheer him up, he was irritable and nervous. It was difficult to make him comfortable, as he was restless and seemed to be laboring under a strain. He enjoyed visiting with such friends as Dr. Calvin Bridges who was leaving shortly for Russia to work with other scientists there, Charles Fort, the James D. Mooneys, Marion and Peter Powys, the Will Lengels, Esther McCoy, Dorothy Dudley, Louise Campbell, Lillian Gish, George Jean Nathan, the Sherwood Andersons, the Wharton Eshericks, Ralph Fabri, the Burton Rascoes, the Henry Poors and others, but when he was alone, he became preoccupied and tense. Occasionally he would provoke an argument over some triviality, and I too became nervous from so much tension. Once when my mother and sister were over in the guest house where nothing of our conversation could be heard, we became involved in such a heated argument the very walls seemed to tremble. Our butler, Frank, hearing the outburst from the second floor, went over to my mother saying: "Oh!

Mr. and Mrs. Dreiser are having a terrible quarrel. I'm sure this is the end."

My mother calmly told Frank to stay away, and after a half hour passed, as Frank related the story, nothing more was heard. Having to go to the village of Mount Kisco a few minutes later on an errand, he was astounded when he walked into the restaurant and saw us happily enjoying Sunday breakfast as though nothing had happened. The storm had broken and spent itself.

During this summer, when he appeared to be passing through a trying emotional episode, I told him not to come to Mount Kisco unless he felt he really needed a rest. I knew he had to emerge from his present dilemma before he could be at peace in the country. So there were many weekends when he did not appear. He called me on the phone, however, quite often, to ascertain for himself how I was. If he sensed a depressed mood in me, I would at once receive an invitation to come into town for dinner or to attend something interesting, for Teddie never wanted me to become too discouraged.

On October 1, he engaged a suite at the Ansonia Hotel, consisting of a writing studio and bedroom, for the winter. In addition, he arranged for an adjoining room with its own private entrance for my use when I wished to be in the city. He maintained an office on the third floor of the hotel for his secretary, Miss Evelyn Light, who took his phone calls. His book *Dawn* had been published and he was nearing the end of *Tragic America*, his book on economics, having been assisted by Miss Kathryn Sayre in the editing and research.

Dreiser's friend, Charles Fort, visited us at Mount Kisco

fairly often during these early fall months of 1931. He had met Fort back in 1905, and as he once wrote:

I didn't discover Fort. He discovered me by walking in on me when I was editing for Street and Smith in 1904 and 1905. Fort came to me with the best humorous short stories that I have ever seen produced in America. I purchased some of them. Some of his writings suggested mental clowning, but they were realistic, ironic, wise and in their way, beautiful. I think I published six or seven. And other editors did the same. And among ourselves—Richard Duffy of Tom Watson's, Charles Agnew MacLean of *The Popular Magazine*, and others, we loved to talk of him and his future—a new and rare literary star. But presently he quit writing them. That was after I left Smith's and became the editor of *Hampton's Magazine*. I sent for Fort and told him that now I could pay him much more—one hundred or one hundred and twenty-five dollars as against thirty or forty dollars. But imagine my astonishment as well as chagrin when most calmly he announced that he wasn't writing short stories any more. No. He was working on a new book "X," and nothing could take him away from that.

Following that I saw no more of him until he came to me in 10th Street one day, and laying "X" on my table, asked me to read it, which I gladly did.

Fort, in his book, saw certain rays, only he did not call them X or Cosmic, for X was the mysterious something from which these rays were emanating. But what these rays did, and wherein it was that their wonder and power lay, I will try to show. These rays were the emanation of something that was capable *through them as a medium* of creating *us*, you, me, all animals, plants, the earth and its fullness, its beauty and variety and strangeness, its joy and sorrow and terror as well as the ecstasy of this thing we call life in all its variety and scope. And it did this quite as we, by the means of light and photography, throw a moving picture on a screen, the sensitive chemicals of a photographic film and the light

THEODORE DREISER

July 25-1929

Dear Fort:

Hail!

All my best wishes to the two
of you. Expect to be in London this
coming winter & will call at
39. Dont move.

I have read your books.
Why not publish X as written.
It is a good book.

Dreiser

Facsimile of letter to Charles Fort.

that causes that film first to receive an impression of something and later to retransmit it as seemingly the very substance of reality. Only to X, the earth is the sensitive film and its speeding rays the light of the modern film camera.

Of course, all this was interwoven with comments on the history of man, or the dubiousness of his recorded knowledge, the unreliability of his so-called facts, together with much data sufficiently substantiated to seem to be well worth accepting or, if not that, of investigating. Yet all of this, as I personally rise to testify, was in its day consistently and irritatingly and even insultingly ignored by those to whom I presented it. Yet so impressed was I by all this that shortly after I read his book I had a dream which seemed in no indefinite way to confirm it. And arising from that dream, some months or weeks after I had read the book, I immediately sat down and wrote out a one-act interpretation of it, using Fort's theory as the thesis or backbone of the action. You will find it on pages 60 to 75 in my book *Hey-Rub-a-dub-dub*. I entitled that one-act play *The Dream*, and later showed it to Fort. It was nothing like his book in action and less so in effectiveness. For his book had the immense and rugged massiveness of a whole natural and physical scene—the world and all its history, no less—and amazingly substantiated by heaven knows what astounding data, whereas my one-act play was no more than an eight- or nine-page conversation between a few characters in real life and in my dream. Yet even so, my dream was a fairly fortunate adumbration of the central idea of his great work.

"X" was an amazing book and at the time, I thought to myself, "Well here at last is something new—a new mind and a new approach. I can sponsor it." So I went to Macmillan, Harper's, Scribner's, John Lane, but not one of them wanted it. "It's not this and it's not that," they said. And so they rejected it. I asked Fort to leave a copy of the book with me and in due time I would interest a publisher. But no, he wouldn't do that. He took it away, and the next thing he told me was that he had destroyed it and was writing

The Book of the Damned, and that he would rather I would interest myself in that, which I did, only still believing that "X" was even more wonderful. However, this time I didn't waste time with scientific publications or their editors or just any publisher. Rather I took it—*The Book of the Damned*—direct to my personal publisher, Horace Liveright, and, laying the book on the table, told him to publish it. And when, after a week or so, he announced: "But I can't do it. We'll lose money," I said, "If you don't publish it, you'll lose me." So the book was published.

Apparently some men are of that sensitive and creative substance out of which spring so many strange things, intuitions, suspicions, imaginings of many and strange varieties, some of such great worth or import as to cause one to try to prove them. And that, I think, is the really great thing about mind at its best, its intuitions and speculative creativeness. For out of all that passes through or before such a mind, material as well as mental or spatial and its own sensations and intuitions in regard to the same, something sticks, some thought, and from that eventually may come some action on the part of a man like Fort. Out of all the things that pass before or through or into such a mind, something, I might say with just the right wave length, clicks with something else in the brain or temperament itself, and there you have a new thing or idea such as Fort's "X." And eventually, by subsequent observation, study and experience, such a mind gathers enough data to more or less substantiate those peculiar intuitions or sensations of the mind.*

Fort disliked mixed company but he loved to visit alone with Dreiser at Iroki, where they spent many interesting hours together. They were men of strong intuition, the value of which they both suspected to be precious beyond measure. Fort told how when he was working in England in a small two-room apartment on the second floor, buried in notes which he had

* Manuscript by Theodore Dreiser at the University of Pennsylvania.

collected on scientific data that had been "damned" or ostracized by scientists, the door suddenly opened and in walked Dreiser. He said: "Life itself with all its component parts came in through the door when Dreiser appeared."

I visited Fort shortly before his death. He was not very old but he was wasting away rapidly with leukemia. Fort spoke of it as a conscious mysterious parasite which had seized on him and there was no possible escape. He held the firm conviction of his passing which became a reality two weeks later, on May 3, 1932.*

In late October, Dreiser, as Chairman of the National Committee for the Defense of Political Prisoners, received a thirty-two-page document from the International Labor Defense, relating to crimes and abuses inflicted on the striking miners in the Harlan County coal mines of Kentucky. The International Labor Defense confessed itself in no position to evoke public interest in this wholesale brutality, and therefore, wanted to know if Dreiser would organize a committee out of the membership of the National Committee, to proceed to Kentucky not only to question the authorities there but to see if by so doing he could not focus public attention and thereby modify if not dispel some of the ills being endured by the miners.

In June, 1931, Dreiser, at the request of William Z. Foster, Earl Browder and Joseph Pass, had visited the mines in the Pittsburgh area, the conditions of which he found appalling. And now in November, failing to enlist the support of several prominent citizens, he finally called a meeting of the N.C.D.-

* Mrs. Charles Fort left a number of literary materials to Dreiser which I turned over to the Fortean Society in 1946.

P.P., asking for volunteers from among its membership. The following responded: John Dos Passos, Adelaide Walker, Charles Rumford Walker, Mrs. Bruce Crawford, Samuel Ornitz, Lester Cohen and Melvin P. Levy. Their first action as a committee was to give notice to the press that they would invade Harlan County and the eastern coal district of Kentucky, and after securing military protection from Governor Flem D. Sampson, they proceeded to Pineville in Bell County and later to Harlan County. Upon his arrival, Dreiser was greeted by the Mayor of Pineville and a Judge Jones. Testimony was taken from the miners as well as the sheriff, district attorney and county judge. The meetings were thrown open to the public and the press, but the investigating committee met with opposition, including threats of violence and its members were followed and spied upon everywhere they went.

On November 10 I went down by boat to meet Dreiser at the Monticello Hotel in Norfolk, taking the car with me. On our drive back he was interviewed at several points along the way. His very life had been threatened in Harlan and Bell Counties, for daring to center nationwide attention on the horrible injustices then being perpetrated on the miners. He, Dos Passos and others on the Dreiser Committee were indicted by the Bell County Grand Jury for criminal syndicalism, and rumor circulated that Kentucky would seek to extradite Dreiser for trial. In fact, a warrant was issued for his arrest, should he attempt to re-enter the Commonwealth of Kentucky. Publicity spread like wildfire. Franklin D. Roosevelt, Governor of New York at the time, indicated he would grant Dreiser an open hearing and John W. Davis agreed to defend the committee. However, due to the widespread publicity, on

March 1, 1932, all formal charges against Dreiser and his committee were dropped.

Returning to Iroki, Teddie was content to work on the ground for a little physical exercise and much needed relaxation. Christmas was approaching and there were visits from many intimate friends. There was snow and a promise of more; every window of the house framed a scene of winterwhite loveliness. Nick, and my sister's wolfhound, Boy, who was now with us, reveled in it. After Nick's first fit of jealousy over his arrival, they became good friends, standing guard together all day and barking furiously in unison each time a strange animal was sighted within a thousand feet or more. A bright fire blazed in the fireplace in Dreiser's studio and in another one directly above in the dining room on the second floor.

There was a visit before Christmas to John Cowper Powys and Phyllis at Harlanville, New York, where they lived. Jack told us of his plan to return to the land of his ancestors—Corwen, Merionethshire, North Wales, which is in that part of ancient Wales that was called "Powys" in the old days. His father had been the vicar in the village of Shirley, halfway between Derby and Ashbourne. His mother was born in Norfolk. Jack, along with the first five of his parents' children, was born in Derbyshire; and the part of North Wales called "Powys" in those former times is about the same latitude as Shirley. We were saddened to lose the companionship of Jack and Phyllis, but as he said, he must have thought a great deal of the United States to have spent almost thirty years here. Not long after this, they left for North Wales.

23

In January, 1932, Teddie received a letter from Jug (Mrs. Dreiser), which he answered at Iroki, dictating the reply to me. As it throws a direct light on this story, I will quote some of it:

MY DEAR JUG:

... When we separated in 1909 it was because our temperaments were not worth anything to each other any longer. . . . When our relationship was dissolved that ended completely the marriage state. You were no longer my wife in any sense of the word and are not today. . . . Yet you have insisted over a long period of years in holding on to a name that to the general public and any thinking person does not really any longer belong to you. . . . Today, as you must know, and if you were truthfully willing to face facts, marriage and divorce are very different proceedings from what they were twenty-three years ago. And I am fairly well satisfied that the time will soon be here when living apart for reasons of incompatability for a period of years will constitute divorce—a relief which you have already refused to grant me—even in the face of your verbal agreement so to do. . . .

At the time of our separation . . . as you know, I gave you absolutely everything I had. What was left for me was what I could earn by my pen—an average of from one hundred and twenty-five to one hundred and fifty dollars a month. And yet, in the face of that, when in 1914 or 1915 the time came when I could not continue the weekly allowance you proceeded to force me to do what I could not do and it was only by showing the representative of the Court of Family Relations, who called upon me to demand action in your behalf, the letter which you yourself had written to me acknowledging all that I had done for you that that action was dropped. For that person herself stated that your then demands in the face of what you had already received were outrageous. I still have that letter. . . .

The money I have been forced to pay you under this *second agreement* [$200 monthly from 1927] has become a severe burden. . . . During the time that you have been receiving this money from me and during the time which you also have worked, and particularly with yourself alone to look after, you should have been able to prepare for the ordinary contingencies of your life. More, you have never favored me in the matter of either public comment or in keeping your agreement to free me.

As I see it the contract between us is specific and final.*

I so often encountered in him a bitterness against marriage that had grown directly out of his own personal experience and which he voiced emphatically, even to friends who were happily married. I was convinced, in the face of such a fixed, idea on his part, that freedom was the only solution. Not only for him but for myself, as I felt a pressing need for freedom in order to meet the complicated problem which living with Dreiser presented. But what appeared to be freedom to him appeared to me as being held with the heaviest of chains, for it seemed as though he was continually involved to some degree. At least I felt if the time came when I could not go any

* Letter in my possession.

farther in our relationship, I was free to leave and start all
over again. And this thought alone was sustaining. It gave me
a kind of security in insecurity. I had the satisfaction of knowing that no strangling legal knot or convention was holding us
together by force or fear. Instead, the entire relationship, with
all of its emotional ramifications, was being held up by a
single thread, but one that seemed to be made of indestructible
material—a little like the cable of a suspension bridge made
up of steel wire ropes or steel links of high tensile strength
calculated to withstand stresses, impact, vibration and the
rest.

One evening Teddie phoned me at Iroki. His voice was taut
and strained. He said he did not know what to do, but things
could not go on as they were. I told him I would come down to
the city the next day and we would talk things over. That night
I could not sleep; I could think of nothing but the necessity of
going into town as soon as possible in the morning. Things had
reached a climax, that was certain.

The following morning, I arrived at his studio in the Ansonia Hotel. He sat behind his rosewood piano desk, facing
me. We talked on several subjects, one being his necessity to
curtail expenses even further than he already had. He was now
thinking of giving up his suite at the Ansonia and doing all of
his work at Iroki. *Tragic America* hadn't done very well and
he wanted to finish *The Stoic*, the third volume of his "Trilogy
of Desire." But then, he said he was doing so much active work
in connection with social reform and liberal causes, requiring
discussion and personal appearances here and there, that he
wondered how it would work out if he were not available in
the city when he was needed.

As we sat conversing on these matters, the telephone rang. Dreiser answered abruptly: "Yes, *very* busy," and hung up.

In about ten minutes there was a light knock on the door. When Dreiser went to see who it was, in dashed Alice Prager. After taking in my presence with one quick glance, she started to speak in spurts which sounded like drops of water touching a very hot stove. She had been here. She had been there. She had had lunch with a man. Dreiser cut her remarks short with calm contradictions. She started to walk about the room wringing her hands, saying: "You drive me *mad*, simply *mad*."

I felt embarrassed watching an intimate scene of this nature, which had a distinctly theatrical flavor, and I had the desire to leave. Then Dreiser said: "Alice, you know you are one of those too smart people. So smart, they are stupid— you know."

At this, she must have conceived another plan, for she quickly left. However, in a little while she called back over the telephone from her apartment on Sixtieth Street, asking to speak with me. Would I please come over to see her? She wanted to talk with me. It was a request I was reluctant to grant, and yet decided to. Yes, I would come over a little later.

When I arrived at her apartment that afternoon she had changed to a red jumper dress and her long blonde hair was plaited into two long braids. There were colored shawls draped about the room, an artist's easel, several paintings which had considerable interest for me. Over a glass of wine, she talked on and on rapidly. She said Dreiser was so jealous he would not trust her two hours alone. She had no influence with him.

And then, a few moments later, she went on to say that whenever she wanted to do anything, she always pretended she wanted to do the opposite. On and on she talked until a half hour later, when Dreiser himself knocked on the door.

We all went to dinner together, but before leaving her apartment, she presented me with a tiny doll dressed in a fancy Bohemian peasant costume. I did not want to accept it, but I did. I still have the doll and I am very glad I accepted it in the friendly way it was offered. At dinner Alice continued to talk about Dreiser and his faults, flaws and shortcomings—criticism that he did not seem to mind at all. In fact, the remarks were taken in good humor by all of us. I refused to allow myself to be drawn into the emotional tangle, and, to my astonishment, was able to remain remarkably detached.

The next day, Teddie drove with me to Iroki where we had dinner together, after which he returned to the city. When I went to New York toward the end of the week to take my singing lesson with Maria Samson, he called me there to tell me that Alice was leaving the next morning for Europe. However, when I called on him the following day, I realized that not only had she departed but the romance was over. I sensed a profound relief in Dreiser although he was nervously exhausted and bore evidence of a psychic wound which was sure to take some time to heal, if it ever did. That evening he took me to dinner at one of his favorite speakeasies, in those days the only place where one could get a good dinner with a cocktail or bottle of wine.

He wanted to talk. He said his work came first in this world and any opposing force was destined to be cut sharply out of his life, if it killed him to do so. And as I looked at him, I thought he would succeed in his effort to guard the survival of his creative urge; but he was capable of being hurt too, and I loved him the more for it.

During the weeks following, Teddie spent considerable time at Iroki. Miss Light came out to arrange his reference library. Hubert Davis, an artist of whom he was very fond, was painting some color panels in the new dining room then under construction. My sister Myrtle was journeying back and forth to New York to study singing with Yeatman Griffith, and taking advantage of the opportunity to attend with me the entire Wagner Ring cycle at the Metropolitan Opera House.

The tragedy of the Charles Lindbergh baby kidnaping had burst upon the country and the whole nation was in an uproar. The depression had settled down over everything and everyone, and the entire United States seemed to be in a state of sleeping sickness. All activity was paralyzed and people everywhere were sharply curtailing expenses. Hoovervilles were springing up all over on the fringe of large cities, including New York, where dejected people were forced to crawl into quickly improvised shelters made out of large wooden packing boxes and scraps of tin. The war veterans had been fired upon in Washington, D. C., when they staged their bonus march.

Dreiser was becoming more and more actively involved in social reform and had finally been persuaded to speak in public here and there. He had something he wanted to say and the force of that desire had at last opened the way. I remember the first time he stood up to speak at a formal gathering, where he had expected to address a small audience in an informal manner. When the door was opened and Dreiser started to walk down the aisle, he suddenly realized he was facing a large group of people eagerly awaiting his appearance. The hall was filled to its capacity of over four hundred. As I sat with Myrtle in the audience, I wondered what effect such an assembly would have on him as he entered. I felt in him the same old nervousness that he had always displayed when called upon to speak. But I was truly amazed this time to observe how soon, after being introduced, he not only recovered himself but developed an arresting poise that was thereafter always with him on any public lecture platform. The audience was interested, sympathetic and responsive, and Dreiser instantly caught its electrifying mobility. He soon had them laughing one moment and serious the next.

After it was over, and he had answered all of the questions addressed to him during the question period, I said: "Why you were not nervous at all. You can speak anywhere."

"Yes," he replied, "I can speak anywhere now before as large an audience as is required. But don't imagine that I was not nervous. I was actually trembling, at first. But when I walked down the aisle, realizing that at last I had to face an audience, my long-standing self-consciousness disappeared and I am sure it will never return. It is over." So it was, and consequently, many public addresses followed.

Earl Browder and several other members of the Communist Party came out to Iroki quite often during this period. There were heated discussions that lasted for hours, and invariably afterward, Dreiser would talk to me about them. I recall his saying many times that while he went along with many of the concepts of Communism, where they applied directly to the enrichment and betterment of the social and economic status of the individual, he felt that the leaders of the Party in this country were without imagination. He could not tolerate their determination to hew sharply to the Party line, regardless of constructive suggestions of any kind. However, he had a genuine regard for William Z. Foster, whom he always referred to as "a kind of saint," in view of the many sacrifices he had made for the cause of his choice. As for himself, he said he would never join any party, believing his influence in the field of social reform would be more effective if he remained free to speak as he wished on any subject.

In May, Teddie left for a trip to Arizona and New Mexico. He wanted to get away from New York for a while. Writing to me from New Mexico, he said he was resting—that he had taken away a lot of mental worries, all of which he was trying to drop, and to a certain extent was succeeding.

"The chief one should pass presently and then I can settle down to writing or just living or vegetating." But as the days passed into weeks, he said he was lonely. We both realized that we wanted to be together. And when, in a letter, he wrote about Iroki: "I see it now and wonder if the grass is showing— and the flowers. It should be beautiful this year—almost complete for the first time," I answered, asking him to please come back. Spring in the country was intoxicating and he should be there.

So in July, just two months after Teddie had left New York, he appeared at Iroki. My mother and sister had been planning to return west, but were reluctant to leave while he was away. Now that he was back, they felt better about it and left in a few days.

That summer Teddie came to me to say that he had drawn up a will in my favor, making me the sole heir to his estate. He had also deeded the Mount Kisco and California property to me. I was utterly dumfounded and said so, for up to then, I had no least security and I could hardly grasp the full significance of his action. He knew and understood, however, that I was deeply grateful and added: "I want you to know how things stand, in case anything happens to me. Life is uncertain, you know."

It wasn't until years later, in 1947, when I was sorting his correspondence, that I learned from a letter to his lawyer, Arthur Carter Hume, that Dreiser had called at his office in Yonkers, on May 6, the day before he left on his trip south, to sign the will which Mr. Hume had been drawing up.

24

Dreiser now settled down to concentrated work on *The Stoic*, large sections being handwritten by him while other parts were dictated to a secretary, Miss Clara Clark.

Toward the end of August, a luncheon was given at Iroki for George Jean Nathan and Ernest Boyd, at which the proposed publication of a new literary magazine, *The American Spectator*, was discussed. It was scheduled to come out in October and was to be a magazine of quality. There was to be no advertising, and consequently, it would be an organ of free expression for the aesthetic, artistic and intellectual temperament, national as well as international—a paper designed primarily as a forum for the interchange of ideas and views on the part of representative writers in Europe and America, which might influence the thoughts and prejudices of less open-minded persons in their own and other nations. For instance, there was Wickham Steed, one of England's outstanding political journalists, whose name seldom appeared in America's magazines. There was Havelock Ellis, pioneer in the psychology of sex; H. M. Tomlinson, the essayist; Frank Swinnerton, Edwin Muir, Sean O'Casey, Ivor Brown, whose names were lined up as possible contributors. Dreiser was to be delegated the task of interesting such personalities as Diego Rivera, Angna Enters, Dr. Calvin Bridges, Karl Radek, Arthur Davison Ficke, George Ade, John Cowper Powys, Sherwood Anderson and others to write articles for the magazine. Richard R. Smith and Ray Long were the publishers, with an editorial board, serving without pay, consisting of George Jean Nathan, Ernest Boyd, James Branch Cabell, Eugene O'Neill and Dreiser.

Dreiser was enthusiastic about the project. He always held on to his recollections of his early editorial career with nostalgic persistence, as if reluctant to relinquish them. So it was not surprising that he entered into this venture with all his heart and soul.

"There is no reason why," he said, "an immense good may not come out of an alliance of thought among the world's outstanding men of letters, however contradictory" At last, so he said, he had an instrument of expression worthy of an effort. He even transferred his very efficient secretary, Miss Evelyn Light, to the permanent headquarters of *The American Spectator*, at 12 East Forty-first Street, New York.

In September, we went up to Harlanville, New York, to secure an article from John Cowper Powys for the first edition which was to come out October 20, 1932. The response to the new publication was heartening (40,000 copies), and Dreiser had the desire to devote most of his time to it. He remained one of the associate editors for a period of two years, and then resigned. The fact that the editors were determined to accept advertising for the paper convinced Dreiser that its policy of free expression would be influenced in some way.

During this time he had a close association with George Jean Nathan, and as Nathan told me years later, one morning he received an urgent call from Dreiser at the Ansonia Hotel, asking him to come right over. Thinking Dreiser was ill, he rushed to the hotel, not even stopping to shave. When he arrived at the studio, he found Teddie in one of his most expansive moods. What did he want Nathan for? Why he wanted him to sample a new beverage concoction he had just mixed which was "tops"!

When a request came from California for him to be the principal speaker at a large mass meeting in San Francisco, being held on November 6 for the cause of Tom Mooney, Dreiser remembered his promise to Mooney to do something for him and at once accepted. Flying to San Francisco, he spoke before an audience of fifteen thousand people in the Civic Auditorium. Before returning to New York, he stopped off in Los Angeles, where on November 10, he signed a contract with the Paramount Publix Corporation for the sale of the motion picture rights to *Jennie Gerhardt*, which was later produced by Ben Schulberg with Sylvia Sidney, Donald Cook, Mary Astor and Edward Arnold in the principal roles.

So versatile was Dreiser's mind that even in the face of his interest in *The American Spectator* and the progress he was making on *The Stoic*, as well as his many activities in connection with social equity, he found time to work on an original realistic American motion picture epic entitled *Revolt*. Its background consisted of episodes in the history of

the tobacco industry in the United States. The scenes were to
be laid around Hopkinsville, Kentucky, where a war of rebellion had been fought in 1905 between the tobacco growers in
the South and the Duke tobacco trust. H. S. Kraft, technical
screen adaptor; J. Fischler, of the Sanitas Fundoshi Company; Emanuel J. Rosenberg, producer; and Joseph Rothman, director, became interested in the story and formed a
corporation for its promotion. Dreiser, Kraft and Rothman
left for the South to collect data for the screening of the picture. I was to drive down later with Hubert Davis, who was
to do a series of sketches of scenes to be used, and Miss Clara
Clark who was to do the secretarial work. We left New York
by car in February but the icy roads over which we traveled
made driving an adventure indeed. Ice formed on the car
windows through which we caught glimpses of dilapidated
and forsaken little farms in the valley far below—glimpses
that were not wasted on the artistic eye of Hubert Davis, for
long after we arrived back in New York, I saw some of those
scenes materialize on canvas as though by magic.

Our destination was Nashville, Tennessee, where Miss
Clark and I stayed while the others went over to Hopkinsville,
Kentucky. On our way North, we stopped off at Winston-
Salem, Durham, Asheville and other places where we went
through several tobacco plants from the beginning to the end,
one of the most interesting phases of American life that I have
observed. At the auction markets, there were auctioneers
musically calling out their wares and selling to the highest
bidder. Large bins were filled with varied grades of tobacco,
carefully sorted leaf by leaf, according to size, color and
texture. Some were segregated for cigarettes. Other varieties

were for expensive cigars. But the men who handled this product knew the moment they set their eyes on a crop that had been hauled into town by some small tobacco raiser just where it would go and how much it would bring.

We were glad to return finally to Iroki where we could relax while the screen technique for the plot and sequences of *Revolt* was worked out.*

The early part of 1933 brought many visitors. Among them was Dorothy Dudley, author of *Forgotten Frontiers*† which had just been published and had created much interest, especially in literary circles. Others were the O. O. McIntyres, Alma Clayburgh, the Diego Riveras, Jerome Blums and Burton Rascoes.

After one of McIntyre's visits, he wrote an article for Hearst's International *Cosmopolitan*‡ in which he said:

> The topics which give his (Dreiser's) conversation a dazzle are the consciously villainous. Rio white-slave traffic or injustices to child workers! He will tinge an apoplectic purple.
>
> After one of these outbursts he asked me to see a ravine that he had dredged and into which he had harnessed a pond of water. He seemed proud of this primitive achievement. He was the docile "Teddy," by which he is known to his intimates. The humble clothcap, proud of toil with his own hands!
>
> It was late, and a moon had hung a thin scimitar in the sky. As the car in which we departed mounted a ridge, I looked back. Dreiser was in his rocker, swaying rapidly and furiously pleating his kerchief in the moonglow. The gray wolf in silhouette!

* The picture was never produced. Script is in my possession.
† Later re-titled *Dreiser and the Land of the Free.*
‡ December, 1933, issue.

In June, we went by plane to visit the Century of Progress Exposition in Chicago. Being my first long plane trip, it was a great adventure for me. But as I slumped down in the seat, feeling I would be airsick, Dreiser teased me, saying: "What is the use of bringing you by plane? Are you going to stay down like that all the way?"

However, after stopping at Cleveland and having a bowl of soup, I was all right again. In fact, I loved the voyage up among the clouds. To me it was the most exhilarating thing I had done in years, whereas Dreiser was a veteran air traveler, preferring to go by plane whenever possible.

The fair with its lighted waterways, modernistic homes and interesting exhibits was a thing of beauty. We spent most of our time in the Science buildings, for Dreiser was by then far along in his collection of scientific data to be used in his volume of philosophical essays which he intended writing and collecting into one volume. He had given it the tentative title of *The Formulae Called Life*. A few of the subtitles are: *Myth of Individuality, Myth of Free Will, Myth of Reality, Myth of Possessions, Transmutation of Personality, Concerning Good and Evil, Necessity for Contrast, Necessity for Secrecy, Change, Equation Inevitable*. When he began the process of collecting scientific data, illustrations, items from newspapers and magazines which threw light on his interpretation of life, or pointed up his own argument, he had many typewritten copies made and placed under several of these subheadings. He intended to choose the data and illustrations that could be used to the best advantage to elucidate his deductions when the time came for the actual writing of any particular essay—a method he used in working out the essays he was able to finish. As he said, only a few of the illustrations should be selected.

Dreiser worked eight years on the manuscript, for once it was started, he could never put it aside or stop collecting notes. Of course, he always thought he would finish it, until about two years before he passed away, when he began saying: "When I am gone do thus and so with the Formulae." He stopped to write *America Is Worth Saving* in 1940 but went back to work on his volume of essays in 1941 and 1942, putting it aside for the last time when he resumed work on *The Bulwark* in 1943. An introduction for this posthumous volume, which will now carry the title *Notes on Life*, was written at my request by John Cowper Powys, in which he says:

His mind was predominantly attracted by the chemical changes and mutations of the elements. It was not only that such chemical phenomena fascinated him. They haunted him. They obsessed him. They were a mania with him. He was always seeing humanity in relation to the mysterious movements and transformations of the various atomic and electric events and occasions and energies and impressions, apprehended by our senses and worked over by our conscious minds, we accept as the palpable shapes and textures of the visible world. For Dreiser the psychic and the physical world were never divided. He was always seeing mountains as men and men as atoms, and men and mountains and atoms as transitory bubbles in an unfathomable flood of Being, of which there was neither beginning nor end, and where reality was always turning into illusion and illusion into reality.

In his own words—and when he is in these cosmogonic moods his words gather to themselves a particular kind of rhythm that makes us think of both Whitman and Melville—"transmutation of personality" is positively the outstanding law of life—so much so that even the mountains and plains, to say nothing of the cities and hamlets, change men—transmute them from one thing to another. Thus the Himalayas, being unlike any other mountain range for size, change those nearest them. For, unlike any other mountain range, they present jagged undulations of enormous height, and they seem to speak to men in deep tones, although occasionally they speak with the roar of their avalanches. And yet at the same time they so loftily ignore man as something puny and unimportant. And they have nurtured and made sure the most important of humble men on our globe. In fact, their overpowering effect has made many men too humble, so that even today they try to efface themselves from an earth looked down upon by clouds that sit on the thrones of Gods.

When I read these words of John Cowper Powys, I think of the words of Gandhi in his autobiography:

The world crushes the dust under its feet, but the seeker after truth should so humble himself that even the dust could crush him. Only then, and not till then, will we have a glimpse of truth.

Each season at Iroki had its own distinctive beauty. I could never decide when I loved it most—in the newness of spring, in the lush greenery of summer, in the bronze radiance of autumn, or when the clean, cold days and nights of winter closed in on us. There were days during the winter of '33-'34, when we were all but snowbound, and a walk to the mailbox, a distance of about a thousand feet, was likely to result in a frostbitten ear or nose. Sometimes the snowdrifts on the steps leading down to the road from the second floor were so deep that the dogs were forced to dig their way through, ending up by sliding most of the way down to the road level, returning later to the house with fringes of icicles hanging on their whiskers.

Nick and Boy were a source of great interest to Dreiser. He was especially amused by one of Boy's idiosyncrasies. Whenever Dreiser remained in his study after everyone else had retired, Boy would take it upon himself to make his way down the winding stairs to the studio where the light was burning brightly as Teddie continued at work, and start circling the long table, whining softly but persistently until Teddie was forced to stop writing and speak to him. At that, his whine would grow louder and louder until Teddie finally pushed his papers aside and put down his pen.

"All right, old man," he'd say, "I'll go to bed; you'll never rest until I do, so come on, let's go!"

At this, Boy would jump for joy as he bounded triumphantly ahead of him up the stairway to the second floor. Boy never failed to round up Dreiser whenever he felt the light was burning too late in his studio.

That summer, the Freda McKechnie-Robert Edwards tragedy of Wilkes-Barre, Pennsylvania, which paralleled Dreiser's *An American Tragedy*, was attracting nationwide attention, and Dreiser was asked by the New York Post Syndicate to write it up. The murder had occurred in Harvey's Lake, a small body of water near Wilkes-Barre, where we went with Teddie's secretary, Miss Henrietta Helston, to cover the case. The Sterling Hotel, where we all stopped, was ablaze with excitement. Edwards was charged with having slugged Freda McKechnie with a blackjack and having thrown her body into the lake to avoid the consequences of her approaching motherhood; Freda was an obstacle to his desired marriage with Margaret Crain, a music teacher with whom he had fallen in love. Dreiser, not at all surprised at the similarity between

the Wilkes-Barre murder case and the plot of his novel, told
newspaper reporters:

> Headlines have referred to the Edwards case as *the American
> Tragedy*. And newspapers all over the country have wired me for
> permission to use excerpts from my book. It proves my original
> contention that I chose a typical case. That was why I gave it the
> title of *An American Tragedy*. I had a bit of difficulty getting that
> title accepted, at the time. Now, I know I was right.*

Asked whether he thought the reading of his book might
have given young Edwards the idea of the action he was
alleged to have performed, he further said:

> It's entirely possible, of course. We can only speculate, since we
> don't actually know. People get ideas from many sources—from
> parents, from friends, from books, plays or movies. It would be
> absurd to say we should refrain from all creative works merely be-
> cause they might inspire people to imitate the plots.*

Following the death of Horace Liveright, Dreiser severed
his connection with that publishing house and went to Simon
and Schuster, who forthwith announced their desire to hold a
huge reception at Iroki to celebrate the union. They agreed to
send out all the beverages needed while we were to furnish
the food. About three hundred guests were invited to attend
the gathering, preparations for which had to be set in motion
a month before. A buffet supper was spread on the second-
floor dining table, and on the large table in the studio on the
ground floor—baked hams, roasted turkeys, patties of all
sorts, and every conceivable delicacy.

It was a very successful affair, with a rather distinctive

* *New York Evening Journal*, August 8, 1934.

touch added by the international flavor of the staff engaged to handle the details of service. There were three butlers—a Swede, a Frenchman and a Negro. The gardener, who was in charge of parking cars, was Spanish; our housekeeper was an American, and, of course, there was our maid Pearl. Only one disturbing incident occurred, a minor argument between France and Sweden or Spain and France, I forget which; otherwise they furnished an excellent demonstration of international solidarity.

Due to the insolvency of the Liveright Corporation, there now began for Dreiser long-drawn-out arbitration proceedings that went on for years until finally he was forced to pay a considerable sum of money to the publishers to disentangle himself from that connection.

This lawsuit was extremely wearing on him and in the spring of 1935 he announced that he wanted to go to California for a change. He longed to see his beloved friend, George Douglas, who was then working for William Randolph Hearst as an editorial writer on the *Los Angeles Examiner*. Douglas had been writing Dreiser that he was lonely for intellectual companionship and welcomed an opportunity to discuss with him his *Formulae Called Life*. He would be delighted to have Theodore occupy a suite in his home and do his writing there, a suggestion which appealed to Teddie so much that we decided to lease our country place and go to California for the summer.

25

The home of George and Molly Douglas was an attractive one which housed the Douglas family group, consisting of George, Molly and their two daughters—Halley, the elder, a motion-picture script writer, and Dorothy, a dancer. George was a devoted husband and father, but he was intellectually lonely in Los Angeles. By contrast, his life in San Francisco, where he had lived and worked so long, had been a colorful, stimulating one, for he had known and circulated with writers, artists and critics. In fact, he had known everyone of importance in the cultural world of San Francisco, having carte blanche to any intellectual center including the famous Bohemian Club.

George Douglas was a man of highly developed mental gifts—scholarly, witty and extremely well informed as to current affairs—a man who delighted all those about him with his brilliance of mind and spirit. Having a marked retentive memory, he was able to quote offhand appropriate lines of verse or prose to fit any and every occasion. Naturally, Teddie loved a man like Douglas, and his appreciation of his temperament kindled a response in George that seemed to expand with each passing day. He was as happy as a child in the enthusiastic presence of Dreiser, who had even persuaded him to buy a new hat and some very light-colored trousers. His associates in the editorial department of the *Los Angeles Examiner*, were aghast when he walked in one morning wearing them. In some ways, he was as conservative as the proverbial Scotchman, but he overwhelmed one with his generosity when it came to giving of himself—his temperament, his knowledge, his appreciation for the finer and worthwhile things of life.

Molly, having business interests in San Francisco, was away from their home in Los Angeles quite often that summer, so Dreiser and Douglas had a magnificent time alone together, the housekeeping problem having been solved by Dreiser's locating a very efficient woman to take care of it. Several nights a week they dined together at home; other nights they went out for dinner. Having no desire to interfere with this glowing renewal of friendship, I took a large comfortable room in the neighborhood where I could work at my typewriter without disturbing anyone. Nick, who was with me, would lie quietly at my feet during the day, because he knew I would take him out in the evening. Frequently I joined George and Teddie for dinner, and on one occasion when their birthday anniversaries happened to occur a few days apart, I cooperated with Molly in giving them a gay birthday party.

The following letter written by Teddie to George a few months later from New York, describes this summer more vividly than I can:

Above: Helen and Theodore in Germany, 1926. *Below:* Dreiser in the Donetz Basin in Russia.

Above: Winter at Iroki, Mount Kisco. *Below:* Helen, Theodore, Rosa Vermonte and Olin Downes at Iroki.

Above: Hollywood, 1930. *Below:* Dreiser.

Portrait of Helen Dreiser by Ralph Fabri.

MOUNT KISCO, N. Y., Tuesday, Jan. 28, 1936

GEORGE DEAR,

Thanks for the letter. I always read your words as I do pages from Plato or Huxley or Spencer or any of my favorite commentators on life and wish that we were in the rear garden in the swing, watching the birds at the pool or the stars in the sky. We were happiest alone, but I dislike thinking of you alone again. You are so appropriately and desirably the center of a Johnsonian table, and it should be prepared for you. Most naturally and affectionately my mind runs to the evenings—walking under the still trees, and saying over and over and over that life is what it is. To return as we did and open Swinburne, or Shakespeare, or Keats, or Sterling, or Shelley! The tall bamboos are outside the window! a mocking bird begins at midnight! I can see the green electric words Gaylord over the roof-tops! And you read or present in your own words what is or was—the mutton birds of Australia, the one-time Bohemia of San Francisco.

Hail, George! Oh, ho! I am grateful. And I could cry.

T. D.

P.S.—We plan to move back to L.A.—most surely. How I wish I could spend more days with you. I have almost enough material for all of the topics I want to deal with.

Whenever Teddie felt the need of a few moments' relaxation from his writing table, he would wander out to the garden at the rear of the house where there was an artistic fish pond. He would sit by the edge of it absorbed in watching the fish and the birds carrying out their pattern of the life process. Later he told stories of the behavior of the mother birds with their young—how they taught them to fly from branch to branch, how to dunk the hard bread which he threw them into the water to soften it, how they called the attention of their little ones to some small worm or insect and how they chastised and scolded when a grave mistake had been made. All animals caught and held Teddie's interest. Years before, when he lived on West Tenth Street in New York, he kept a tiny mouse in a little cage on his desk, giving it water and food and making a pet of it for a few months. Then one day he decided it was cruel to keep it caged, and he and the mouse rode in a taxicab to the first open field he saw outside New York, where he turned it lose. However, the mouse, by this time robbed of all initiative and undoubtedly preferring confinement to the hazards of a free way of life, simply followed along behind him squeaking as he walked away. For a long time he talked about this, questioning the wisdom of his action, pondering on the fate of the little mouse.

Brenetta Yerg, a charming young woman whom we had met in Mentone, France, in 1928, took care of Dreiser's secretarial work. Tom Treanor, a young journalist who was killed in an airplane crash over Europe in World War II, while he was in the midst of writing some brilliant war articles for the *Los Angeles Times*, was living next door and came over occasionally to visit with Dreiser and Douglas. Dr. D. P. McCord, brother of Peter McCord,* was another frequent visitor that summer, as was Dr. Calvin Bridges, then connected with the California Institute of Technology.

During the course of the summer, Douglas arranged through the courtesy of Dr. Edwin P. Hubble, distinguished astronomer, for a visit to the Mount Wilson Observatory, on an evening when no one else was to be present. After driving to the top of Mount Wilson, where we arrived at dusk, we were

* "Peter" of *Twelve Men*.

taken through the great Observatory, at that time the largest in the world, before actually viewing the stars on which the huge telescope was directed that night. What impressed me most was the way in which photography was used in the study of astronomy. An enormous geared wheel, turning slowly through the twenty-four hour focus on any particular star or galaxy, was gauged to the most minute fractional measurement in order to keep the telescopic view steady and unblurred, so the photos would be clear. Enormous time and labor was being spent constantly on this vast geared wheel to keep its rate of revolution accurate with that of the earth, fixing the eye of the telescope on its chosen star of the evening which appeared to the eye about the size of a plate four or five inches in diameter. The double star Antares looked like a ball of fire, and the Cygni with fluted spectrum, looked like a brilliant blue-white diamond. The Milky Way and other galactic circles looked like filtered cosmic star dust scattered across the sky by the hand of God in some lavish moment in eternity. The thought that each speck of light represented a celestial body made one feel more insignificant than a grain of dust on this infinitesimal planet.

As we drove home we were strangely silent, thinking, no doubt, of the wonders we had beheld. In the weeks to follow there were other excursions to points of interest, including such educational centers as the California Institute of Technology and the Huntington Library at San Marino.

After seeing a small bungalow for rent on Rosewood Avenue, Teddie expressed the desire to take it for the balance of the summer. The task of getting settled in the little house was an easy one for we had little to encumber us with the exception of several large bags and a few boxes filled with Dreiser's *Formulae* notes on which he had continued to work. But the little temporary home was attractive to George as well as others, and it soon took on the warmth and hospitality of Dreiser's temperament. In his spare time, Teddie watered the badly neglected garden containing a few dried-up rosebushes, which responded to his loving care with the most beautiful blossoms.

One day as I was driving along Wilshire Boulevard, I approached a corner where all traffic was forced to stop while a car was making a huge U-turn against traffic. I looked, as did everyone else, to see who could be doing such a daring thing, and there I beheld Dreiser guiding his Buick roadster in this most amazing manner. I will never know how he escaped being served with a traffic violation summons, but I am sure all the traffic officers were far from the scene. I made no immediate mention of it, but it was too amusing to be kept a secret very long. When I finally did mention it, he said: "Well I'll be damned, did you see that? I thought I had gotten away with it, or hoped so, and now you saw it." We had a good laugh over it, and Dreiser continued to drive.

As October drew near, we became conscious of approaching fall in the east and found ourselves contemplating our inevitable return. Dreiser was sad about leaving George, as he realized fully what they had meant to each other in the way of intellectual companionship. George's life would not be the same—ever. One could see it in his expression as he put his arm lovingly about Dreiser and began to recite a few lines from one of his favorite poets. Teddie had been extremely stimulating to him; in fact, he was everything George had been seeking for a number of years. How well Dreiser knew it! And it was only a few months after we left Los Angeles, that we heard the sad news of his sudden death, and recollected those poignant words he had prophetically recited that last fleeting moment before we drove away: "There is a taste of death in every parting."

A few weeks later Teddie received a poem written by George about their last evening together:

FOR THEODORE DREISER

(The night we said nothing. Oct. 14, '35)
Now is the test of all our reasonings;
  Of dialectics as defensive art
  In vain endeavor to divert the dart
When you must take tomorrow morning's wings,
Leaving me "Kismet" and "the scheme of things"
  That brought us mind to mind, then heart to heart,
  Only to prove, when comes the time to part,
That every joy its equal sorrow brings.

Oh what a little thing is man! Still less
  His power to reason when compelled to feel
    The pangs of parting from his dearest friend:
  His ego shrinking into nothingness
    As o'er his senses sadly, swiftly steal
    The taste and terror of all things the end.

GEORGE DOUGLAS

On our way back east, we decided to take the southern route due to threatening weather. All went well until we reached the state of Arkansas where they had been having torrential rains for days. One entire day we traveled through driving and almost blinding rains until we felt compelled to stop for a while. Teddie was worried about his notes which he was carrying in boxes in the back of his roadster. He wanted to examine them to see if any dampness had penetrated the boxes. After we procured a cabin in the town of Little Rock, Arkansas, consisting of two rooms and bath, we unpacked the boxes. The notes *had* absorbed dampness and there was only one thing to do—spread them out in one of the rooms in which there was a hot wood-stove fire brightly burning. Never will I forget that night with the heavy downpour outside, sounding like a cloudburst, and the hundreds of notes spread and strung all over the cabin—on the beds, chairs, boxes, over little lines that Teddie had made out of twine and strung back and forth across the room. It was a fantastic night and a discouraging one indeed, for we were literally buried in notes and were considerably worried about them. However, we determined to make the best of it and remain in Little Rock until the notes were thoroughly dry so we could safely repack them.

There was nothing to do in such weather, but we were fortunate in finding an attractive restaurant where we were offered country fried chicken and a very good bottle of wine. The roads through the countryside were flooded in many places and there was only one direction in which we could go when we were ready to leave, so we were told. In fact, as we drove about the town, we had to turn back from some streets as we sank into water two or more feet deep. We welcomed the opportunity to settle down for the night and the following day.

Teddie's thoughts naturally turned back to Los Angeles and George Douglas, and his prospects for a satisfactory if not a happy life. He began reminiscing over their summer together, their long intricate philosophical discussions and the many happy hours just being in each other's company. Dreiser said he knew George would not be happy working day after day on an editorial job. He longed to be independent, as any first-rate writer does, in order to be able to express himself freely on any subject of his choice. Often Douglas had expressed his dissatisfaction in writing editorials for any paper, and confided to Dreiser his deep desire to escape from this kind of work; but being forced to earn a living for his family, he was deprived of the range of the free-lance writer. And with this point of view, no one could have been more sympathetic than Dreiser, for he had waged a fierce fight all through the years for himself and other writers to retain freedom of expression and a clear vision in a world of prejudices, worn-out traditions, customs and beliefs that stifled the progressive mind.

Dreiser did not agree with Douglas' employer, William Randolph Hearst, on much of anything. However, he did admit that Hearst was a very able newspaper man, and when, several years before, he had been invited to Hearst's huge estate at San Simeon, California, he had accepted and we had started out in our car to visit him. And now, as we waited in Little Rock for the floods to subside, we recalled this trip to mind.

The journey to Hearst's medieval castle, which stood on the top of a mountain commanding a beach front along the Pacific Ocean of about twenty miles, had been a fascinating experience for both of us. When we turned away from the ocean and started to encircle the mountain approach to the great stone mansion on the crest, we drove through three gates a few hundred feet apart, that lifted above the car when a rope was pulled. Continuing to drive 'round and 'round the mountain, we were startled by two beautiful gazelles, gracefully leaping off the ground in sudden retreat. At the top we came to the huge stone residence which for size alone was an overwhelming spectacle. We were ushered into a palatial guest room in one of the many stone wings of the castle—a castle that included even a private theater. A little later we entered a reception room where we were greeted by Marion Davies. She was very cordial. As we chatted with her, several young movie starlets passed in and out—some in riding habits on their way to the stables, and others obviously bound for hikes or tennis. Both of us were struck with the good humor and smartness of Marion Davies, who did not look a day over twenty. Soon Mr. Hearst, a raw-boned man with large features, sort of trotted into the reception room and welcomed us in a most friendly and hospitable manner, quickly joining in the light badinage. When luncheon was announced we proceeded to a dining room befitting a baronial castle of the grand order. It was not only a vast room but an impressively beautiful one. The fireplace alone was so large that mules with rubber shoes hauled logs two feet in diameter to the grate.

Not more than six people were seated at the center of the dining table which was at least fifty feet in length. It seemed strange to be one of this small group sitting in the center of a great room conversing easily about current world affairs, the newspaper business, and the movies, as though we were all accustomed to lunching in baronial castles. Of course, there had been our visits to the museums and castles in Europe, but they were hardly a part of one's everyday American life.

I was particularly struck with the way in which Mr. Hearst solicited Miss Davies' opinion on practically everything, and by his affectionate and considerate manner when addressing her. It was obvious that he had a great affection for her. Also, I noticed his courtesy toward all those present. Miss Davies was witty, gay and vivaciously attractive, which helped to make the luncheon pleasant and interesting. And although Dreiser was diametrically opposed to Hearst in most of his views, yet they got on exceptionally well together, and Dreiser even commented to me afterwards on his good manners and tact, as well as his knowledge of the newspaper business, something Dreiser, being an ex-newspaper man himself, could well appreciate. He himself had written human interest articles for *Cosmopolitan* and the Hearst Syndicate, but they had always been on subjects of his own choice, expressed in his own way, which Hearst probably felt contained interest for his readers at the time.

And so we spent most of our marooned day in Little Rock, Arkansas, discussing Douglas, his future prospects, Hearst's past record and our visit to San Simeon.

The following day the *Formulae* notes were dry, and after carefully gathering them together, we repacked the car and started north through Tennessee, Kentucky, Ohio and Pennsylvania toward Iroki.

26

The year 1936 brought few significant happenings with the exception of the March 13 production of the Erwin Piscator-Lena Goldschmidt dramatic adaptation of *An American Tragedy*, which they called "The Case of Clyde Griffiths." It was produced at the Ethel Barrymore Theatre in New York by Milton Shubert and The Group Theatre Players, and was an outstanding artistic achievement that attracted wide attention. Translated from the original German into the English language by Louise Campbell of Philadelphia, it was first presented by Jasper Deeter of the Hedgerow Theatre in Moylan, Pennsylvania, on April 20, 1935. In the original Patrick Kearney version, staged when the book was first published, the leading roles were played by Morgan Farley, Miriam Hopkins and Katherine Wilson; whereas, in the Piscator-Goldschmidt version, the leading roles were performed by Morris Carnovsky, Alexander Kirkland, Phoebe Brand and Margaret Barker.

As the thirties progressed, Dreiser's financial situation was growing steadily worse. Traveling expenses, salaries for secretarial and research work, taxes, the upkeep of Iroki—all were drawing heavily on his income. An idea for a motion picture story based on the life of Paul Dresser, Teddie's brother, and using his famous songs began to take root in my mind. I started to reread all the biographical material Dreiser had written about Paul, contained in such volumes as *Twelve Men* ("My Brother Paul"), *A Hoosier Holiday, A Book about Myself* and *Dawn.* Mame, who had been closely associated with Paul through his creative years, was extremely enthusiastic about the idea and was able to furnish me with interesting anecdotes connected with his life. When I discussed my plan with Theodore, he thought it would be a fine thing to do, but doubted that I would be able to bring the different members of the family into agreement; also, as Paul had left no will, there were song royalty rights to be considered. This prospect did not subdue my spirits, for I was sure I would be able to convince the family of the advantages to be obtained from a successful picture.

I then decided to visit the Paull-Pioneer Music Corporation and the Edward B. Marks Music Corporation, publishers of the songs of Paul Dresser, to outline my idea of using his songs in a motion picture adaptation of the story of his life. The publishers were enthusiastic and offered me great encouragement, drawing up the contracts at once. The other parties to the contract, besides myself were Theodore Dreiser and Mary Frances Brennan (Mame).

Finally in 1937, having concluded most of the legal arrangements, I decided to go to California to proceed with the further promotion of the picture which was to be entitled *My Gal Sal,* one of Paul's songs. How the sale and production of the story became a reality three years later in Hollywood, with Rita Hayworth and Victor Mature in the stellar roles, and how much thought and effort went into its promotion is a story in itself.

While I was in California, Theodore accepted an invitation from the League of American Writers to attend the International Peace Conference* to be held in Paris. It was the time of the Spanish Civil War, and Dreiser was deeply disturbed as to the outcome of this struggle. He wrote me from Paris that he was amazed to note such marked indifference to the cause of the Loyalists from democratic representatives at the Conference. Many of the delegates, he told me later, were so entirely out of sympathy with his views that they attempted to block his programmed speech by placing him toward the end of the long list of speakers. He defeated their purpose, however, by rising to his feet and calling out to the people who were leaving in rather large numbers, having grown tired of a long evening of speeches and being under the impression that the meeting was about over: "Don't go! Don't go! I have something of importance to say!"

At this, many of the people filed back to their seats. Stimulated by the attempt to muffle him, he delivered one of the most impassioned speeches of the Conference on the subject of the unjust predicament of the Spanish Loyalists, and the necessity to cease the bombing of open cities. The result was that Dreiser's speech made the front page of the evening papers.

Later, at the instigation of a group of Loyalists, he con-

* Sponsored by the *Resemblement Universal pour la Paix*, among whose leaders were Lord Robert Cecil, Georges Bonnet and M. Pierre Cot.

tinued on to Barcelona, where, with bombs falling in the streets nearby and even on the hotel in which he slept, he risked all to observe at first hand the sufferings of the Spanish people. Such degradation and starvation, filth and poverty as he described when he returned to America had its effect upon many people who became devotees to the cause of the Spanish Loyalists, although it was a little late. He even went to visit President Roosevelt one afternoon aboard his yacht, the *Potomac*, and, while cruising up the Hudson River at luncheon, laid before him his chart for proposed aid to the Spanish Loyalists. After Roosevelt scrutinized the scheduled chart, he exclaimed: "Now that's what I call a well prepared paper. If everyone would bring me a chart as well laid out as this one perhaps I could get things done."

While Roosevelt said he was not in a position to favor either side in the struggle, he did promise to do what he could —a promise he later fulfilled in a substantial way by sending two or three heavily laden ships to the aid of Spain, for which Dreiser wrote him a personal letter of thanks and appreciation:*

GLENDALE, CALIF., Jan. 5, 1939

DEAR MR. ROOSEVELT:

I was so greatly gratified to read in the *New York Times* of your move in connection with the plight of the women, children and aged in Spain—the impartial relief you are providing.

After approaching you with the facts I did my best to enlist a really powerful and impartial committee. Without naming anyone I can assure you that twelve distinguished Americans of great wealth and influence, while they lauded the idea as a new humani-

* Dreiser-Roosevelt correspondence in the University of Pennsylvania.

tarian instrument destined not only to be useful now but in the future, nevertheless, because of the possibility of their being identified with either the Fascists or the Communists, declined to serve. Everyone suggested some other. However, to them I actually worded the value of the idea this way: "The waste material alone of any competitive period will be plenty to alleviate the sufferings of the victims of any war or disaster, and from now on I think it will be used that way." I did not stop trying until Mr. Rufus Jones assured me that you were moving to do something through the Red Cross.

That you should have applied the mechanism of the plan suggested so accurately and effectively, and particularly in the face of the stalemate that any ordinary citizen was certain to encounter, makes still more clear to me the enormous value of a great executive in the Presidential chair at all times but most particularly in periods of stress and change.

I am deeply grateful to you. You did what I so much would have liked to do for you.

Very truly yours,
THEODORE DREISER

Before sailing for home, he went to Wales to visit John Cowper Powys at Corwen, Merionethshire. From Corwen, he wrote me describing their wonderful walks through the woods together, and how extremely happy the visit had made him.

When he passed through London, he went to visit the prison cell in Reading Gaol once occupied by Oscar Wilde, and there wrote on the wall:

> Tie your spirit to a sail
> Call for sky and wind
> Fly in mood to Reading Gaol
> To a cell bound mind

HELEN DREISER

Write a message on a wall
To a heart that died:
Yet today shalt thou with me
In Paradise abide!

THEODORE DREISER

In the meantime in Hollywood, the idea of doing a story on the life of Paul Dresser was very well received, but an actual sale was difficult to consummate. A period of reorganization throughout the entire motion picture industry had slowed up negotiations. In view of this, I decided to go to Portland to visit my mother for a few months and to await a healthier condition in Hollywood. It was there in November, 1938, that Teddie journeyed all the way from New York to tell me he had the desire to change his entire mode of living, that is, to simplify everything to the bare necessities. He said he was tired of his complicated life in New York and felt, if I would go with him, we might make a fresh start in California.

I agreed, and on December 3, 1938, with the temperature reaching a mere ninety-three degrees, we returned to Los Angeles. Our first task was to locate a suitable but reasonable apartment, something hard to find at that time. Teddie was inclined toward Glendale where we had begun our life together eighteen years before, so when we found a small apartment in an attractive court on Lorraine Avenue, very near the neighborhood of our first little home, we took it.

Teddie resumed work on his *Formulae Called Life*, but he was so torn with the desire to do something about the instability of the world—European economics, threats of dictators, the deplorable state of the starving populace in Spain, the part imperial England was playing in world affairs—that he decided to accept a lecture tour on the Pacific Coast.

"The world situation right now is the most treacherous set-up I have ever seen, heard or read about," he said. "There is no question about war coming. The most pitiful thing about it, though, is that the United States is not ready for war. The people are taking in the movies, dancing this 'swing' stuff and reading the funny papers instead of preparing to offer a defense in case of conflict.

"Awake, get ready for war. Snap out of it," he warned the people everywhere he went.*

In Oakland he said, in answer to direct questions as to what he thought about life: "My original concept of life was that it was cruel, unjust, a devastating process in which happiness was only an illusion. Perhaps that was because of my early environment. It did not seem right to me that my family should be giving tithes to the church when we didn't have potatoes to eat. When I went to work as a reporter in New York I was disgusted with what was regarded as important—the interest in everything that was abnormal in the lives of wealthy socialites. When I brought in stories about the suffering and oppressed poor I was laughed at. I quit newspaper work and began writing about social injustices. I had a long struggle. It left me not bitter but greatly depressed."†

And when asked if "religion" was responsible for his about face, he replied: "Religion be damned! No—something that replaces the need for religion. About ten years ago I decided to re-educate myself—I had only one year of college. I studied

* *Salt Lake Telegram*, February 20, 1939.
† *San Francisco Chronicle*, February 10, 1939.

science and philosophy, visited laboratories, talked with people who knew about such things. Why no one of us is anything, nobody is the author of anything—all we are capable of being is the substance through which the forces of the universe act and express themselves. Our five senses are not enough to tell us whether these forces are the emanation of a conscious divine brain far greater than our own, or merely fortuitous. I do not profess to know. With the universe as vast as it must be, it is ridiculous to think that we in this little earth shell could have the faculties to even begin to suspect the nature of this acting force or intelligence. All we can do is to adjust ourselves to it. But nobody, rich or poor, can escape sorrows and scratches; it's all about fifty-fifty. . . .

"I am glad to see, however, that the time is passing when aristocrats can set themselves to one side and look upon other human creatures as ants, servants or slaves. That problem is now on the carpet, and I believe we will have it out . . . And unless there is some more generous gesture on the part of the *haves* toward the *have-nots* we may eventually get into the streets and settle it hand to hand. . . . If we are going to pull apart this thing we call civilization I would just as leave perish in that fashion as any other. It really makes very little difference however. Man does not make civilization; it is natural forces acting through him, compelling him to do what is needed. We have had civilizations as satisfactory to their own people as this one. We shall have civilizations as satisfactory to their times, even though this one is destroyed tomorrow."*

Asked, as he so often was, what he thought of President Roosevelt, he said: "He's the only president who has done
* *Ibid.*

265

anything for the country since I was born. He's done a helluva lot."*

While his lecture was billed as "What I Think About Life," he occasionally switched his speech entirely to cover current economic evils riding the world, especially if he had taken part in a stimulating conversation or debate the day of his lecture, as he had in Portland, Oregon. By the time he was to speak at the Masonic Temple (February 16, 1939), he delivered a relentless tirade against England which will be long remembered in that conservative city. It resulted in most unfavorable criticism of his address.

For the sake of convenience, we decided to move to Hollywood, after finding for a very moderate sum a duplex apartment on Hayworth Avenue near Sunset Boulevard. Mrs. Dreiser's lawyers were pressing him very hard for overdue payments amounting to $5,000, on her contract dated 1927, which called for $200 dollars a month. Dreiser explained to them that he was awaiting an opportunity to sell one of his books—a sale he expected to take place any day—at which time he would bring the account up to date. More letters passed back and forth, the lawyers insisting on payment or legal action would be taken against him in California. Dreiser became angry and wrote a letter, excerpts from which follow:†

* *Salt Lake Telegram*, February 20, 1939.
† Letter in my possession.

HELEN DREISER
1026 North Hayworth, Hollywood, California
June 23, 1939

Dear Mr._____ :

I have your letter and note the contents.

In the first place, taking this thing on the moral basis, which stand, you, as Mrs. Dreiser's representatives, take, the moral injustice is all on my side, and there is no mistake about that.

I would like to review this thing.

Mrs. Dreiser and I broke a long time ago—30 years to be exact. At that time she was comparatively young and could have made a life for herself . . . I gave her the most of everything I had at that time—materially. I chose a different life—the life of writing, for which sacrifice is the predominant symbol. . . . I worked on. Not with the satisfaction, however, of a big salary and security. I went along another road—the creative road—which is no easy road, as you know. I did *not* make money.

Then much later, in 1925, after four years of intense work— existing on very little money—I published the *Tragedy.* I had help in my struggles, but not from her. To whom does my moral obligation really belong? To the person or persons who helped me over this period, I should say . . . Now I am in a low period, financially, in my life. I am 68 years old. I have to devote considerable attention to my health. I have to have the help of others to do it. . . .

What, pray tell me, can I do for a woman who has been out of my life for 30 years and only in it 10? I have had the help of another woman for twenty years through my creative life and that woman has asked nothing. She makes no demands. But she helps. To whom is my moral duty, I ask you.

The only reason I am telling you this is because you, as representative of the law, and justice, should know it. . . .

If I sell something—yes—I will give her what she unjustly demands. I say unjustly because she made an agreement with me that she never kept. Why all the yelling about an agreement that I

---

never kept? I kept mine as long as I had the money. And I will continue to pay her if I can get it. . . .

You can do what you will about this but as I see it you cannot get blood out of a turnip. If I sell anything you will probably be the first one to know it. And I might add that I am trying everything to bring that about.

Yours very truly,
THEODORE DREISER

The answer to this letter dated June 28, 1939, began as follows:*

DEAR MR. DREISER:

I have your letter of June 23rd. You were apparently very low when you wrote it. . . .

Disregarding his own personal problems, however, he began to expand his sociological interests in earnest. He traveled to Washington, D. C., and to New York to lecture for the Committee for Soviet Friendship and the American Peace Mobilization. He addressed the people from Washington and New York over the radio. He got out pamphlet after pamphlet on his own volition and at his own expense, which he distributed by the thousands to friends and liberal-minded people all over the United States, on any subject he thought of enough importance and which he felt should be brought to the attention of the American people. Following is one of them written in April, 1940:

WAR

This war business is very like the sword that, up to the arrival of gunpowder, it wielded. It has two edges. Personally, I still believe

* Letter in my possession.

in self defense which is obviously the proper answer to predatory war. But I also believe in the defense of others against inequity either by themselves or by the social and legal forces which they erect in order to see that they are legally and honestly defended. Hence I believe in Constitutions, Bills of Rights and their fulfillment by just laws, honest representative bodies, honest courts, honest juries and an honest and decent police system designed to protect all of the people in their constitutional rights—not in any sense to misuse or prey on them. And I have always held that these things are worth fighting for.

I also believe that it is not only human and natural for the strong, if they chance to be strong, to come to the rescue of the weak when and where they feel them to be the victims of predatory crooks, robbers and murderers. And where the strong are either absent or indifferent to the ills and sufferings of the weak I believe it to be the proper wisdom as well as the duty of those who are weak individually to combine in order to be able to resist and drive off their powerful and predatory enemies. That to me is human and natural and legal.

Life is and ever must be an equation or balance between all sorts of contending forces—a fair and maintainable balance. Neither chemically nor physically nor socially nor financially can it be workably run off into unbalance. In chemistry and physics explosions follow—disastrous and frightful to behold. And of humanity collectively and socially assembled under forms of government the same thing is true. Where financial or social unbalance sets in and a few, because of extorted wealth, set themselves apart and above the many, and fail to see how necessarily interrelated they are either for good or ill, you have either (1) revolution and so a restoration of balance or (2) where equity is defeated and inequity prevails you have death of that land or nation. If you do not believe this, consider Rome that declined and fell with the arrival of the Caesars; Italy that plundered up to the days of Mussolini; France, Monarchial France, that ended with the French Revolution;

Autocratic Russia that ended with the Russian Revolution; completely Autocratic England that ended (for a time) with King John and Magna Charta; the Roman religious autocracy that ended with Martin Luther; Autocratic China that ended with the Boxer Rebellion. No equity or social balance—no peace and finally no government.

Wars spring from the greed and the inequity of individuals and the oppression and a little later the enforced ignorance and so the weakness of the masses. Yet the individuals of greed and subtlety, but no real wisdom, who seek to set themselves apart from the welfare and the education and the reasonable comfort of the masses, and by so doing hope to prosper and parade in luxury indefinitely, do nothing more than bring about the misery and the inefficiency of the masses as well as their own and so most certainly their national and individual decay and death. Read history and see. And wars—and by wars I mean predatory wars—are never anything more than brigand adventures. And where they succeed for a time, as quite frequently they have, they bring about nothing more than rival brigandage on the part of others who are fools enough to believe that stolen goods are better than earned goods, and that some decent form of life can be based on that. They have not brains enough to know that it never has worked so for more than a time and it never will. The government that truly succeeds and lives is an orderly government and an equitable one—the one in which ability and weakness—the mentally strong and the not so strong strive to bring about an approximation of the Golden Rule. And where that lives and works that nation prospers. And where it does not it will surely die. For an unjust war of a class upon a mass or of a predatory nation upon another nation will result *only* in more war, until all that is worth having is frittered away. Look at Asia. At Europe. At Africa—and after thousands of years of life and of decayed governments. "They that take the sword shall perish by the sword." But it is also true that those nations that will set the Golden

Rule above oppression and robbery and will not tolerate a predatory class above an oppressed and cheated mass will live long and prosper.

THEODORE DREISER

Even this outlet did not satisfy him. He wanted to write a book on economics. People everywhere were demanding another novel from his pen, but he said: "How can one more novel mean anything in this catastrophic period through which the world is passing? No, I must write on economics."

And so *America Is Worth Saving* came into being. Not a novel, but a fighting factual book that dealt bluntly with America's crisis: Should we keep out of the impending imperialistic war? Emphatically we should, he said. He took as his platform the Declaration of Independence and the Constitution of the United States.

"America is worth saving," he cried. "Stay out of this imperialistic war."

As one review stated:

He does more than merely protest our participation. With the skill of a lawyer, the research of a statistician, and the analysis of a historian, he marshals a vast array of evidence that proves that this war is not a fight for democracy but just one more mad imperialistic scramble for profit and power. In this book, in fact, Dreiser has written a text and an encyclopedia for the peace of America:

Practical reasons for keeping out of war?

Dreiser gives us a chapter full.

Does England love us?

How democratic is England?

Has England democratized the people of its empire?

271

Without slandering the people of England, he gives chapter and verse of the brutal, undemocratic, arrogant history of the British ruling class that has only paid lip service to democracy while it has plundered the world for profit. Nor does Dreiser spare Hitler, nor the Fascists of France, nor enemies of the people anywhere, at home or abroad. They're all in this book, named by name, with all their cunning, criminal trickery exposed; the vicious parisitic millionaires of England, France, Germany, America.*

But, of course, events were happening fast at that time. After Germany attacked Russia and we ourselves were attacked at Pearl Harbor by Japan, Dreiser was for our all-out prosecution of the war to a successful conclusion, and he contributed his services to that end.

The limiting financial situation Teddie was experiencing at this time had a telling effect upon him. He was stricken with a heart attack and was forced to remain in bed for two months under the care of his regular physician and a heart specialist.

One morning after he had been ill for six weeks, Mr. A. Dorian Otvos, who had been working on the sale of *Sister Carrie* for some time, called on the phone to say that it had been sold to RKO Radio Pictures, Inc. The sale of *Sister Carrie*, forty years after it was written,† added another chapter to the interesting and unusual history of that book. In fact, the difficulties surrounding its publication have become a legend in publishing circles.

---

* Article by Richard Ramsey, in the *New Dealer*, May 1, 1941.

† Fifty years after the writing of *Sister Carrie*, Paramount Pictures, Inc., took over the motion picture rights, to produce it under the direction of William Wyler with Sir Laurence Olivier and Jennifer Jones in the principal roles of George Hurstwood and Carrie Meeber.

It was late in 1899 when Dreiser began writing *Sister Carrie* with the encouragement of a long-time friend of those days, Arthur Henry. Early in 1900, with Henry's help in the final revision, it was finished and sent to Harper's, who refused it. He then took it to Doubleday, Page and Company, where it was received in manuscript by Frank Doubleday himself. As he was leaving with his wife for Europe, he turned it over to Frank Norris, author of *Moran of the Lady Letty*, *McTeague* and other stories, who was then proofreading for Doubleday. Norris became wildly enthusiastic about *Sister Carrie* and advised publication. After the manuscript was read by Henry Lanier and Walter Hines Page, partners of the firm, a contract was drawn up and signed and the book was well on its way toward publication when Frank Doubleday and his wife returned from Europe. He took a set of proofs of the highly praised forthcoming novel home with him to read, where they naturally fell into the hands of Mrs. Doubleday. She was horrified. To her the book was not only vulgar but immoral, and impelled by her own particular moralistic principles, she vehemently insisted that Doubleday withdraw from their contract. Of this she was able to convince her husband, and Dreiser was notified. He hastened to the defense of his book and his contract. The Doubleday lawyer, Thomas H. McKee, advised the firm that they would have to publish a small edition but would not be required to sell or promote it. So 1,000 copies were printed, and although Norris sent over a hundred copies out for review, no advertising to proclaim its publication on November 8 was provided. As a result, only 465 copies were sold.

Among the publishers who received review copies from

Frank Norris was Heinemann of London, who published it in his Dollar Library of American Novelists.* The English reviews were enthusiastic in their praise of the book and Dreiser's spirits lifted. Later, Joseph Taylor, president of the J. F. Taylor Company, bought the plates and sheets of *Sister Carrie* from Doubleday, Page and Company, but failed to publish it. Charles Agnew MacLean of Street and Smith, for whom Dreiser went to work to help edit thriller stories and dime novels, purchased the plates and sheets from Taylor for five hundred dollars. MacLean was a Scotch Irishman in good standing with Ormand Smith, a man Dreiser came to know and like. It was while there that they worked out two new thrill journals called *Smith's* and *The Popular Magazine*. As Teddie humorously described it to me, many times he took a long, bloodcurdling manuscript and simply cut it in two, putting a new ending on the first half and a new beginning on the last half.

When Dreiser went to work in 1906 as editor for Ben Hampton of the *Broadway Magazine*, he purchased the plates and sheets of *Sister Carrie* from MacLean. Then, in 1907, Ben W. Dodge of B. W. Dodge and Company reissued the book for Dreiser, who became associated with that firm. Afterwards, when Dreiser made a deal with Harper and Brothers for *Jennie Gerhardt* and *The Financier*, they took over the rights for *Sister Carrie* from B. W. Dodge and Company and published it in 1912, advertising it with the quotation from Arnold Bennett to the effect that here was "perhaps the great American novel." This twelve years from the day it was first submitted for publication.

* Published July, 1901.

The news of the sale of *Sister Carrie* to RKO was so encouraging to Teddie that he began to mend immediately. In two weeks he was on his way to recovery. Soon after this, a letter came from Jug offering to get a divorce if Theodore would give her five thousand dollars in addition to the five thousand due. However, after discussing it with me, he refused her belated offer. Nevertheless, as he was then in a position to settle back payments, he brought the account up to date.

27

In December, 1940, while driving along North Kings Road in Hollywood, we saw an attractive house for sale, and stopped to inquire about it. As we walked into the living room, we knew this was what we wanted, and immediately made arrangements for its purchase. A month later three large vanloads of furniture, literary materials and the Dreiser library arrived from Iroki to find lodging in their new surroundings. A moisture-proof storeroom was already under construction, and the garden at the back of the lot was being landscaped in accordance with Dreiser's taste. All shrubs and flowers were moved to the borders of a plain lawn, broken only by two avocado trees with long, graceful branches. Other parts of the garden contained a lemon, a plum and a walnut tree as well as several banana-bearing palms. The house, of white Moorish design, was built wholly of cement blocks, creating solidity as well as insulation against heat in the summer and cold in the winter. The living room opened into an adjoining dining room and music room, creating an atmosphere of spaciousness. Teddie liked the place because of its accessibility.

We found ourselves relatively happy on "the Kings Road." Teddie had his cherished rosewood piano desk back again in a northern suite consisting of writing room, bedroom, bathroom and patio with private entrance into the garden. Here he worked on several original motion picture scripts, short stories and lectures, along with his *Notes*.

During the summer of 1941, Robert H. Elias, of the Department of English at the University of Pennsylvania, came out to Hollywood to do research on the Dreiser correspondence and manuscripts in order to write a dissertation and obtain his degree at that university. After discussing the subject at length, he interested Dreiser in contributing a part of his literary effects to the University, with the provision that suitable arrangements would be made for their safe preservation and proper use—a gift that I later augmented in 1946.* The original dissertation of Robert H. Elias, now Professor of English at Cornell University, evolved into the very able biography entitled *Dreiser: Apostle of Nature*, published in 1949.

Teddie took advantage of every opportunity to visit the California Institute of Technology, witnessing experiments, entering into discussions with scientists and probing into their latest findings. Once we visited Dr. Edison Pettit, a prominent astronomer of the Mount Wilson Observatory. At his home and private laboratory in Pasadena, he showed us his astounding pictures taken at the McMath Hulbert Observatory, Michigan. They were among the first moving pictures taken of the sun, showing it spewing forth its great solar promi-

* In 1949, through the direct influence of Dr. Charles W. David, Director of Libraries, the University of Pennsylvania came into possession of the complete Theodore Dreiser collection which resides in a special Dreiser room there.

nences four or five hundred thousand kilometres into space,* and then sucking the most of it back again into its molten self in the most fantastic manner of fiery attraction and consumption.

Dr. Theodore von Karman, aeronautical genius who directed wind tunnel experiments, also discussed his technical scientific problems of air flow with Dreiser. There were many other interesting visits to laboratories engaged in the process of discovering some of the secrets of the universe.

The pattern of Dreiser's life during this time was a harmonious blending of work and intermittent social activity. Mrs. Elizabeth Coakley, sister of Patrick Kearney, playwright, was doing secretarial work for him as well as Mrs. Byron Smith of Glendale, who was also engaged in research work. She had been collecting old magazines containing Dreiser articles and short stories for years, a collection which, after his death, she presented to the Los Angeles Public Library during the administration of Miss Althea Warren, Librarian.

A ballet was being composed for *The Spring Recital,* one of Dreiser's *Plays of the Natural and Supernatural,* by Ivan Boutnikoff, distinguished conductor and composer from Europe, who later performed it brilliantly at the Hollywood Bowl.

Lillian Rosedale Goodman, composer of *Cheri, I Love You,* and other songs including musical settings for several of Dreiser's poems from his volume *Moods,* had moved her vocal studio to Hollywood from Chicago. Her friendship with Ted-

* According to Dr. Pettit, this calculation of distance has now been stepped up to a height reaching one million five hundred and fifty thousand kilometres.

die dated back to the writing days of *Jennie Gerhardt*—a
friendship he was able to renew with her and her family.
Many enchanting evenings were spent at her home and studio
in Pilgrimage Trail, and I found in her a new, deeply affectionate friend and appreciative artist.

We enjoyed an inspiring last visit with Eleanor and
Sherwood Anderson when they passed through Los Angeles,
spending a long evening in dimly lighted old Chinatown listening to Sherwood and Theodore reminisce. They had once
been near neighbors in Greenwich Village and had much to
talk about. However, we both thought Sherwood looked
strained and tired and when the news came of his death on
March 8, 1941, at Colon Hospital in Panama, we were not
greatly shocked. A tribute to Anderson by Dreiser was read at
his funeral by Stanley Young:

> Anderson, his life and his writings, epitomize for me the pilgrim-
> age of a poet and dreamer across this limited stage called life whose
> reactions to the mystery of our being and doings here,—(our will-
> less and so wholly automatic responses to our environing forces)
> involved tenderness, love and beauty, delight in the strangeness
> of our will-less reactions, as well as pity, sympathy and love for all
> things, both great and small. Whenever I think of him I think of
> that wondrous line out of the Ancient Mariner—"He prayeth best
> who lovest best all things both great and small." And so sometimes
> the things he wrote as well as the not too many things he said, to
> me personally, had the value of a poetic prayer for the happiness
> and well being of everything and everybody—as well as the well-
> outcoming of everything, guided as each thing plainly is by an
> enormous wisdom—if seemingly not always imbued with mercy—
> that none-the-less "passeth all understanding." He seemed to me to
> accept in humbleness, as well as in and of necessity in nature,

THEODORE DREISER

Christ's dictum: "The rain falleth on the just and unjust." Also
that we are to "take no thought for your life, what ye shall eat, or
what ye shall drink; nor yet for your body, what ye shall put on.
Is not the life more than meat, and the body than raiment?"

As I see him now there was something biblical and prophetic
about him. Through all his days he appears to have been wandering
here and there, looking, thinking, wondering. And the things he
brought back from the fields of life! Dark Laughter! Many Mar-
riages! The Triumph of the Egg! Mid American Chants! Wines-
burg! in which is that beautiful commentary on the strain of life
on some temperaments called "Hands"! It is to me so truly beautiful, understanding and loving, and weeping, almost for the suffering of others.

Well he is gone—wise, kind, affectionate, forgiving. And I wish
he were not. To me, amidst all the strain of living and working,
he was a comforting figure—never in any sense a slave to money,
or that other seeming necessity to so many—SHOW—or pretense.
He was what he was and accepted himself in just that sense—"I
am that I am"—"Take me or leave me for what I am to you."
And I, like millions of others, I assume, have taken him in just
that sense. And other millions will, I feel, for the duration at least
of our American literature.

THEODORE DREISER

We renewed our friendship with Esther McCoy, who was
now living in Santa Monica where we often went to visit her
in her cottage-by-the-sea. A great liberal and humanitarian, as
well as a warm and friendly woman who always welcomed
her guests in the most gracious, simple manner. She was passing through a strenuous financial and emotional period of
her life at that time, but she was able to express great beauty
in her artistic but unvarnished way of life. I always waited
eagerly to read her latest short story, and although she had not

Above: Dreiser and George Douglas, Los Angeles, 1936. *Below:* Dreiser and Charles Fort at Iroki, 1931.

Above: Dreiser in Paris, 1938. *Below:* Dreiser speaking before representatives of the International Peace Conference, Paris, 1938.

Above: Rustic "wishing" bench in Stevenson, Washington. *Drawing by Ralph Fabri. Below:* Last photograph taken of Dreiser, December 21, 1945.

The Dreiser Memorial

been stamped with public approval, Teddie constantly prodded her to keep on writing and sending out her stories to editors of magazines, over and over, no matter how many times they were returned, for he believed in her as a writer and was ever a source of inspiration. Esther took his advice, and the faith that her friends expressed in her ultimate victory was justified, for she finally made a considerable success with her stories, wrote a novel and successfully completed a large amount of worthwhile writing.

I received a terrible shock in the news of the suicide of my beloved friend and singing teacher, Maria Samson. After the death of her husband, Dr. Bella Vass, in New York, she had moved to California where she built up a most valued following of students and friends. Her untimely death was a mystery to all who knew her, for Maria had beauty, health and a fine voice. Teddie, whom she loved dearly, delivered an affectionate eulogy at her funeral.

We attended numerous soirées at the Russian Consulate where we met many of our friends. Here we came to know intimately Oona and Charles Chaplin. Teddie had a deep regard for Chaplin as artist, intellectual, humanitarian, world citizen and comedian.

So often young ambitious writers looked Teddie up to talk with him, seeking advice, or just to see him. Many times they were completely overawed. One day he explained to me that the last thing he wanted was to have young literary people or any people overawed by him. "That would make me lonely and very sad indeed," he said. "Always make them feel perfectly at ease and free to approach me at any time. That's the way I want it." And I knew this to be true, for how many

times had he not chosen the unannounced approach, preferring to remain unnoticed as he gathered his own fresh impressions free of observation?

In September, 1942, when Dreiser was invited to speak
before the Toronto, Canada, Town Forum, he was not inclined
to accept. Finally he agreed to make the trip, not being aware,
however, of the bitter feudal political factions existing in that
part of the country. No sooner had he arrived in that city
where he gave out advance interviews, than a few of his
"grossly misquoted remarks" flashed with the speed of lightning around the entire globe. Rumors flew that he was pro-
Nazi. He was barred from speaking in Canada, threatened
with arrest and attacked bitterly by the Writers' War Board,
to which, upon his return to the States, he made the following
answer in Indianapolis, Indiana:

> Recently I was invited by the Toronto Town Forum to be one of
> the speakers. I neither had the time nor the inclination to make the
> journey from Los Angeles to Toronto to accommodate these good
> people. But, after several appeals on their part, I reluctantly ac-
> cepted their offer and agreed to address their Forum. I took it for
> granted that the people of the Toronto Town Forum were well
> aware of my views on public questions in general and Russia in
> particular. My views are not a military secret, and in this spirit I
> made the long journey to Toronto to fill the engagement. On arriv-
> ing there I was interviewed by a group of reporters, and, in sending
> out their report, they attributed to me an expressed desire to have
> Hitler defeat and rule the English people. On the basis of this re-
> port the supposed Department of Justice of Canada ordered my
> banishment. This did not surprise me in the least. What did sur-
> prise me was the fact that the Writers' War Board, on the basis of

the misrepresentation, and without taking the trouble to inquire of me what I had actually said, flew into print with the denunciation of me implying that I had suddenly become an ally of Hitler. In this way they set themselves up as prosecutor, court and jury and condemned me to the newspaper hell prepared for the anti-capitalistic class. Ordinarily I would have dismissed this for its servility to British Toryism were it not for two important facts: First, the great danger of our relations with the only peoples who have thus far thwarted the Nazis in their effort to conquer the world; the other, the denunciation by you, Pearl Buck, who also signed the Writers' War Board statement after you had travelled far and wide through the Far East and truthfully and graphically reported the results of our policy of business as usual. By that I mean the bombs and gasoline that we have furnished to the Japanese for over four years which have enabled them to burn the cities of China and murder their women and children. You also have seen and truthfully reported the brutal rule by the British Tories of the colonial peoples of the Far East.

How does it happen that you would sign your name to a document of this kind without inquiring as to what was actually said by me? Instead you join the chorus that we need unity in our war effort. Unity around what? Unity around the whipping post? And this brings us to what was said in Toronto. What essential difference is there between Hitler's firing squad in the conquered countries and Churchill's whipping post in India? Should we permit, by our silence on this subject, the natural assumption by the people of India, Russia and China that we approve of it when we do not? Is this in accordance with our history, traditions and ideals? But you will say that we are at war and cannot offend our allies. What allies? The British Tories, who were more responsible than any one else for bringing this holocaust on the world, or the great masses of India, Russia, China and the common people of England, who heroically fought against Munich in the first place and are today giving their lives by the millions on the altar of freedom? I did not say that I'd be delighted to see Hitler rule the English people as a whole. I yield to no one in my love of our country or that of humanity. My record in the struggle against Naziism is too clear to be repeated but I see in our continual tagging along behind the British policy of business as usual the ultimate defeat of our country.

Many informed Americans assert and believe that if a balance sheet were struck at this time we have lost the war. As I see it there is only one way we can win this war and freedom and peace for everyone and that is by joining our forces quickly with the people of Russia, India and China. Another thing, the time has come when we must boldly speak against injustice and perfidy wherever it may appear and from whatever source it may come. We must repudiate the whipping post of Churchill. And right here, I would like to ask: Why did all mention of India suddenly disappear from American newspapers the moment the American people became sincerely interested in its freedom as an honest and sensible interpretation of the Atlantic Charter, and their conception of what we are fighting for—the Four Freedoms for all the peoples of the World?

As to the Churchill interpretation of his agreement with Stalin regarding a second front, I do not know of any American record when our country has welshed on an agreement, or explained it away by an interpretation such as that made by Churchill to the effect that an understanding that had been reached between Russia and England looking toward the opening of a second front in 1942 did not mean that at all.

In view of these facts, I think it would be gentlemanly, or let us say just decent, for those who spread the assertions of which I complain, to render me a public apology. Private letters will in no way cheer me.*

* Printed letter in my possession.

284

HELEN DREISER

The statement below appeared in *PM*, Sunday, September 27, 1942:

SHAW ON DREISER

George Bernard Shaw said Saturday in London that the press reports he had seen concerning Theodore Dreiser's remark that he would prefer to see Germans in Britain than the "horse-riding snobs" who are here now were insufficient for comment, but he added:

"To say that Dreiser's comments regarding the war are furiously inaccurate is only to say that they are like everyone else's comments regarding the war.

"In England we denounce crimes against the German Reich because we do not know that our British Empire has committed so many of these crimes itself that it does not become us to give ourselves moral airs unless we sincerely repent our past, a change of heart whereof we have given the world no assurance whatever.

"Although the English do not know their own history, Americans know it, the Irish know it, the Indians know it to their cost. There is no reason to suppose the Germans do not know it. Dreiser evidently knows it and reacts explosively when we pose as Herrenvolk exactly as Hitler does.

"There's nothing to fuss about. If Dreiser is soundly determined to see Adolph Hitler damned first, he can say what he likes about wicked old England. We can take care of ourselves with America's help, or even without it, at a pinch."

Dreiser's answer to Shaw was:

October 10, 1942

MY DEAR SHAW:

Thanks for the kindly lifeline to the presumably drowning critic of dear old England. Only I hadn't gone down for even the first time. And I think it would do the dear mother-land a lot of good

285

Oct. 10 - 1942

My Dear Shaw:

Thanks for the kindly lifeline to the presumably drowning
critic of dear old England. Only I
hadn't gone down for even the first
time. And I think it would do the
dear mother-land a lot of good if
we followed your hint and allowed
her to save herself in just one real
finish. Besides I think we'd like
her better. This "hands across the
sea" stuff - constantly conveying
supplies eastward to the
dear motherland, - well, - you know,
Even children occasionally turn on an

Facsimile of letter to George Bernard Shaw.

if we followed your hint and allowed her to save herself in just one real pinch. Besides I think we'd like her better. This "hands across the sea" stuff—our hands for instance—constantly conveying supplies eastward to the dear mother-land,—well, you know. Even children occasionally turn on an over exacting parent.

The Irish ought to know.

In fact I think I know one Irishman who does know and I feel that I don't need to give you even one guess.

With unchanging admiration and affection—

THEODORE DREISER

When Teddie finally returned to California after all the disturbing and annoying excitement had died down, he was noticeably quiet. The trip east with its accompanying notoriety had taken its toll in spite of his well developed immunity to criticism. The desire to settle down to work in a deeply creative mood was again stirring in him. He had had his say on economics. He had traveled all over the country lecturing here and there. The war was in hand and great preparations were being made. In view of this, he decided that the pressing urge for his personal economic activities was over and the desire grew in him to concentrate on his long resting novel, *The Bulwark*, which his publishers and many of his followers had been demanding of him for years. Consequently, he dug the manuscript out from his vast literary effects, saying: "Damn it all, I am going to work on a novel, and I would like to see anyone take me away from it."

With this, he quietly but determinedly settled down to work.

28

The manuscript of *The Bulwark* that Dreiser took from his storeroom covered about two thirds of the book as he planned and wrote it years before. There were two versions, and after studying them carefully he decided to make an entirely new start. He began writing chapter one and continued writing every day until he had forty chapters written, which were finally cut down to the twenty-four comprising the first part of the book.

As he sat describing the charming Quaker atmosphere that he revered and respected, building up the background, traditions and customs of the lives of his characters in Segookit, Maine, and Dukla, near Philadelphia, I could feel and see Teddie, in spite of himself, becoming more and more detached from the world and its distracting war sickness as though this book was casting a spell over him.

He took to writing in the swing in a small court outside the music room, where he set up a card table for this purpose. It was there he could be seen every day working contentedly and happily on this book which lay so very near to his heart.

For was it not a study of his father that he was building in his character, Solon Barnes? Only, his father had been not merely a conforming religionist but a narrow one who, according to Theodore, demanded that his children follow blindly the tenets of the church.

Theodore had been a child of unusual mentality and sensitivity of which his mother naturally was well aware. She knew the intensity of his curiosity when it came to learning and reading. Theresa, who was better read than any of the other sisters, was his favorite, and helped him in his selection of good literature. But she died when rather young, and Theodore then had no one to guide him in his reading and was thrown back on his own intuition. However, one day he went to confession and was told by the priest that he would have to discard his varied reading, including scientific books of all kinds, or he could no longer attend Communion. Theodore studied and pondered for days over this ultimatum. Walking past the door of the church on the opposite side of the street on the day of Communion, he indulged in a lengthy soliloquy: "Shall I go in and forget the books of my choice, or shall I never enter the door again?"

Being an honest boy and a serious one, this question lay heavily upon him. He thought of his father and the unreasonable demands he had always made on the entire family to contribute to the church, even when they had not had enough to eat. And then he thought of how a boy or young man could advance himself by reading and training his mind, and thereby develop a capacity to absorb knowledge. His thoughts returned to confession and Communion. And, as he told me, his decision had to be in favor of his books.

But the effect of his father's violent opposition to his thirst for knowledge lingered in him all his life. Many times he quoted him as saying: "You will go to hell with your books. You will come to some bad end with them."

Opposed to this lack of understanding between father and son was the great love Theodore bore for his mother—a love that sustained him to the last day of his life. A "poetic mother" as he so often called her, who understood and stimulated the narrative in him. But in the years after the death of his father, he recalled traits in him, too, that he admired: his honesty, his austere Germanic way of living— and there grew in his mind the desire to build a story around him. However, from the time he described the story of *The Bulwark* to John Cowper Powys and Edgar Lee Masters, around 1913, he had come to know Quakerism and the high ideals and inspiring ethics of John Woolman, George Fox and others. It was then that he decided to change the background of his religious story to that of the Friends. In this way, he believed he could psychologize the limited religionist and yet allow no bitterness to enter his story, which would have been impossible in the depiction of the Catholic background of his father's life. Having become intimately acquainted with several Quaker families, he had come to love the scrupulous and simple ethics of their faith, and as time passed, his story was fused into one harmonious pattern against which he could delineate his beloved character of Solon Barnes.

Naturally, Teddie used the Bible extensively in the writing of *The Bulwark*, as he had already done in many of his writings. Bible quotations had always interested him, and

I would say that not ten days passed in which he did not quote from The Sermon on the Mount or some of the other sayings of Christ. There were some things about Teddie that made me wonder if he had not inherited some of the qualities of his mother's brothers who had been great Bible students. One uncle was the Reverend Henry A. Snepp,* born in 1830 in Montgomery County, Ohio, six miles west of Dayton, who served the church of his choice, the United Brethren, for forty years and died at the age of sixty-five. Another uncle was the Reverend Aaron W. Snepp, born in Preble County, Ohio, in 1842, who also joined the United Brethren and was baptized in the famous Tippecanoe River in Indiana, in 1865. Ordained to the office of an Elder in the year 1876, his ministry covered a wide area; he traveled to the Pacific Coast where he was assigned to various charges, presiding as pastor in Washington, Oregon and California Conferences.

One day, while Teddie was doing a little spading in the garden in the shade of an overhanging avocado tree, he came into the house to announce that he would stop working on his book for a few days in order to write an essay on life, to be entitled *My Creator*, an appreciation of the life processes as expressed by the creative force working in nature. The result was a twelve-page essay which he concluded with:

> . . . and so studying this matter of genius in design and beauty, as well as the wisdom of contrast and interest in this so carefully engineered and regulated universe—this amazing process called living—I am moved not only to awe but to reverence for the Creator of the same concerning whom—his or its presence in all things from worm to star to thought—I meditate constantly even though

* Snepp, a contraction of Schnepp.

it be, as I see it, that my import to this, My Creator, can be as nothing, or less, if that were possible.

Yet I have. And, at long last, profound reverence for so amazing and esthetic and wondrous a process, that may truly have been, and for all that I know, may yet continue to be forever and forever. An esthetic and wondrous process of which I might pray—and do— to remain the infinitesimal part of that same that I now am.*

While he was working on *The Bulwark*, he consented to sit for the Italian sculptor, Edgardo Simone. With the exception of a portrait of Dreiser by Boris Chaliapin, commissioned in 1939 by Josiah K. Lilly of Indianapolis, this was the only work of art for which Teddie posed during his stay in California. The Chaliapin portrait was one of a collection of Indiana writers to be presented to the Indiana State Library.

Twice a week Teddie went to Mr. Simone's studio. The result was an arresting study of Dreiser's head. It won several first prizes for the sculptor, and Teddie then purchased the original. Later I had a bronze copy made and presented it to the Metropolitan Museum of Art.

One day Mr. Simone invited us to one of the picture studios to see the making of *A Night in Paradise* where some of his oversized sculptures were being used on one of the sets. It was an exotic picture with swans floating on lakes, colored birds, flower girls, handsome slaves and golden chariots. Pictures were taken of Teddie with Turhan Bey. When the publicity men insisted upon an expression of opinion, Teddie wound up his statement with the genial comment: "It is

* Unpublished manuscript, November, 1943, in my possession.

mar—vel—ous! but meaningless," a remark that found its way into all the local papers the next day.

Teddie was beginning to worry again over finances, as he had spent a good portion of the money he had received from the sale of the motion picture rights to *Sister Carrie*; the money had paid for our Hollywood home, the enormous shipment from New York and had erased his debt to Jug. His normal income from the sale of his books had almost stopped, because they had been out of print during World War II. When he inquired about the possibility of having them brought back into print, the answer was that *The Bulwark* had to come first, to act as a spearhead for his other books. This pressure irritated him to the point where he decided to repay the publisher the $3,000 advance on *The Bulwark*, so that he could work unharried by the thought of a deadline. The effect of this repayment was immediate release from tension, and he set to work with renewed vigor.

But then something happened which changed the entire financial picture. For some time Dreiser had been reading reports of the enormous sales of his books in Russia. Wherever a tabulation of book sales in that country was made in print, he found his name among the first five best-sellers. And while he had not received any payment from the U.S.S.R. since he first drew up a contract with the state publishing house in Moscow in 1927, he did not care to demand an accounting because he had such a desire to see Russia succeed in its experiment. He felt that now her position was different and an accounting should be made to him. Upon making inquiries about payments to other authors in the United States, he was told confidentially that payments were indeed being made by Russia to several authors in this country. Immediately he came home and dictated a long personal letter to Premier Stalin, explaining the situation and stating that an accounting should be made to him for past-due royalties.

Two months later a notice arrived from one of the leading Los Angeles banks. As Teddie had now turned over his financial records to me for attention, I opened the letter. He was out at the time, but when he returned I handed it to him. There was no indication of the country nor any other information except the amount to be transferred, and since we were accustomed to receiving small statements now and then, Dreiser read aloud: "Three dollars and forty-six cents. Why do they bother to send me such statements?"

"You're putting in a decimal that isn't there," I said. "Why don't you read it correctly?"

Looking more closely, he read: "Thirty-four thousand, six hundred and—what is this? Call the bank. Find out!" he exclaimed, very excited. Whereupon I called the bank which verified the payment as coming from Russia. Dreiser's face was aglow with exhilaration. I can't imagine anything pleasing him more than such a prompt response to his letter.

"I refuse to worry any more. This will carry me through to the end," he said.

The next day we went to the bank to collect the money. But that was not the last accounting to be made by the U.S.S.R. In 1946, about three months after Teddie's death, three representatives of the Russian government called on me and, after satisfying themselves by reading the will that I was the rightful heir, personally delivered to me the next day the sum of seven thousand dollars in cash.

During this time I became conscious of a gradual change in Teddie's attitude toward me. He was noticeably mellowing, and was extremely considerate, thoughtful and solicitous of me. I had always understood his affection for me. He was not a demonstrative man, but he had ways of conveying his love. Now he was going out of his way to impress the fact upon me. He told me things he could never have told me in the past, having too much masculine pride to let a woman know what he thought. I became embarrassed at some of his compliments and told him so. But he merely said: "I want you to know, that's all."

True enough, he was telling me things I had perhaps always longed to hear from him, but now they worried me, for I had the feeling that he was building up in me a treasure of memories to sustain me when he was no longer here.

In the spring of 1944, a letter came from Dr. Walter Damrosch, President of The American Academy of Arts and Letters, in which he said that once in each five years, the Academy presented to an American novelist, not a member of the Academy or the Institute, the Award of Merit Medal, together with a cash prize of one thousand dollars, for extraordinary achievement in his art. In that year, 1944, Dreiser had been chosen for the distinction of such books as *Sister Carrie, An American Tragedy, Twelve Men,* and a long list of other volumes, as well as for his courage and integrity in breaking trail as a pioneer in the presentation in fiction of real human beings and a real America.

When he informed Dr. Damrosch that he would accept the Award, he was invited to attend the ceremony personally. He expressed the desire that I go with him, and I wanted very much to do so, especially as I felt that he was not overly strong and feared the New York trip might further deplete his vitality. But having received news that my mother was quite ill and that there was a possibility of her dying, I thought it unwise to go east at that time.

Before packing his bag to take off for New York, Teddie told me one day that he thought, for convenience sake, it would be a good idea for us to be legally married on his return.*

"Of course," he said, "there will be a lot of publicity and all that, but does it really matter very much?"

"No," I replied, "I don't think it matters very much—at this late date, anyway. But I think I can arrange it so there will not be any publicity." I said this without the slightest idea as to how I could bring it about.

"All right, you're a wizard if you can," he said, "but go ahead and arrange it, and let me know. I'll meet you anywhere you say. Just wire me."

So Teddie and I went our separate ways—he to New York to personally accept the Award of Merit Medal from the Academy of Arts and Letters and I to Oregon to see my mother. His stay in New York, with all its pressing social engagements, had an extremely tiring effect on him. I encouraged and welcomed the secretarial services offered by Marguerite Tjader Harris, while he was there, and when he wrote me that his niece, Vera Dreiser, a consulting psychol-

* Mrs. Dreiser had died on October 1, 1942.

ogist in New York, had insisted on taking him to Dr. Shailer
Laughton for a thorough physical check-up, I was deeply
grateful to her.

When he arrived in New York, he found his sister Mame
seriously ill in a hospital. Spending some time at her bedside, he was with her shortly before she closed her eyes for
the last time. Later, when he returned to Hollywood, he often
described to me how beautiful she had looked as she lay
in her casket. He could not get over her last words.

"What do you think Mame said to me just before she
died?" he asked. "She said, as she gently touched my hand
with hers—'You know . . . Theo . . . all the men in the world,
together, cannot create one blade of grass.' "

Upon my arrival in Portland, I learned that my mother
was not fatally ill and realized I could have accompanied
Teddie to New York. However, I used the time to good advantage by working on a prospective sale of the Mount Kisco
place. Many telegrams and letters were exchanged before
the deal was consummated and Iroki finally changed hands.

I then began to make inquiries about a place where Teddie
and I could be quietly married. To my surprise, I was informed through an attorney friend of Myrtle's that this
could be accomplished in the unobtrusive little town of
Stevenson, Washington. A few days later Myrtle and I
visited Stevenson on the Columbia River, commanding a
superb view of the hills of Oregon on the opposite side. I
was overjoyed with the idea of meeting Teddie in such a
romantic spot.

When I received a letter from him announcing the time of

his arrival, I wired him to get off at Stevenson, fifty-three miles east of Portland, through which his train would pass on its way to the West Coast. Then I engaged two front rooms across the hall from each other at the Sampson Hotel, a quaint old-fashioned place that had been very popular in its day.

Teddie's train was arriving at 5:55 A.M. the next morning. When I went down to the station to meet him, I was informed that it was a long train and that he would probably get off far down the track. I walked quite a distance and then I saw him alighting.

We walked arm in arm over to the sloping lawn in front of the Sampson Hotel, where we sat on an old rustic "wishing bench" on which many couples must have rested in the past.

Suddenly, becoming self-conscious and almost bashful, Teddie reached into his pocket and brought forth a small package which he handed to me.

"This is for you. I brought it to you."

I opened the package to see a large, round, gold, coin-like medal which had been presented to him by the American Academy of Arts and Letters.

"But Teddie," I exclaimed, "this is yours!"

"No!" he said, "it is as much yours as mine. I want you to have it. I am only sorry you were not with me when I received it." I was overwhelmed.

Tears filled my eyes as I read the inscription—*Opportunity, Inspiration, Achievement*—around an Apollo-like figure holding a lyre in one hand and extending a laurel branch with the other. On the opposite side, encircling a wreath of leaves and flowers, was engraved: *The American Academy of Arts and Letters—Award of Merit.* Around the edge of the disc: *Awarded to Theodore Dreiser 1944 for Distinction in the Art of the Novel.*

As we sat and talked, he told me all about his trip and I related my own activities. Then we went to the Eagle Café on the corner of the main street and talked some more. What a youthful mind he had, and what a privileged woman I was to have had such a companion! Here we were at the end of a long journey, to stand before a justice of the peace who would place an official seal, like a period, on a long relationship that had withstood many trials.

"After the fact," as Teddie said, "but necessary for legal reasons in this world of man-made rights, codes, decrees and all that."

At our hotel, Teddie became fascinated with a rubber plant growing out of a large pot. It was about sixty feet in length and consisted of not much more than one long root supported by wires along the ceiling of the enclosed veranda. Mr. Sampson, the proprietor, had planted it thirty-five years before, when he first came to Stevenson.

We decided to have a ring ceremony performed by Gertrude Brown, Justice of the Peace, and the next day, Saturday, Teddie went to file the application and make all the necessary arrangements. Myrtle came up to visit us and witness the filing of the application. She agreed to return with her fiancé, Chester Butcher, to stand up with us, three days later, Tuesday, June 13, 1944.

During the three-day waiting period, we spent most of the time touring the adjacent countryside. One place we visited was a famous Indian sulphur spring, to which thousands of

299

people migrate every year. Another was the Columbia River Gorge Hotel, with its incomparable view of the entire country, reminding us so much of Norway.

When the appointed day finally arrived, Myrtle and Chester appeared in great spirits. Beautiful white orchid corsages and champagne toasts created an atmosphere of gaiety before leaving the hotel. On our way to Mrs. Brown's we were surprised by being vigorously pelted with great quantities of rice which Myrtle and Chester had brought along for the occasion. I became nervous at the last moment about the possible sudden discovery of Teddie's identity, although he had decided to sign his name Herman Dreiser instead of his full name, Herman Theodore Dreiser, as he was originally christened. I think this did the trick, for Mrs. Brown, though quite a reader judging by the books on her living room table, obviously attached no particular significance to the name.

When it was over, we motored across to the Oregon side for a special wedding supper, after which Teddie and I went to the Congress Hotel in Portland for a few days before returning to Hollywood.

Two years later, Chester and Myrtle retraced their steps to Stevenson and to the Justice of the Peace, Mrs. Gertrude Brown, where they went through the same ceremony.

29

Many telegrams and letters of congratulation on his receiving the Award of Merit were awaiting Teddie on our return to Hollywood. After two weeks of rest, he resumed work on *The Bulwark*.

I received a letter from Marguerite Tjader Harris in New York, saying Dreiser had expressed the wish that she come to Hollywood to work with him on the book; she wanted my approval. I wrote her that I knew he needed editorial assistance, and I would be very glad to have her.

She and her son Hilary arrived in Hollywood in August, just in time to attend a garden birthday party I was having for Teddie.* Although he had given his consent to have the party if I would confine it to a few intimate friends, upon observing the preparations, he came to me every little while with a statement such as: "Well, if we are going to *have* this party we might as well invite ――――――."

The list soon grew to nearly sixty persons. Teddie loved his friends, of which there were many, and he could not bear to

* August 27, 1944.

leave one out. The guests included Mr. and Mrs. Will Durant; Clare Kummer and her daughter Marjorie; Mr. and Mrs. Clifford Odets; Lillian Goodman, her husband Mark and her mother Mrs. Rosenthal; Mr. and Mrs. Byron Smith; Lt. George Smith; Mr. and Mrs. Berkeley Tobey (Esther McCoy); Ivan Boutnikoff; Mr. and Mrs. Edgar Ward (Jane Wyatt); Mr. and Mrs. A. Dorian Otvos; Mr. and Mrs. Harry Yerg; Dr. Chang the Chinese Consul, Mrs. Chang and their fascinating and brilliant concertist daughter, Rosita; Marcia Masters, charming poetess daughter of Edgar Lee Masters, and her equally talented composer daughter, little Marcia.

Teddie was in one of his happiest and most expansive moods, which always kindled a warm responsive glow in those who loved him. Howard Ross, one of Lillian Goodman's students, sang Theodore's favorite song—*Jeanie with the Light Brown Hair*—from the music room stairs leading into the garden. Toward evening, all gathered in the dining room where the candles were lit on his birthday cake, the icing of which formed an open book representing *The Bulwark*. When the time came for Teddie to cut the cake, it revolved on a circular music box playing *Happy Birthday to You*, a refrain that was taken up by everyone. It was one of our most successful parties and the last one of any size.

He was soon absorbed in the completion of his novel and often discussed scenes and characters as he progressed. However, I noticed whenever he talked of his principal character, Solon Barnes, his eyes would fill with tears, and I knew he was thinking not only of his father but of what he considered his own shortcomings. I knew he was putting a lot of himself into this story of the Quaker, and I saw in his eyes the realiza-

tion that his own life might end at any time and that he felt
he might have done differently at times in the past. Often he
quoted: ". . . this night thy soul shall be required of thee."

At night when he was tired, I read from Carl Sandburg's
Abraham Lincoln, a magnificent work that he loved as much
as I did. We were cooperating in every way to conserve his
strength for the task of finishing the book, and Mrs. Harris
put in long hours editing and working on revisions.

Often Teddie accompanied me to the Christian Science and
other churches and seemed to enjoy the services. While I did
not wish to join any particular church, I liked to attend
occasionally.

One day I showed him a comprehensive bibliography on
which I, with the aid of Mrs. Byron Smith, had been working
for some time, and noticing the title "Chicago Drainage
Canal, Ainslee's, February, 1899," he exclaimed:

"My God! Did I write about that, too?"

"Why yes," I said, "it's one of your early articles."

"Well," he went on, "this last time when I passed through
Chicago on my way west, I was fascinated thinking over the
engaging possibilities of the Chicago Drainage Canal, as we
rode alongside it. I thought to myself: 'What an excellent article it would make—this canal—I must remember to write
it up one day soon.' And here, I see that I have already written
the article—and that, forty-five years ago. Well I'll be
damned!"

By the following May, *The Bulwark* was finished and Doubleday and Company contracted for it through Teddie's literary agent in Hollywood, Alvin Manuel. Marguerite Harris

returned to New York and Theodore sent copies of his manuscript to James Farrell and Louise Campbell for comments and possibly more editing. Louise returned a cut version which was submitted, along with the original script, to Doubleday and Company in care of Donald Elder, Editor. Mr. Elder restored some of the original passages, and the final result was a compromise between the two versions which pleased Teddie very much.

Being a prolific and voluminous writer with a tendency to repetition, Dreiser was convinced of the need for cutting, and although he himself had had wide experience as an editor, he often said a fresh eye to scan a manuscript on which he had worked a long time was refreshing and helpful to him. However, before he ever gave a piece of work to any individual, he was familiar with the temperament and literary taste of that person and knew his or her artistic defects as well as talents. But he was not quick to make changes in his style or structure, as H. L. Mencken pointed out in his introduction to *An American Tragedy*.* I have seen him patiently re-edit chapters after they had been edited by someone other than himself, often rewriting long passages on all the marginal space of a page.

During the month of June, Dreiser was considering the possibility of applying for membership in the Communist Party.† Up to that time, he had always said he would never join any party. But he was convinced that they would succeed in stamping out Fascism throughout the world. As he said:

* Memorial edition, The World Publishing Co.
† Application dated July 20, 1945.

"Theirs were the first and clearest voices raised against the march of aggression in China, Ethiopia and Spain."

Knowing that the final chapter of his life was approaching, and soon he would no longer be able to speak out against Fascism and inequity in the world, he felt that joining the Communist Party would safeguard his position on the side of the common man. But to say he was informed as to the internal political workings of the Party in this country would be a false statement. He was looking at the problem from the world humanitarian point of view, and said: "Belief in the greatness and dignity of man has been the guiding principle of my life and work."*

Teddie was exhausted and knew he needed a rest, but he said: "My time on this earth may not be long and I want to finish *The Stoic*.† I know now that I will never be able to complete my *Formulae* but *The Stoic* is a definite part of my literary program."

His determination to finish *The Stoic* at once distressed me, as I was deeply concerned about his health. Therefore, I suggested: "Well then, take at least a month's vacation, and when we return, I will help you all I can."

He agreed to this and we started off in our car toward Portland for my mother's place. While we were there, Teddie rested considerably and every day he seemed a little stronger. However, he set up a card table in the shade of the trees where he carried on with his notations for his approaching task, and no amount of persuasion could keep him from it.

One evening my sister sang a number of songs before a

* *Ibid.*
† *The Stoic*, third volume of his "Trilogy of Desire."

spellbound audience gathered in the living room. She was in better voice than she had ever been in her life. First she sang an operatic aria, then interpreted a cowboy song, followed by a ballad and several light encore numbers, demonstrating a versatility and freedom of technique beyond even my expectations. I realized she *had* progressed as I saw how sure of her interpretations and artistry she was. Perhaps her audience that evening was made up of just the right combination of personalities. But Teddie, as well as the rest of us, was amazed.

He came to me afterward to ask if she really *knew* what she was doing artistically, or if it was just an accident. I said I thought she knew what she was doing—she had always been an artist—and I had always known it.

"Well," he replied, "I would like to discuss it with her."

"I think that would be wonderful, honey," I answered, "why don't you do that?"

The next morning he had a long talk with her in the garden, and later came to me saying: "That girl certainly does know just what she is after artistically, and I stand ready to finance and promote her if she wants to come to Hollywood."

But Teddie did not know Myrtle as I knew her. I was doubtful from the beginning that she would ever come to Hollywood. She was in love with her fiance, a rancher and cattleman, and was as much interested in ranch life as she was in singing. I had a premonition that the ranch life would win out. And so it did.

Back home again, Teddie lost no time in settling down to work on *The Stoic*. After having completed a book of the nature of *The Bulwark*, it was not an easy task to turn back to his "Trilogy of Desire," two volumes of which had been written and published years before.* But I knew that once he started, he would continue in the same vein in which he had written the two preceding novels, his only object being to finish a great story.

He had about the same amount of work ahead of him that he had had on *The Bulwark*, the manuscript of *The Stoic* being about two thirds completed. But he had spent about all his creative energy on *The Bulwark* and had not recuperated sufficiently to tackle another book. While he dictated much of the writing which I took down directly on the typewriter, there was always the necessary discussion about scenes, action, structure, and he tired easily. I felt his great need for strong support, so I mustered all the strength I had to give him in this final struggle. Day after day, we worked on opposite sides of his long work table, Teddie in his old-fashioned yellow-winged rocking chair and I at the typewriter. Sometimes when we needed more room to spread out chapters, we would go into the dining room to work on the large Spanish table where he would pull his rocker after him, settling down again to his rocking and dictating. It was incredible the way he persisted in his job; in fact, it was all he wanted to do with the exception of an occasional diversion.

In the morning while I was preparing breakfast, he would bathe, shave, and then, immaculately dressed, walk into the kitchen to pour himself a small drink before sitting down to the table. Every time I saw him appear in this way, I mar-

---

* *The Financier*, 1912; *The Titan*, 1914.

---

veled at the miracle of his presence; it was always inspiring to me.

Two sets of galley proofs and the final typescript of *The Bulwark* were received from New York. Marguerite Harris, who had been back in California for a time, working on some things of her own, had expressed the desire to check them with Teddie when they came. Being notified over the telephone that they had arrived, she said she would be right over. When I hung up the receiver and went into his room, I noticed him carefully putting the galleys away in a drawer. Coming to the house a few minutes later, Marguerite said she wanted to check the galleys with him at her own place. Teddie refused, as he wanted the three of us to check them together in his study. This, she did not care to do, and an argument started between them. I was quite surprised at the resolute stand he took when he told her firmly that he had no intention of checking them anywhere else.

"Helen is a part of this as much as you are," he said, "and I want her to be present at the checking."

Marguerite continued to argue, but he was immovable. At that point, I became involved in the argument and several sharp words were exchanged. After she left, Teddie went quietly back to his study, and taking out the galleys again, determinedly set to work on them. I assisted him, and when the checking was completed, he mailed the proofs back to the publisher, at once resuming work on *The Stoic*.

Never in our long relationship of twenty-six years had we ever been so close, mentally, spiritually and physically as we were this last year of his life. If a woman ever experienced a complete renewal of her love life combined with a new depth of spirit, I had that joy. And no one could have been more surprised. Teddie flooded me with his love. He praised me for things I had long forgotten, and expressed many little tendernesses I didn't know he was capable of. When I went upstairs to my own room for a little meditation, he would occasionally follow me there, sitting in my rocker, discussing everything with me from the dress I was to wear that evening for dinner, to the next phase of his book. I was filled with happiness that I knew would carry me through to the end. For my life had become whole, and as I looked at Teddie, I could see that he, too, was content at long last.

On Monday, August 27, we celebrated his last birthday at home, with about fifteen intimate friends. A dark shadow that dimmed the usual buoyancy of the occasion was the absence of his very good frend, A. Dorian Otvos, who had died two days before and was not to be seen and enjoyed in his familiar role of humorist and punster.

The services for Dorian were held on Tuesday, August 28, at Forest Lawn, and while it was a private service limited to close relatives, Teddie and I were invited to attend. As often in the past, he was asked to say a few words at the side of the grave before the casket was lowered into the ground. He stood beside his friend, speaking so simply and movingly that one felt warmer and easier, as though all present were merely bidding a good friend an affectionate au revoir. As we were walking back to our car along a ridge in this picturesque Whispering Pine section of Forest Lawn, Teddie remarked to me that he had never seen a more beautiful resting place.

He was invited to speak on a panel at the University of the City of Los Angeles on December 8, but I was uncertain as to his ability to keep the engagement. However, he accepted the invitation and they went ahead with the printing of his name on the program. When the day arrived, he told me at breakfast to telephone and cancel the engagement, that he was not up to it. Knowing how disappointed the faculty at the University would be, I reluctantly went to the phone to notify them. The following morning, as we were seated at breakfast, I was surprised to see tears in Teddie's eyes as he gently hit the table with his fist saying: "I may not be strong enough to speak in public now, but I *will* speak again about the things I wish to talk about."

"Why Teddie, I didn't think it mattered that much to you!" I replied.

"Yes," he said, "it matters."

On the night of December 12, I had a most peculiar dream. I was sitting next to Lillian Goodman, at a large table with about thirteen or fourteen other people, when suddenly I noticed she was crying. Her tears were flowing in a steady stream to the floor underneath the table. I took her hand in mine in an effort to comfort her, but the tears continued to flow. The following morning I called her on the phone to find out if everything was all right with her. And then, though ordinarily I would not have done so, I told her of my dream.

"Well," she said, in a most cheerful tone of voice, "dreams always mean the opposite, you know, so I'm sure everything will be all right." Feeling better about it, I put the dream out of my mind.

About a week later, I had another strange dream. Teddie and I were operating an open plane of peculiar design. He was sitting in the rear, steering it with a rudder like that of a boat. We were flying over water toward a shore on which there were hundreds of people and I was concerned with the problem of gliding into a safe landing over the heads of the crowd. Glancing back to see if all was well with Teddie, I became terrified when I saw he had fallen over to one side. I went back quickly to where he was sitting and kissed him on the side of his mouth. Then I realized I must rush back to my place or we would crash. We glided to safety on the shore, but by that time, Teddie had revived and all was well. When I told him in the morning of my dream, he said: "Well, it came out all right, didn't it?"

On December 21, we attended the wedding of Bernice Dorothy Tucker, daughter of Mr. and Mrs. Ernest H. Tucker, to Lt. George B. Smith, son of Mr. and Mrs. Byron Smith, where the last photograph of Teddie was taken. The wedding ceremony was performed at the Wee Kirk o' the Heather Church in Forest Lawn Memorial Park, after which there was a reception at the home of Mr. and Mrs. Byron Smith, in Glendale.

Christmas morning we joined the Goodmans for breakfast at their home in Pilgrimage Trail. It was a family affair and everyone seemed to be in a happy mood. In the afternoon, we visited Clare Kummer and her daughter Marjorie. Clare, distinguished playwright and composer of many lovely songs including *Dearie*, had been the wife of Arthur Henry, Teddie's friend of *Sister Carrie* days, and there was a great bond of friendship between them. We always loved to visit Clare, and Teddie sat beside her on the piano bench that Christmas day as he always had before, listening intently as she sang her

latest song in her charming little bird-like way. Teddie loved
her songs and it made her very happy to sing them to him.

The next day we attended a tea in Beverly Hills, at the
home of Barbara Vajda, producer and director of legitimate
stage plays. That evening, Teddie and I had dinner in a small
cocktail lounge on Santa Monica Boulevard. He talked of
Greenwich Village and how he used to meet so many of his
friends and contemporaries every time he went out. I could
see he was homesick for the old New York he had known in
those early days. We decided we would go to New York the
following May for several months, but as we were talking, I
wondered how disappointed he might be if he were unable to
recapture something of the atmosphere he had known so well.
After making this decision to go to New York in May, we
both cheered up considerably.

We were now revising certain last chapters of *The Stoic*. He
had sent a copy of the manuscript to James Farrell for criticism, and Farrell had made a few suggestions with which
Teddie fully agreed. In fact, he had intended to add two addi-
tional chapters to the book before sending it to Farrell, but
had been so physically exhausted that he had stopped writing
for a while to rest. However, when Farrell returned the manuscript, he started to work out the ending which was to include
a soliloquy, summing up the three books of the Trilogy, and
on December 27 he was writing the next to the last chapter.
Having worked until five o'clock, he suggested we go out to
the ocean for a breath of fresh air, and off we went to the
beach. We drove to the end of Washington Boulevard and
watched an exquisite sunset—all blended in neutral shades
of grays and blues with streaks of turquoise and cerise. As

we walked along the boardwalk, I noticed Teddie's magnificent silhouette against that background.

"He looks pretty well," I thought. "I guess he will be all right. All he needs is a little rest."

After we were in the sea air for about an hour, he suggested, as he invariably did whenever he was anywhere near the ocean, "Let's have a hot dog."

Going to a stand at 8 Washington Boulevard, we were attracted to the cheerful and chatty man who was running it. He told us all about his family of five children he supported out of his little hamburger and hot dog stand, and how they came in so often to visit him that he was forced to send them home to get the good food prepared by his wife. When Teddie and I left, we commented on the happy effervescence of this man who could be grateful for so little in life as a hot dog stand out of which he supported his entire family.

Arriving home about 7:30 P.M., I felt so refreshed I decided to continue working for a while. But Teddie announced that he would "turn in" and went to his room. I went ahead with the revision of the chapter we had worked out that day, and at 9:00 P.M. I was finished. When I took the chapter in to read to him, I was startled by the glossy appearance of his skin combined with a certain pallor revealed by the light of the lamp.

Not letting him see my surprise, I said: "No, honey, I think I'll read it to you in the morning when we are both fresh."

"*No!*" he said. "I want to hear it right *now!*"

So I read the chapter through. He was pleased, saying it was much better. I then put the radio on so he could hear

the ten o'clock news, and went up to my room to get ready
to retire. When I came down, Teddie complained of a pain
in the kidney area. I suggested he try the infra-red ray lamp,
and after a half hour, he said it was a little better and to
please put out the light.

I knew nothing more until suddenly I was awakened out of
a deep sleep and saw him standing in the middle of the room
in his dressing gown.

"Helen," he called, "I have an *intense* pain."

I jumped up immediately, but at that moment he crumpled
to the floor, groaning and twisting in pain. Frantically, I
grabbed pillows and blankets, straightened his legs out and
tried to get him to lean against the bed. I ran for a little
brandy, but when I offered him some in a spoon, his teeth
were set. I managed somehow to get to the phone to call
Lillian Goodman, sister-in-law of Dr. Hirshfeld, Teddie's
physician, telling her he was very ill and to please call the
doctor for me at once. She said she would and that she and her
husband, Mark, would be at the house in a few moments.

Hurrying back to Teddie, I finally made him a little more
comfortable. Then he said he would like to get into the
bathroom. How I achieved this, I will never know. Before he
left the bathroom Lillian and Mark were at the door, followed very shortly by Dr. Ruben Chier, assistant to Dr.
Hirshfeld, who was out on another case. They helped him
into bed, and Dr. Chier gave him an injection to stop the
pain. In a few moments, as the pain was lessening, Teddie
said: "Why, a pain like that could kill you!"

Lillian and Mark and Dr. Chier stayed on with him through
the night. Toward morning I went upstairs to dress, and

shortly afterward Dr. Hirshfeld arrived. He and Dr. Chier
made an examination, and as they came out of the room,
Dr. Hirshfeld said to me: "There is a slim chance. He is
very ill. He must have an oxygen tent at once."

Two male nurses, an oxygen tent and other necessary
supplies were arranged for immediately. Early that afternoon, although no one had been notified of his illness, Esther
McCoy dropped in. Teddie greeted her, and when she asked
him how he felt, he replied: "Pretty bum." Dr. Hunter of
the Hollywood Congregational Church was another caller that
afternoon. Teddie was perfectly rational and seemed somewhat better, but warned me not to leave the room for a moment. Shortly, Dr. Hirshfeld returned. He remained in the
room some time and when he came out, I walked to his car
with him. He said:

"Well, I wouldn't have believed it. He is *much* better since
the oxygen came. *Much* better. He may even pull through."

"I *knew* it," I replied. "I know his constitution. Oh thank
you, doctor." I went back into the house very hopeful, and
told Lil that she might as well go home to rest, as she had
been up all night. By that time, one of the male nurses had
arrived and I told all those present that the doctor said
he was better, and I thought I could handle everything for
a while; they could come back later. I then called Marguerite
Harris and left word with her son for her to come right over
as soon as she got home. They all left and the nurse and I
were alone with him. He lay quietly, but I noticed his hands
were cold; they had been cold from the moment he fell and I
could not warm them.

Suddenly he said: "Kiss me, Helen." I did, *on the side of*

*the mouth,** and then I kissed him again. He looked steadily into my eyes saying: "You are beautiful." He had always said that to me, but I was frightened because he had asked me to kiss him, and I wondered if he expected to die. If so, he did not want to alarm me even at that stage, for he said nothing more.

The nurse watched him closely. He was resting. Two hours passed. Suddenly the nurse hurried to the phone to call the doctor. I heard him say: "Can you come right over? His breathing is becoming shallower and his fingertips are turning blue."

I looked and saw that it was true. I held his hands; they were cold and damp, and I felt his life slipping away through them. I felt desperately helpless; he was going fast. His eyes were closed and there were deep shadows around them. But there was such a hallowed peace enveloping him, which was reflected in his face! The peace that passeth all human understanding had clothed him and he seemed elevated to another dimension. There was something magnificent in the dignity of his departure as though every atom of his body was in complete repose.

His breath became shallower and shallower until I felt it stop. He was gone. The doctor arrived and pronounced him dead at 6:50 P.M. I still could not believe it, but sat there an hour and a half longer until he began to grow cold. Soon, representatives of The Forest Lawn Association came to take him away. I went into the living room. But as they wheeled him out the same door through which he had walked so many times, I experienced the cruelest and most agonizing

* Weeks later I recalled the strange dreams I had had a week or so before.

moment I had ever known. The biggest and best part of my life went through the door with him. I simply crumbled. The others had returned, but I was not conscious of when they returned. All I knew was that he would never walk in and slam the door again, and yet, as they wheeled him out, I felt so deeply that he had not gone with them—that if I found him again, it would be right in the house where he had left so much of himself—near his desk, in his room or in the garden. And as I have written this on his beautiful rosewood desk, I have often felt his presence strong and near, especially when I have been in difficulty of some kind. His vibrations were so powerful they must have registered on every inanimate surface in the house, for I think as he always did: Matter is nothing. . . . Spirit . . . all.

EPILOGUE

Memorial Services for Theodore Dreiser were held in the Church of the Recessional at Forest Lawn Memorial Park, in Glendale, California, on the third day of January, 1946. Dr. Allan Hunter, of the Hollywood Congregational Church, was the presiding minister.

The opening musical number was *Largo* by George Frederick Handel, played by Mr. Harold Dick, organist. Other selections included:

Arioso	Bach
Ah, let me weep, Lord!	Handel
If Thou Be Neur	Bach
Come Kindly Death	Bach

Honorary pallbearers, chosen from Dreiser's friends, were Charles Chaplin, Will Durant, Dudley Nichols, Lt. George Smith, Dan James, Leo Gallagher, Berkeley Tobey and Mark Goodman.

John Howard Lawson, a friend of long standing, paid tribute to Dreiser in an eulogy on his life and works. Charles Chaplin recited Dreiser's poem, "The Road I Came":

> *Ah, what is this*
> *That knows*
> *The road I came*

319

And go again?
Matter?
Instinct?
Energy?
Nature?
That whispers of paths
Beyond these
Which now I seem to know
Yet do not;
Wastes,
Planes,
Immensities,
In remote consciousness,
Where is no breath of self,
Such as I witness here,
Yet of which
To be conscious
Is wisdom—
Power, perhaps,
Creative strength.

Oh, inorganic
Yet breathing
The organic,—
Inarticulate,
Yet voicing itself
Articulate
In heights,
Depths,
To which we rise
Or sink—
Yet infinite
And from which we take our rise.

Oh, space!
Change!

Toward which we run
So gladly,
Or from which we retreat
In terror—
Yet that promises to bear us
In itself
Forever.

Oh, what is this
That knows the road I came?

The indescribable expression of peace on the strong contour of Dreiser's countenance pervaded the entire atmosphere and had the strange effect of comforting all those present.

He was laid to rest in almost the exact spot he himself had chosen four months before as we had walked over it returning from the grave of our friend, A. Dorian Otvos, when he had turned to me saying: "Could there be a more beautiful resting place than this?"

Just before the casket was closed, I placed the poem I had written to Theodore beside him:

TO A POET

If I did touch the margin of your soul
In its swift moving earthly seeming plight,
And but beheld its burnished aureole
That shed a brilliance to the inner sight,
And opened up the windows of the mind
To rarer beauties far than most men feel;
Then I have sung the lark's sweet song designed
To fuse our senses with celestial seal
As once on grassy sward we lay enthralled;
But moved as quickened spirits to the birth

THEODORE DREISER

Of other joys to which our hearts were called:
To ride melodic wings above the earth
Where you, the song and I are now afloat
In that one crystal clear immortal note.

INDEX

INDEX

INDEX

INDEX